MW00526405

Graham Ward is Regius Professor of Divinity at the University of Oxford and a canon of Christ Church, Oxford. A former editor of the journal *Literature and Theology*, he has written numerous books which explore varied topics in religion, theology, literature and literary and cultural theory. These include *Barth, Derrida and the Language of Theology* (1995), *Theology and Contemporary Critical Theory* (1996), *Radical Orthodoxy: A New Theology* (edited with John Milbank and Catherine Pickstock, 1998), *The Certeau Reader* (2000), *True Religion* (2002), *Cultural Transformation and Religious Practice* (2010) and *Unbelievable: Why We Believe and Why We Don't* (I.B.Tauris, 2014).

'*Unimaginable* is a book of wonders. It is an interdisciplinary excavation of imagination, its "palaeontology, archaeology, biology, physiology, psychology [...] and how it engages with the world". Yet it is far more than this: it is an exploration of language and art, of life itself, through enchanted prose and a weaving together of ideas, layers and cultures – "the stark, ungraspable beauty; the raw, defenceless horror" – that makes for compulsive reading. *Unimaginable* is a unique and powerful contribution to our understanding. Not to be missed.'

MAGGIE ROSS, author of *Silence: A User's Guide*

'Our contemporary world has seen a great rift between so-called religious fundamentalists and an enlightened liberalism which wishes religion would simply go away. Both sides are woefully failing in that deep human quality: the imagination. Graham Ward's new book *Unimaginable* is a profound and richly enjoyable journey towards the ground of our being. I know this is a text which I shall often revisit.'

A. N. WILSON

GRAHAM WARD

Unimaginable

What We Imagine and What We Can't

I.B. TAURIS

LONDON · NEW YORK

Published in 2018 by
I.B.Tauris & Co. Ltd
London • New York
www.ibtauris.com

References to websites were correct at the time of writing.

ISBN: 978 1 78453 757 9
eISBN: 978 1 78672 408 3
ePDF: 978 1 78673 408 2

A full CIP record for this book is available from the British Library
A full CIP record is available from the Library of Congress

Library of Congress Catalog Card Number: available

Typeset in Garamond Three by OKS Prepress Services, Chennai, India
Printed and bound by CPI Group (UK) Ltd, Croydon, CR0 4YY

For Rachel & David

CONTENTS

ACKNOWLEDGEMENTS

A book like this is written through a thousand other voices besides my own. My friend David Moss (deep in Devon) read each chapter as I worked, reworked and reworked it again from a mountain retreat in South Africa. He came up with the idea of the imagination as a suture and that really opened some doors for me in describing the relationship between the animal and the human. My friends Martha Reeves and Peter Davidson read the whole reworked copy when I thought I'd finished it. Each, from the wide differences in their experience and expertise, made invaluable comments that shaped and improved the final text – and saved me from embarrassment. They suggested modifications with patience, tact and courtesy. Then A. N. Wilson agreed to read an unedited draft. Chapters and sub-chapters were crafted with the help of other friends labouring on their distinctive intellectual projects: Marcia Polly who introduced me to ways of thinking about dance; Jeremy Llewellyn who went over what I had to say about music, correcting and adding observations; Carol Harrison who read through what I had to say about Augustine and offered insights I have certainly profited from; Tiago Garros who walked me through what was going on in the Acampamento Farroupilha, and read and then revised what I had to say about it; discussions with John de Gruchy and Wentzel van Huyssten that fuelled my enthusiasm for the archaeology of southern Africa; and Irwin Said who, while he was a post-doc at Christ Church, helped me understand current research into the origins of life and made me realize Agamben was deeply mistaken in believing ζωη could be separated from βιος. And there are many others, including colleagues and my graduate students, whose contributions are in here but I can't quite separate from my own voice.

I need to thank the Oppenheim Fund at Oxford that helped finance my stay in the Western Cape; the diocese of Edinburgh and their bishop, John Armes, for encouraging and supporting my delivery of early material at their diocesan conference; and Alex Wright at I.B.Tauris who urged me to write this volume and then urged me to revise the draft I sent him. I also want to thank my research assistant, Travis La Couter, for his work on the copy-editing and index. The Christian community at Volmoed, Western Cape, have a trailer out on the edges of their land in the mountains above Hermanus and inching towards a lush but treacherous gorge. It was here that I wrote and rewrote this text with the baboons, the stars of the southern hemisphere, the rock dassies and the mousebirds. They all welcomed me and I flourished in their friendship on a spacious south-facing *stoep* that makes several appearances.

The book is dedicated my children – no longer children – David and Rachel, for whom my love, pride and admiration have no words, only gratitude.

INTRODUCTION

Deep Dreaming

It's August and I'm eighteen. This is the summer vacation and, for once, the summer is gloriously, amazingly hot. A group of us from the industrial north of England go down to Norfolk on a fuggy train. Five friends swaggering like men along a dusty road laden with backpacks. We're heading for a place called Walsingham, driven by a desire to be by the sea. We went youth hostelling in Cambridge, we went youth hostelling in Norwich, and the plan is to end up youth hostelling in London. But then the heat got to us and, collectively, primitively, what we wanted was water; great stretches of water with heavy waves and fine, fawn sand. None of us had heard of Walsingham before. In a pub in Norwich with the maps of East Anglia spread across a table and one of us holding open the *Youth Hostelling Handbook* we scanned the coast from King's Lynn to Dunwich, and discovered a hostel in a place called Walsingham that looked about five miles inland from the sea and a place called Wells. So the next morning we boarded a train and set off. Only, without a car there's no way to get to Walsingham except by walking miles from a sleepy mediaeval town called Fakenham.

We're dropped off by a local bus; dropped into a landscape none of us have ever been in before: acres of corn and sugar beet whitening under the relentless glare of the sun and a sky of petrol blue. It's late afternoon or early evening. We're trekking along a single-track asphalt road; no cars come one way or go the other. The sun is on its descent, a large flaring disc on a silver arc. Hungry and thirsty, we trudge, engulfed by light, overawed by the enormous sky, with the silence that presses in upon us making us silent too. And eventually we arrive at a tiny village of stone weathered cottages and walled gardens overflowing with apple, pear and plum trees. Ripe fruit hang so low our faces can brush their bodies and smell the sweetness of the sun and rain that fattened them. We eat large Victoria plums, their purple skins splitting and oozing, looking about to see if someone is going to accuse us of stealing. But they are in abundance and rotting on the pavement.

From the back-to-backs and high-rise flats north of Manchester, Walsingham seems to us an ancient village of sudden and unexpected grandeur: low Tudor yeomen's houses with exposed black beams split and dry; stone pillared porches crusted in lichen; a huge wooden facade to a ruined abbey in which a smaller door is inserted; and an inn beside it with an impressive oak tree overshadowing a scatter of Formica-topped tables, each empty except for an aluminium ashtray. The door to the pub is closed. Not yet opening time. So we turn at a signpost with a green triangle enclosing YHA to the youth hostel. It's in a cobbled side street. There is one room left in the roof of a converted barn. We take it. Four beds, but we'll toss for who sleeps top to toe. We roll out our sleeping sheets and head for the inn. The sun is still setting in unearthly scarlets.

We eat, I think; we certainly drink outside: pints of dark East Anglian ale as the stars flower and other drinkers arrive. These are stars like we have never witnessed before: thick and bright and throbbing in a deep, sultry darkness. The skin on our arms, legs and foreheads glows with the sunlight we have absorbed throughout the day. At some point, closing time is announced by a bell and we start walking, but away from the village, along a lane. And then somehow we're on the other side of a stone wall, helped by an overhanging tree, and in the enclosed grounds of the abbey. Ruined gothic windows stretch up into a night that is moonless. Rain-eaten pilasters lie on the ground, and lintelled doorways, carved and free-standing, are entries into nowhere. The beer and a day of fresh air make us stop in a field looking down on the relics of a past we have been told nothing about at school. Instinctively we lie upon the ground. It too shares the warmth of our bodies, runkled and spiky under our backs, and heady with the sweetness of cut, dry grass. The day is over, limbs ache, bellies are full of beer, minds are swirling with fantasies of seascapes, and the dizziness of sleep is descending. Above us the constellations turn about Polaris with awesome grandeur and startling detail, and the Milky Way, the first time we have ever seen it as such, spreads out like a cloud, high and misty in the density of its stars.

'Up there,' Ian says, his arm upraised – a lad who will eventually go on to Edinburgh University to read astronomy. 'Up there, on the very edge of the Milky Way they say there's a great black hole.'

No one says anything in reply; we just look. The words don't mean much even though they sound technical. But we see 'black', powerful and distending, and we know what 'hole' is. In the vastness of space and the infinite enormity of hole my mind shatters, upwards. And I stare, stare, stare – in the direction of that great dark cavity in the universe. Not seen. Impossible to see. Unimaginable. But I know it's there, because somehow it's also inside of me.

I walk, mainly, on my own now. Down bracken sheep tracks in summer in the Hebrides, the sea below me, the ground strewn thick with clover, daisy and yellow pimpernel; along winter chalkscapes the hawthorn black and pencilled on my right and left, bounding the sweep of churned fields of heavy clay and knuckled flint; by rivers in spring, on towpaths trodden in the past by horses and muddied now by the bicycled coaches called out across the swollen water to rowers whose bodies steam in the early morning. And always when I walk I imagine, for imagination is a walk, a journeying; and that's where the stories come from, the narrative paths where dreaming, daydreaming, fictional tellings and autobiographical retellings pick up and rethread the traces of those who have walked this path before and those who will walk it afterwards. And they all meet in thought that strays and, in straying, heals ... somehow.

GRAVITIES

So what connects my first encounter with black holes to the imagination? Me. Us. Us as human beings thrust continually beyond ourselves in a desire to grasp the ungraspable. It's not just curiosity that propels us. That's too intellectual. It's more some half-recognized affinity between the vast strangenesses within and the vast strangenesses without. And imagination swells and sparks within those strangenesses. Imagination feeds upon the ungraspable; the not-known but yet still felt . . . somehow. It conjures and creates and transforms – bushes into bears, trees into shrieking banshees, star-patterns into constellations and zodiacs. Self and land and sky and cosmos work upon each other in and through the imagination and memory.

Wordsworth would have seen my account of the summer's night in Norfolk as a 'recollection in tranquillity'. He recognized, as he lay on his daybed in Westmoreland, in pensive mood and scenting the onset of the poetic, that such imaginative recollecting was transformative. It is transformative in multiple ways. It transforms that Norfolk memory of mine, for a start. For there are other memories, such as the awful sunburn to my legs that late afternoon walk caused which meant a week of smearing them with calamine lotion so they looked like bloated, pink marshmallows. I walked down the streets watching dogs and children salivating for a bite. Of other things I have no memory whatsoever. What happened to the sea, for instance? I have fragments of memories of walking down a disused rail track, between banks of yarrow and buddleia, but none of reaching the sea. None at all – as if, for me, that wasn't the point of what we were about. My account is washed down with the beer and the camaraderie to some very bare, narrative bones held together with muscular bright memories.

But the bones betray what was transformative about the memory for me. It certainly wasn't my first exposure to the deep English countryside, but it was my first experience of such overwhelming skies, the way light falls and drenches the landscape, and the way darkness make shadows portentous and clear, mild nights awe-inspiring. The recollection in tranquillity focuses and abstracts what most affected me. And who can say what effects follow from such an experience – or from any experience? The memory has been worked upon by imagination; but the imagination now of a much older man. I can't recall what I imagined exactly when that school friend spoke those words 'black hole' and pointed with an index finger to a vicinity of the heavens in which no stars shone. I have a book on my shelf that I picked up in the late 1990s by John Taylor called *Black Holes: The End of the Universe*. I no doubt picked it up because of that Norfolk experience. But this event took place twenty years before I discovered something about the nature of black holes from cosmologists. I don't know where my school friend even picked up the idea. There was no consensus among cosmologists and theoretical physicists such things existed until the 1980s. But, in February 1974, six months before our Norfolk trip, two American astronomers, Bruce Balick and Robert Brown, first detected the black hole at the centre of our galaxy using a radio telescope. It's now called Sagittarius A.

Memory is deeply implicated in imaginative processes, and that's to be explored. But the recollection of those few days in Walsingham is not just of a black hole. The black hole formed what cosmologists would call an 'event horizon' (the bright plasma ring edging a black hole) for a series of experiences. Maybe a lifetime of experiences. And just as my imagination now works with a different set of understandings of black holes, so my imagination brings now to that recollection other secret workings upon my mind and affections; other imaginative immersions and appreciations: the different mystical lightscapes, cloudscapes and landscapes of Turner of Oxford and Samuel Palmer, Shakespeare's *A Midsummer Night's Dream*, and Vaughan Williams' settings of English folk songs. These verbal and nonverbal evocations enrich not just the language that saturates and conjures the recollection, but its tone, sensibility and power to stir. Deep, concealed immensities, not just of the cosmos but in me, emerged as they did in Wordsworth on that night he borrowed a rowing boat and stole across Ullswater to encounter first the 'craggy ridge' and then the 'huge peak, black and huge' towering above him. The effect is haunting:

> huge and mighty Forms, that do not live
> Like living men mov'd slowly through my mind
> By day and were the trouble of my dreams.
>
> (*Prelude*, 127–9)

Dreaming too cannot easily be separated from imagining – one seeps into another. Dreaming is the imagination in default mode. The couch in Wordsworth's study where he lay in a pensive mood between past event of the dancing daffodils and his present articulation of much that is half-expressed connects the two. It is in interweaving of encounter, imagination and remembrance that the mountains meld into 'living men' beneath rational thinking. In the subconscious and preconscious, time bends like light under the pressure of gravity; a star dies and another star, in a different vicinity, is born. The point here of beginning with the memory of an evening in Norfolk is that maybe we have always been searching for black holes in outer space because they resemble the dark, chthonic gravities of our own imaginations.

EXPLORATION

This book *explores* those gravities that open fundamental questions about what it is to be human. For we are far more than little islanded egos, and our capacity to imagine shows us this. So, caught in these subtle webs of relation between earth and sky, cosmos and mindfulness, what are we – we who imagine far more than we reason? This book mines that question by exploring the evolution, nature and work of our *need* to imagine; a human activity more primitive and more powerful than belief or knowledge, calculation or certainty.

Since the early eighteenth century there have been many books written about the imagination: its history, its workings, its impact on certain cultures (like Romanticism), and the various forms it takes in the arts and sciences. The recognized exercise of the imagination in theoretical physics and cosmology can be compared to its exercise in music, in mathematics, in dance and architecture. But this isn't a book like those books. I have very little to say or add to that already said about Romanticism. Rather, this book informs by performing; by persuading the imagination to explore something of the *gravitas* of its own force field. To appreciate the power of the imagination it seeks to stir, evoke and prime that power. The book is *being* imaginative, and so it works across and associates any number of fields of enquiry from archaeology, literature, psychology and film to the captured minds of suicide bombers. It does not argue so much as excavate; excavate the way self, land, sky and cosmos work to make us what we are.

That summer evening in Norfolk showed me that the imagination is powerful and transformative, and textures every awareness of what is in us and outside us. In Chapters I and II we will look at its evolution, tracing its emergence from its animal beginnings to its early development in the various species of hominid that anticipate *Homo sapiens*. That way, we get at how primitive imagination is as it tunes into the instinctive and turns it into the intuited. The imagination evolves as creative and embodied minds evolve; as being human evolves. Animals exhibit degrees of imagination – levels of imaged experience that stir in *their* dreaming. But through the long aeons of evolution and adaptation hominid species and human beings discovered and unlocked imagination's potential. How and why did they do this? In all the cut, thrust and inseminations of survival how and why was the cultivation of imagination so fundamental? Why does the erratic course of adaptation blow gently, over millennia, on the spark, the filament of fire, which will encourage the conflagrations of the imagination? And with what consequences? These are the questions that will preoccupy the first two chapters that delve into what it meant to stand upright and become a migrant, to grasp with two hands and begin to manipulate and make sense of the world. From the formation of feet and advances in manual dexterity we enter the caves of northern Spain and southern France. We will examine the painting and carving and stencilling of exquisite forms that give tangible expression to the powerful and transformative working of the imagination.

Once we have understood something of the evolution of the imagination and how it relates to the development of the brain, in Chapters III, IV and V we will look closer at how it works. Through the research of biologists and neuroscientists we can appreciate the ways in which the imagination is deeply woven into our physiologies, desires, emotions and cognition. But far from being a mental process, it is rooted in sentience itself. We are barometers of atmospheres, tones and rhythms of which we are barely, if ever, conscious. And in this way imagination folds out from and folds into memories locked not just in our brains but our bodies. It saturates dreams that are inseparable from the inner workings of our physiologies and from the emotional content of what we desire and what we hope for. Imagination relates us to the worlds we inhabit and fashion around us.

Where, in Chapters I and II, we come to recognize the primitive nature of imagining, in Chapters III, IV and V we come to recognize the profundity of its power over us. It is a power not easily rationalized because it emerges deeper than mind in embodiment, and the complex interchanges between body states and mental states. We *live* imaginatively. Forms we register upon our flesh are transformed; figures are transfigured. In this lies the unbounded creativity of the imagination; but in this also lies its destructive attraction. It can work for good; it can work for evil. If it stretches out towards intuited truths of experience that forever elude its grasp, imagination also ferments lies and delusions, conjuring tricks and projections. It can work what Wordsworth described as 'the first and last of all knowledge'; it can also be the mark of madness. It fosters emotional health and balanced human development; but it is also the source of every psychosis.

In Chapter III we look at imagination's close association with our senses, the way our physical sensing cultivates our sensibilities and the way those sensibilities helps us to *make* sense of our experience. Imagination is a fundamental aspect of all perception; there is no perception without it (even among those who are blind). Which means that all our sensing emerges from and is impacted by imagination. In this way memories are laid down in our bodies and in our brains. But we are also the bearers of memories we have never lived as such. These are memories sealed into our evolution, adaptation and development; memories bequeathed to us by generations that preceded us. Imagination can tap into these primal, instinctive awarenesses. Being a more primitive aspect of our embodied consciousness, imagination bears traces, tracks and tendencies laid down in the remote past of our human species.

In Chapter IV we plunge with St Augustine into the abyssal depths of memory and with it his fear of the phantasms generated by the images that give shape to our understanding of the world. The imagination has a long history of being venerated and feared. Often viewed as a form of memory, imagination was also viewed as the seat of all deception. We observe the uneasy negotiation in Shakespeare's dramas of the imagination as something to be guarded against and the imagination as having the potential to mend the world.

In Chapter V we plumb Shakespeare further to understand the imagination's mercurial work in dreams, imaginative expression and the creation of knowledge. From exploring *A Midsummer Night's Dream* we move into the films of Alfred Hitchcock, and what psychology tell us about dreaming, hallucination and the way imagination bends, extends, sprains and breaks with our notions of reality. The imagination is the unbounded, dynamic play of filaments of sense from which is fashioned all we believe about ourselves, our experience and the world around us. And from the sheer persistence over time these beliefs become knowledge, but a knowledge that is continually morphing. It is knowledge constantly open to correction and amendment, modification, cancellation and approval. And this is because imagination is at work in all perception and the *production of knowledge*. It is an ever-shifting and deliquescent domain where images cluster like galaxies. As such, imagination is the 'event horizon' circling the gravitational pull beyond which no resistance is possible on the edge of a black hole. Here, for cosmologists, matter evaporates in pure folds of space, time and energy. So imagination makes possible all our accounts and cognitions of what is real while pulling that reality towards the ungraspable. Beneath reasoning and only partly, feebly, under the control of a conscious will, it makes both reasoning and willing possible. The will bends under the pressures of desire and curiosity; the reason warps. Active day and night, invoking moods and memories, imagination fashions both our dreamscapes and our waking world. Rooted far beneath consciousness, it is written into our biologies and somatic rhythms, the emotional tones and textures of experience that far exceed our capacities to clutch. At this point, being human sheers off into mysteries material, animal, possibly even religious.

Where, in Chapters III, IV and V, we explore *how* and *why* the work of the imagination has such a powerful effect over us, in Chapters VI, VII and VIII we shift our excavation of the mechanics of the imagination to its potent exercise. Here we enter the different domains in which that potency is manifest culturally and socially. These are domains in which any individual is situated, where the shared and public exercise of the imagination can crush or create us, destroy us or heal us, pitch us into battles with demons or set us among the songs of angels.

In Chapter VI we will begin by examining one of the roots of this communal power in myth and the power of mythic resonances to stir latencies and potencies deep within the cultural and the social. Language (or communication in its widest sense) is always a cultural product with a history. The signs and symbols whereby we communicate rest upon profound layers of shared memory and communal experience sedimented in mythic formations. These shape both cultural expression and the way we picture our common lives socially. We are continually captive to myth and mythic resonances in all attempts to make our lives meaningful, understand our shared existence and organize ourselves. Myth's hold upon us can take stronger or weaker forms, but the imaginative force of myth and mythic resonance cannot be erased.

In Chapter VII we will explore how, from myth and mythic resonance, the cultural imagination emerges. Since no one can overleap the times in which they live, all of us live within the ever-shifting cultural imagination. We produce and reproduce it. It forms our values, fashions our ethos, and permeates all the possibilities for our social lives. It cannot be separated out from the multiple forms of cultural memory, so we examine that relationship. Then, taking specific examples of its expression – a building in Singapore, Christopher Nolan's makeover of the Batman franchise – we explore how the cultural imagination gives us access to the hopes, desires, fears, convictions and threats circulating not just individually but corporately, globally. The cultural imagination is the subconscious within which we move and from out of which we try to make sense, even cope, with of our collective experience.

In the cultural imagination lie all the possibilities for the way we live or might live, act or might act, socially. So, in Chapter VIII, we explore how the mythic lives powerfully at the level of suggestion and affect in politics, religion, economics and all the relations that bind and oppose us, one to another. Here the terrifying force of the imagination is unveiled in human atrocity and systemic violence on national and international scales. Shakespeare's madman, under the sway of imagination's lunar dominance, takes on Leviathan stature. And yet, as Shakespeare also recognized, it is the same dominance that inspires the lover and the poet.

So we end the exploration into the imagination, its evolution and its power, by reflecting on what the imagination reveals not about *who* we are, as human beings, but rather *what* we are: *ecce homo*. We who are planted in sand and hope it's home; we who live like other animals between the land and the sky – prey to the bestial and open to the cosmic.

And where am I in all this? Certainly no privileged overseer. I am aware that conducting an exploration into the imagination is conducting an exploration into *my* imagination. *I* am the one making the connections here, whatever the facts. But this exploration is only partly autobiographical. Beyond and beneath describing and examining and analysing the work of the imagination, this book excavates the imagination by stirring and stimulating it through the act of writing. And an act of writing is always an act of faith – a stepping out and into resonances that lie *within* words, *between* them and *beneath* them; sounding their depths. When imagination is effectively communicated it can take on a life of its own beyond the individual who has given it expression. That's the aim: to express something of the evolved profundity of our capacity to imagine that it might resonate in others who will give it even greater depth.

Despite the elements of autobiography, then, this exploration is not all in my head. It's in all our heads as we grapple with what we *imagine* we know; what it is possible to know, even about ourselves and the world we experience. 'When you set out on the journey to Ithaca,' the Greek poet Cavafy advises, 'pray that the road be long/full of adventures, full of knowledge.' Freud's greatest achievement, to my mind, isn't to be found in his theories of complexes and drives or the structures of id, ego and super-ego – however insightful these have been in enabling us to understand the human person. His greatest achievement was his own journey to the Ithaca of the unconscious; to chart the unchartable, navigating an inner *terra incognita* for which there were no maps – only the sensitive listening to hesitant, wounded voices on a couch. He entered into his patients' dreams as a cartographer in order to dream them more deeply. Because only in dreaming them more deeply might he begin to understand. Perhaps only Augustine had made this voyage before Freud. This book too is an exercise in cartography and in dreaming more deeply.

I stand elsewhere now: thousands of miles south of Norfolk in the mountains that surround the small town of Hermanus in the Western Cape of South Africa. And there is no warm, stubbled earth beneath my back. I have learned to name and locate the stars – Alpha Centauri, the Southern Cross, the constellation of Carina. On a clear night (and there are many) I can stare into the centre of our galaxy, with its 300 billion stars, and towards the occluded spinning of that black hole. And I know now that this galaxy is only one of a group of fifty-four local galaxies dancing and whirling around each other through stretches of space and time that are ungraspable. We live, apparently, in a rather quiet part of the universe – on the inner rim of a spiralling arm at the edge of the Milky Way. I like that. Not too close to a monster that would suck us down in nanoseconds and evaporate all our chances for anything. We live, life has flourished, because of a narrow band of balanced possibilities. But I can look out on a summer night like this, in the southern hemisphere; I can look up and appreciate its vast unfolding all around the tiny spot on which I stand. Now all this space, time and darkness is unimaginable; and yet here I am, undaunted, trying to grasp it in and through the imagination. I am silenced by its frightening, dizzying, dazzling vastness – and ours.

PART ONE

ARCHAEOLOGIES

I

Landscapes

PURSUING A DECISIVE MOMENT

I t isn't a moment we know anything about, but it must have occurred. It's a moment we can only deduce from the traces and tracks that all animals leave. We are in the borderlands here between the animal and the human, piecing together bits of information that would enable us to reconstruct the moment when the imagination is born. The traces may be middens of fossilized shells on raised beaches, spoil heaps or rudimentary tools. These begin to speak of the moment, but only after it has occurred. The moment itself still remains silent, brittle, carbonized – like a skeleton. We can only get the silences to stutter as we make tentative, imaginative connections. The question is *whose voice is being heard*?

What is curious about the skeleton of an early hominid from around 3.9 to 4.2 million years ago is not the cranium and the estimated brain size. The increase in the size of the brain from an ape's is small. What is curious are the remarkable physiological changes to the legs, feet, hands and spine. Though short, Lucy *A. afarensis*, discovered in Ethiopia, walked (though probably no quicker than her scampering cousins). She also climbed. From a jaw here and a molar there, it has been suggested that *Ramapithecus*, an ancestor going back ten to fourteen million years, may also have been bipedal, but the skeleton of Lucy also shows that she was able to grasp differently shaped objects. She had some control over her environment through the joints of the hand at the fingers, changes in the wrist bones and the lengthening of her thumb. Lucy could throw and pound stone with better precision – although, at present, there is no entirely convincing evidence that tools were produced. The earliest stone tools date to 2.4 million years, were found in the Omo Valley in Africa and are thought to be the work of *Homo habilis*.

We developed our hands and feet among the trees as primates, evolving nails and jointed fingers from claws. More developments followed. To stand upright, when it offers no greater speed of movement, is risky: too much of the body surface is exposed to an environment that is as likely to be hostile as it is to be friendly. So the environment has to be manipulated better by *seeing* more clearly ahead and around. Having greater height helps, along with an ability to grip primitive weapons. But the environment can be surveyed now, and this will wire and rewire the circuits of sensing in that small but plastic brain. Hearing and smelling remain important; sight is even more important. Our first clue to the moment of imagination's birth comes with the new attention to seeing.

Imagination is a very visual operation, although not entirely, as Marcel Proust recognized. Tasting, smelling and hearing are also key senses in the activation of the imagination. But even people born blind imagine visually. Modern brain-mapping experiments show that blind people picture their world, and imaginary worlds, by employing the neural circuitry of the visual cortex through other sensory inputs. In other words, they rewire their senses. Then they generate spatial maps through touch or sound.

The ancient track we are picking up is formed in the plasticity of the swelling brain as environmental conditions change. Pre-existing connections, buried deep within our evolving sentience, are remoulded. The physiological changes in Lucy *A. afarensis*, effected by standing and moving on two feet, required neurological changes to the visual cortex and the temporal parietal lobe – areas of the brain fired by the imagination.

THE DEPTHS WE DON'T KNOW ABOUT

Our exploration begins here, with imagination as a suture marking a line between two tissues stitched together: that which is animal and that which is human. We developed this capacity to imagine in order to survive in a world turned upright (and countering the force of gravity). But because of the continuities that exist in our biologies, the traces and tracks we follow point to where we have come from as *Homo sapiens*. And how we arrived here. For we are bearers of genetic and epigenetic processes that left those tracks and traces deep within us. We have lived many other lives, and we live them still.

This is the basis for the body's knowledge, and it is knowledge much older and more primitive than any of our acquired knowledge through schooling. Certain circumstances, certain landscapes, certain words or smells can evoke connections of which we have no conscious memory; older pathways of responding to the world emerge from the drifts and mouldings of pasts we never ourselves lived. But they still live in us. Our ability to see a range of colours goes back, probably, to our tree-dwelling ancestors' need to choose between fruits and leaves at different times of the season. Our fear of snakes and physiological responses to them has a mammal lineage lost in the deep time of our evolutionary development. So our bodies are like the compact snows in a glacial landscape – recording layer upon layer of experience, each written upon my time and circumstance. Our DNA and RNA has been coded and recoded through adaptation, as what the weather brought the weather took away. Our prehistories and histories stipple the texture of muscle, bone, viscera and the mechanisms of response locked in our brains and spinal columns.

Like dark pools and cavernous grottos beneath the clints and grikes of a limestone pavement, our bodies have reservoirs of experience we have no access to. And when we connect with them, under certain conditions, then we begin to behave differently because we are apprehending and processing what we sense from deep-rooted sources. Darkness deepens as night falls, light becomes grainy in a solar eclipse, clouds descend, a blizzard hits and a white-out leaves the land blanketed in snow – and suddenly the familiar becomes unfamiliar and ways of perceiving, modes of experiencing, are awoken from our somatic pasts. The eerie is evoked, senses are heightening, adrenaline pumps, flesh creeps. But from out of such instincts an intuition emerges: we have been here before. We have, we *are*, histories we know nothing about but which nevertheless mark us. And those markings stimulate our imagination.

Imagination issues from these unfathomable and embodied knowledges written into the emergence of the embodied mind in *Homo sapiens* from the astonishingly plastic fibrillations of the brain. And sometimes it forages these ancient awarenesses like Sparrowhawk and Tenar feeling their way to escape through subterranean passages in Ursula Le Guin's story *Tombs of Atuan*. The power of the imagination, over us and others, lies in our human and, more profoundly, animal condition – and how it has evolved.

WALKING INTO HISTORY

Back to Lucy *A. afarensis* and the inferential steps we can take towards the decisive moment of an imaginative awakening.

In the opening of the twenty-first century there was much excitement – anthropological, philosophical and scientific – concerning the hand, and we will be picking up some inferences based on that work later. Lucy had amazing hands. But less attention has been paid to the feet; to what bipedalism effects. In standing and walking the whole weight of the body is placed on the feet. As we know from children learning to walk this demands a new orientation to the world, the body located in that world, and the development of balance (which is a feeling for where we are with respect to the force of gravity). This spurs our education in spatial mapping, which in turn stimulates modifications to the inner ear. The way we process sound (through the cochlea nerve) also advances our vestibular sensing, responsible for balance. That sensing feeds directly to the spinal cord, the brain stem and the oldest part of the brain, the cerebellum. Whenever we move, the orientation of the head to the rest of the body changes with the terrain (flat? inclined?), wind and gravity. Standing upright, Lucy's head is now exposed to the environment and navigating it is highly dependent upon the accuracy of vestibular sensing. And vestibular sensing is connected laterally in the brain to the temporal parietal lobe responsible for memory, recognition and emotional experience.

Why this anatomy? Well, the biopsychology of the imagination has its physiological structure here, and imagination digs down into our bodies, delving the environments they encounter. If we want to reconstruct the moment when the imagination is born then we have to look to the anatomical and its neural architectures. Only then might we understand not only how intensely imagination affects us, but also how radical and startling an aspect it is of being human. Other animals dream (cats and rats, for example), so there are vestiges of the imagination that are shared across species. But we are only just beginning to appreciate the extent to which they can deploy the creative imagination in the way human beings do. There are other animals that habitually walk upright rather than hop (gibbons and large birds like the ostrich), but walking is a more determined and focused activity. From that focus comes attention and with attention a sense of agency.

All life is animated. It moves. Movement is foundational for our understanding of what it is to be alive. But with walking, agency emerges beyond the kinetic and kinesthetic nature of movement written into our biological origins. Moving becomes a way of knowing; it structures our understanding of the world in the way walking around sculpture is our way of grasping the form before us and enquiring into its significance. We construct the three dimensions. So walking is one of the traces we must keep our eyes on because the capacity to walk upright has governed and changed our sense of space, time and our self-understanding as agents. With bipedalism we are literally on the road to an observation made by the British writer Robert MacFarlane – offering us a foretaste of imaginative landscapes to be explored later: 'The compact between writing and walking is almost as old as literature – a walk is only a step away from a story, as every path *tells*.'

With our australopithecines we are not necessarily intentionally path-forming yet. In fact, they probably remained partly arboreal creatures. But the increasing ability to stand on two feet, and move forwards, backwards or sideways, generated a whole new set of spatial maps as they negotiated distance, foregrounding and backgrounding. The attention that bipedalism requires sharpens our powers to observe and learn. This, in turn, hones certain proprioceptive senses that govern our bodily awareness. Lucy may not have had the olfactory acuity of most animals. She may have lost some of the agility of what are now feet because their power to grasp and clutch are much weaker than a chimpanzee's. But with more agile fingers (and the tactile sensitivity of their tips), heightened visual abilities and rewired auditory system, she was alive to the world around her and negotiating it in terms quite different from the apes. Spatially attentive, she could centre that attention to her advantage.

Consciousness becomes key to hominid and human survival, and from the fossil remains found scattered throughout eastern Africa it's evident that bipedalism spread and walking became wandering. Whether for food, for sexual partners, being pursued or because of climate change – as an ice age deepened creating savannah plains – our adaptation continued to find advantages for us. The tracks of this adaptation are still tendentious. Did *Australopithecus afarensis* become *Australopithecus africanus* (3.00–2.3 mya) or are they separate species? *Australopithecus africanus* were more slender, with strong legs for walking greater distances and a developed thumb opposition to the index finger, allowing for more precise tool use and manufacture. The gorilla has a long opposable thumb, but doesn't make or use tools. The chimpanzee does make and use tools but has a short opposable thumb. The baboon comes closest to human manipulative skills and employs it extensively in grooming. I watch baboons from my *stoep* in the mountains of the Western Cape. For a time they watch me. And then they're indifferent because this is their world. A grown male baboon has three to four times my strength. *He's* the one who struts round here.

Then, following the australopithecine adaptations, we have differentiations in the hominid lineage. Again, there's no consensus. Is *Homo ergaster* different from *Homo erectus* (2 mya), the African version of a species that subsequently colonized Asia, or the ancestor? Where do *Homo habilis* (1.8 mya) and *Homo rudolfensis* (1.5 mya) fit into the hominid lineage? There's even a new fossilized skeleton on the Pleistocene scene: *Homo naledi*, discovered near Johannesburg in 2014, and dated, according to some, to around two million years old. Dating and speciation aside, increasingly these hominids had less body hair, larger brains, kept cool by sweating and, importantly for hunting, they could run. If these were different species then they roamed Africa together.

But in 2013 discoveries in a remote part of Georgia, on what became the Silk Road, radically revised the idea of several branches of *Homo* and swerved the opinion of some towards a single species from which we all evolved: *Homo erectus*. Archaeologists working on the excavation of a walled mediaeval town in Dmanisi in the Caucasus – a town that looks like the ruins created for a vampire film set – came across five skulls dating to 1.8 million years ago, the fifth and most controversial only being discovered in 2013. These are the earliest traces of *Homo erectus* outside Africa, and what they seem to indicate is the variety within *Homo erectus* as a single species. Debates still continue over whether this discovery indicates a Eurasian origin for *Homo sapiens* because of the association with *Homo erectus* and, indeed, whether the fossils in Dmanisi are *Homo erectus* or *Homo ergaster*. The debates themselves are imaginative traceries formed from various inferences: the brain size of the skulls at Dmanisi are smaller than the famous example of *Homo erectus*, the Turkana Boy, found in Nariokotome near Lake Turkana in Kenya in 1984, and dated to around 1.6 million years; and the tools found at Dmanisi, along with other sites across Europe and Asia, are of the early Pleistocene type: pebble pounders and choppers. The oldest tools, called Olduvian, are linked to creatures like Lucy who show some *Homo* but also ape characteristics. If the *Homo erectus* theory holds, then *erectus* becomes the superhero of the hominids, with an existence stretching from more than two million years ago to what is thought to be its extinction around 700,000 years ago. If *Homo sapiens* date from 150,000 years ago, then as a species, to date, we have existed only between a ninth and a tenth of that time.

Whatever the outcome of the debates, what the Dmanisi findings have changed is the dating of the 'out of Africa' thesis. And that bears upon developments in bipedalism. *Australopithecus africanus* is associated with southern, not eastern, Africa, so long-distance walking skills were already in evidence. And the Great Rift Valley, running through Ethiopia and Kenya and down to Mozambique, is over 3,500 kilometres in length; 6,000 kilometres if we extend it upwards into Lebanon. Southern Africa is entered once the Zambezi is crossed in what is now Mozambique and the Nyanga highlands are entered. The terrain covered is varied with plateaux, desert, *karoo*, mountain ranges, savannah, coastland, escarpment, river systems like the Vaal and Limpopo, and cliffs soaring 1,900 metres in parts of Kenya. The paleoanthropologists' problem is that the earlier 'out of Africa' theory for the colonization of Asia and Europe dated the exodus to around one million years ago by *Homo erectus*, now characterized (after the Turkana Boy discovery) by a larger brain, more sophisticated, bifaceted, tool production (called Acheulean) and the intentional use of fire (for cooking meat that is easier to digest). Now we are talking about a movement out of Africa by bipeds around two million years ago, possibly earlier.

This is of enormous significance and interest, and has a bearing on the origins of the imagination. Early hominids, with quite small brain sizes, not only walked; they were migratory. Why? Why risk leaving a known landscape that had become a habitat for an unknown, perhaps even alien, landscape in which the basic essentials of food and water had, again, to be discovered? Do we just put this down simply to climate change and following the food source? Some have suggested that by advancing one kilometre a year with the herds being hunted, then over a quite a short period of time these hominids would have dispersed themselves throughout Africa, Asia, Europe and Australasia. But this is a reductive and unimaginative conjecture. It bypasses entirely a fundamental aspect of proto-human beings that emerges with walking and knowing the environment is shared with other creatures: curiosity. What is behind that bush, beyond that hill, across that water? Is it better? Is it worse? Is the grass greener?

It's not just a matter of negotiating distance. It's a matter of the landscapes and environments encountered, foraged. It's a matter of fluctuations in moods: expectation, disappointment and anticipation. It's also a matter of exposure to experiences with epigenetic consequences that get registered corporeally. These experiences change the processing of what is newly perceived in ways that will change perception itself. Our knowledge of the world is restructured. Technically, this is known as 'exaptation', where behavioural phenotypes impact upon and modify genotypes (DNA). We will encounter it again when we turn our attention to the hand. But I have focused on the feet, in the first instance, rather than hands because feet *must* touch. Hands *can* touch. There is a significant difference. Bipedal capabilities seem to be in advance of the developments to hands (evident in *Homo erectus*) that made possible the production of better, more precise, tools. Balance requires the divergence of the big toe and that probably preceded divergence of the thumb. Bipedalism requires constant contact with the ground being walked on and constant exposure of the body's full length, resting upon those feet, to the conditions it is immersed in. The feel of walking on well-watered savannah, walking on sand, walking on granite, walking on chalk, walking through shallow water, walking on snow, walking on scree and walking on shingle (and the geological and climatic environments that have provided each of these surfaces) is very different – as any experienced walker knows. A walk through a forest has an entirely different feel to a walk through a canyon. A climb through a mountain pass has an entirely different feel to clambering over dunes or wading through swamp. Moods are affected, dispositions changed and mind-states altered. Changes in terrain and climate require changes in attention. In the spirit of the English poet, biographer and travel writer Edward Thomas, the walker and writer Robert MacFarlane concludes, 'inner landscapes [are] powerfully shaped by outer'. Those spatial maps that are internally created are affected by location and transit through a multiplicity of very different locations. MacFarlane again, on walking the old ways of Britain: paths offer 'not only means of traversing space, but also ways of feeling, being and knowing [...] [W]alking is not the action by which one arrives at knowledge; it is itself the means of knowing'. Each kind of landscape requires a different form of concentration; a narrowing or widening of field vision. A slip on a wet rock rounding a peninsula and an ankle is twisted or a bone broken; fail to notice the cobalt folds in the snow ahead and you may be lost entirely in a crevasse. There is a continual exchange of touches between the feet and the land, and you learn how to read these touchings. You fail to learn at your peril.

Furthermore, walking, particularly walking that is wayfaring, requires continual improvisation. Maybe, on an open plain, footfalls can become autonomic, with low-grade thought levels. But in any other landscape each footfall is different; a new adjustment between the body, gravity and the land. A different contact is required and a different somatic experience arises from the necessary touch of surfaces. In this way the land is interiorized and externally the body is orientated. The early migrants were path-makers and wayfarers. The ancient trade routes like the King's Highway from Egypt through the Sinai desert to the Gulf of Aqaba (where it runs north through Syria); the Via Egnatia from Turkey through Albania and the mountains to the Balkan peninsula; the Persian Royal Road offering passage from the Mediterranean to the Persian Gulf; the Amber Road between Russia and Italy; and the Silk Road travelling across central Asia from the Middle East to China – were all discovered, formed and walked by these Pleistocene hominids in their grand migrations and in their increasing curiosity to find out what or who might lie ahead. Going by the size of those skulls at Dmanisi maybe the brain volume didn't increase much, but I venture their minds grew. And there is still a debate among neuroscientists on the relationship between brain size and mental facilities.

Aeons in the future, the spatial and geographical possibilities opened up by trekking into what lies ahead and unknown would become 'adventure' and 'exploration', and from it a million oral narratives would spool. Treading in the tracks of fleeing herds, pressing footprints into hoof marks in imitation and perhaps identification, turns walking into dancing, and dancing into summoning, and summoning into becoming the plants, the trees, the birds and the mammals themselves. Mind and land, creatures and weather, interact, altering each other's behaviourial contours, and, at certain points, fuse.

Becoming bipedal required a deep sensitivity to the tensions between ground and gravity; the balances between different wind variances of open and enclosed landscapes; and air, as it travels down into muscles to give them tone. The spine becomes a tree and the tree is on its way to becoming an *axis mundi*. The Khoi Khoi of southern Africa have a giraffe dance that is deeply responsive to these necessary associations of body, mind and land. The spine and even the arms are rigid, only the feet move, rhythmically to a beat. The whole body channels its energies into these two complex cores of bone and muscle through which the dancers mark out a circle. What is discovered is a reasoning deeper than cognitive processes; the body's own reasoning as it calibrates and recalibrates, adjusts its balance, shifts its weight, breaths in at this point and out at that point, uses up energy, screams out for nutrition and educates the senses as they inhale the world and exhale a response. 'Dance is incarnation', the South African novelist J. M. Coetzee writes. In all this the imagination is active, nurtured and engaged.

24

HANDS

As I said earlier, much work has already been done on hands and their evolution – in philosophy, anthropology, physiology and cognitive science. The work was pioneered in the nineteenth century by a Scottish surgeon writing a book that set out to demonstrate that the architecture of the hand was proof of the existence of God. He was a son of the kirk. The book was to fulfil a bequest made to the Royal Society of £7,000 by the Earl of Bridgewater for sponsoring treatises of original inquiry. George Bell was writing before Darwin, but he clearly saw the close relationship between organ design, function, behaviour and environment. The subject was taken up in 1980 when the British anthropologist-physician John Napier published his book *Hands*. His book opens with a remarkable statement summing up a fascination and awe that is given lucid expression in the material that follows: 'There is nothing comparable to the human hand outside nature.'

Then in 2003 two books appeared, the authors unknown to each other, and differing in their approaches, both entitled *The Hand* – one with the subtitle *How its Use Shapes the Brain, Language, and Human Culture*, by the American neurologist Frank R. Wilson, and the other with the subtitle *A Philosophical Inquiry Into Human Being* by the British neurologist Raymond Tallis. Both books gather together and sum up the debates, discoveries and investigations in the field, and both are speculative in distinctive ways: Wilson is more attentive to learning processes intimately related to touch; Tallis is more attentive to current debates in the philosophy of mind and inserting what he knows about human embodiment and its development into those debates. Tallis went on to take his speculations further, and in 2010 published a most insightful book about the development of the index finger, pointing and the shift from the material to the intellectual: *Michelangelo's Finger: An Exploration of Everyday Transcendence*. We will keep returning to that phrase 'everyday transcendence'; it's highly suggestive.

Like the foot, the anatomical structure of the hand is intricate, flexible and strong, with skin well adapted to hard usage, and the chief organ for the sense of touch. As it develops so a number of grips develop which facilitate tool making and handling: precision grip, power grip, hook grip and scissor grip. Primates have partial grips, which enable some species to take up an object like a stick and use it to extract termites from their nest. But human beings have a variety of grips enabling us to fashion tools to fulfil specific functions. Why is the evolution of the hominid hand important for understanding the origins of the imagination? How does its development provide us with inferences to understand that 'decisive moment'? To answer that let's turn to a beautiful novel written by the British writer Alan Garner. *Boneland* (2013) offers itself as an imaginative account of a primitive moment and a path along which our quest can proceed.

In the novel a Neanderthal hominid in Britain, the last of his kind, finds a 'Motherbone' or what archaeologists call a 'core'. It is the bone not the blood that is the root of life. The woman he seeks and desires needs to be cut from a rock face with living rock blades. The Motherbone contains his 'blades' and he has to extract them with 'hammer stones'. So, first, he 'sings to the Mother that the bone should not break'. And then holding hammer stones in each hand he 'sang to them the story of the world and how they came to be'. In the song he tells them their names and how 'his hand would help and his fingers teach' them so they wouldn't wound the Motherbone. He moves them around 'to make them know how they would sit and take knowledge from his palm'. He doesn't want the blades he cuts to break for then he would be unable to release the woman in the rock veil 'and the world would end'.

Boneland is an extraordinary piece of imaginative writing that reaches back into the mind and the world, and the shifting boundaries of each with respect to the other, in a being preceding *Homo sapiens* by hundreds of thousands of years. The writer's world is scraped away as he too hunts for the bone, the structure, the true. Garner is foraging to remember something he could never have consciously remembered, but something nevertheless buried deep within his own human condition: the memory of rhythmic sounds (song), of names and naming, of tactile objects (their weight, their hardness), of primitive skills that are also dance movements, learned and honed, of stories told and retold orally, and of a time when all things lived, each in relation to everything else. The writer is pushing against the rock veil of his own modern consciousness and reaching into the somatic unconscious. The woman is a figure in a dream, a memory and the shape of a desire. She too is buried and bound, but nevertheless her presence is discerned, her release from the earth is hoped for, needed – like the shaping of the material that will form the book.

In and through his writing Garner binds landscape, consciousness, imagination and verbal communication. It is a sensuous account of knapping with coordination between the visual, the tactile and the auditory; a kind of knapping where the 'core' is the imagination as it seeks to find form. In 1911, the French archaeologist, Lalanne, discovered the form of a woman carved in bas-relief into the stone wall of a rock shelter in the Dordogne. It belongs to the Gravettian period (27,000–24,000 years ago) and is the work not of Garner's Neanderthal, but *Homo sapiens*. She holds in her hand a bison horn, she is probably pregnant, and like all our examples of early figurines the face is a blank lozenge, its features never worked upon. The absence of character is both mysterious and disturbing, and we will say more about this absence in Chapter II. But here a certain equivalence is captured: a woman in a novelist's imaginary journey through the dreams and memories of a hominid stands there – 46 centimetres high and, in former times, painted red.

Neither of these figures, imaginary or real, would be possible without the hand: the hand that writes about a hand that strikes blades from a flint core, blades that were used for the 'deep pecking' that brought the Venus with the Horn from the wall of a Palaeolithic rock shelter.

There's a relationship between the hand and the mind. Lively hands reflect a lively mind. It has also been known for some time that an area of the brain related to speaking and language processing (Broca's) is also activated by movements of the hand. Casts made of the inside of fossilized craniums found in the 1960s point to the development of Broca's area in hominids like *Homo habilis* from 2.5 million years ago. And it has its homologues in chimpanzees and marmosets (where it's called F5). This suggests the neo-cortical architecture for Broca's area (and vocalization) goes back 35 million years – 28 or 29 million years before the separation of a species that became human from the monkey genus.

Be that as it may, PET (positron emission tomography) and fMRI (functional magnetic resonance imaging) scans taken during the modern production of stone tools clearly show the activation of those areas of the brain in and around Broca's area. The frontal and parietal lobes and the visual cortex are activated. The inferior parietal lobe integrates information involved in auditory, visual and tactile motor process. And these are also areas associated with language (its understanding, articulation and communication). Hence the same area of the brain is processing what the blind person feels through Braille and what the deaf person sees through sign language. What this means is that the sensory input is *made sense of* abstractly through a mental representation. It is not simply observed, but it is observed *as something* – it comes with and in a specific form.

When Garner's hominid finds the Motherbone in which are hidden the rock blades he so desires, the novelist recreates this distinction that will play so important a role in the development of the imagination. This isn't seeing a chunk of quartz or chert; it is seeing the quartz or chert *in terms of* some other goal he has set himself to achieve. Various goals in fact: first creating the 'stone-flakes' from the core using a 'hammer-stone', and then the carving of the woman which he *sees* behind the veil of a rock-wall. And throughout the process the hominid sings to the Motherbone and to the hammer stones (which he also names) in each hand. The process of tool production involves seeing beyond the sensed; negotiating the invisible and abstract *in* the visible. Current research suggests that such creative and imaginative *making sense* has only a low level of what some call 'semantic content'. But it also points to a new way in which we appreciate what they are doing as imaginative acts. In those stone tools, and particularly those tear-shaped hand-axes, there is activation of the imagination and working memory. The tools and weapons of Fred Flintstone and his friends show complex, abstract practices that go beyond anything observed.

With the development of the hand by a tool user we are closer to understanding the emergence of a species of hominid who thinks symbolically. Garner's hominid *intentionally* sets out to find the Motherbone and to achieve a number of tasks to carve the woman who is locked in the cave behind a veil of rock. We know from early hominid finds by caves and rock shelters, the right kind of stone was imported from elsewhere in the region and brought back for knapping. There is a level of organized planning involved and consciousness of stages in the attainment of a specific end. As Garner's hominid sets to work and sings there is a knowledge in his palms that his fingers will teach the hammer stones. The hand itself is extended and attuned to the tool and what the tool is working upon.

The scientific language found in studies of the hand, the arm, in fact the complete body as a 'tool', reduces the nature of what is active here. The creative employment of the body, through the hand, increases a sense of agency; it hones cognitive attention while always looking beyond the immediate to a future, more abstract goal. As I said earlier: the foot touches by necessity, the hand touches by choice. The body becomes aware of itself, and the making and then wielding of a stone hand-axe of flint or quartz yesterday prepares the way for the making and the wielding of the stylus or the quill or the pen much, much later. In both forms of tool use the mind is seeing what is *beyond* the visible; it is working towards the releasing of that which is visible *within* the mind. It works in and through the body at the border of the instinctive and the intuitive. For Garner's hominid, the body already knows, but in knapping the 'core' the knowledge now finds external expression.

Or that's just one way of putting it. Another way would be avoiding the division of internal and external altogether, allowing the imagined and the real to flow into and out of each other. Who knows where each begins and ends anyway? We might say that this coordinated and nonverbal communication between body, hand and tool *represents* objects in the outside world like the figure of a woman. But that is not how Garner's hominid conceives what he is doing. He sees his act as freeing the woman from the rock. He makes her appear. He is not representing the world outside. He is creating something within that world. He is worlding the world (as the philosopher Heidegger puts it) in which he will continue to dwell. That's what imagination does, and that worlding of worlds, that *making appear*, has an origin in the processes and practices of perceiving what is in the landscape before us and labouring, with feet and hands, with it.

To watch dawn break and twilight fall; to watch the light drain away and the stars appear; and to watch the light return and the stars fade: these are primitive things. Starscapes opening beyond landscapes; landscapes issuing from starscapes. These events are not just seen — they are felt; where to feel is not simply to register a drop and a rise in

29

temperature, but to experience changes in mood as the world contracts and the world expands. There is a hearing, as all creatures slip towards rest. There is a weight to the silence when the only sound is the wind siffling through the trees or the rhythm of the tide washing upon shingle. The hearing changes as that granular silence is broken gently with the predawn stirrings of the magpie and the blackbird, the seagull and the guillemot. There is a smelling too as the damp rises, the dew settles, and the woodsmoke from a low-burning fire thins. These experiences are primeval and perennial; affirming that we are alive − that we *are*. All things from bacteria to archaea and the single cell respond to, in sensing, the diurnal turn of the earth into and out of its hunger for the sun. This is not just sensing, but knowing we are sensing, and what is sensed is meaningful for us because it is life-giving.

That is what I mean by the world 'appearing'. The hand worlds us the world; it allows us to dwell. It can touch its other hand, touch the face, comb through the hair, feel down the body's side, brush the nipple in a movement down to the belly and beyond. It can also touch another's hand, another's face. The hand gives us to each other as working the land or walking the land gives the land to us. A scenario has been constructed through inferences drawn from one of the skulls found at Dmanisi. It's the skull of an old man and it has no teeth. Through sophisticated dental technology they have calculated he lost his teeth two years prior to his death, which indicates that he was being fed and cared for by the others in his group. His food would then have been chewed first by one of them so that, softened, he might consume it himself. That giving is rooted in an exchange of touches (going back to the feet) that relates us profoundly to all others things in our world, organic and inorganic, the weather and the smell of rain on dry rock. The world that appears is a shared and common world enriched with care, intimacy, empathy and imaginative entering into the minds of others. Garner's prehistoric 'core' is a 'Motherbone'.

MONKEY INSIGHTS

This is also a world in which, for those animals with consciousness, imagination is in play. Imagination is not just in the ability to image − vision and the other senses all image *and* map the world. Sensing is *image-forming, image-formation.* All conscious creatures image, from the bird who sees and picks at the cherry to the monkey who grasps at the fruit being offered or begs it from a trainer. Chimpanzees access perceptual information and have similar perceptual-motor skills to us, and that isn't surprising given that their DNA and ours differs only by just over one per cent. Their visual-cognitive processes are also similar. Like a number of other animals they learn through association and can mimic the behaviour of others. Much of the learning is innate; from a primordial and instinctual level of memory. They do not need exposure to the experience because the experience is already hardwired neurologically – as much of our experience is more hardwired than we might intuitively think. In other words they are *disposed towards.* Chimpanzees are *disposed towards* the manipulation of objects, as we are. They are *disposed towards* belief formation about how the world works, but they don't create abstract 'systems' of these beliefs; they don't create a 'world picture' through abstractions.

In some remarkable experiments done in the mid-to late 1990s, the primatologist Daniel Povinelli and the evolutionary anthropologist Michael Tomasello independently set out to examine the kind of mental representations guiding chimpanzee behaviour. Of course, they use and even make simple tools, but how do they understand what they are doing? Several sets of interrelated tests were performed to develop a comparative psychology with children of a similar age. Povinelli concludes that chimpanzees do have a visual imagination, but they cannot handle the unobserved and form concepts from non-perceived processes (like gravity, causality, force). They don't see each other behind rock veils and start finding ways to release these figures they *see*, because they can't access abstract processes. So while they may have concepts about the world, consciousness is more closely tied to what is sensed through sight and touch. They may well then have better visual imagery than we have, imagery that has a finer grain, because our vision can get far too caught up, too quickly, with the abstract and conceptual.

This may have some bearing upon those imaginative processes of our own that operate below the well-lit consciousness of conceptual thinking and are invoked through rhythm, tone and word association. *Our* imaginative processes, though, draw upon a more retentive memory.

These open wider domains, derived from free play between old and new images and creative syntheses. So, probably, our dreams are more wild and wide-ranging. But what might happen if chimpanzees had a language they could use to communicate? Would their writing let things be? Would it disclose a level of the immediately sensed nature of things? What the poet Jane Hirschfield describes as 'the chilling nonnegotiability of the wild'? What would happen if language became 'an organ of perception' rather than conception such that 'the world of objects beyond human consciousness may speak, in poetry's transparent and active transcription'. Imagination, rooted in the kinetics and kinaesthetics of pounding a landscape and pounding a rock, forages these forgotten, primitive receptions/perceptions.

Tool making becomes more ingenious and inventive because of imaginative connections. Not every kind of rock will make a stone tool. There is an exchange of touches between the hand and the boulder and you learn how to read them and their potential, and to understand the skill and patience needed to allow their shape to emerge. All this requires imagination, as Garner shows. Every stone tool is an act of imagination.

But perhaps we can go further. Perhaps these hominid stone tools are more than artefacts and objects collecting dust in museum cabinets. Perhaps, as articulations and acts, they are also poems (from the Greek *poieō* – to make, create or fashion); material poems born of a response to the world; crafted communications expressive of a line crossed between the aesthetic (from *aesthesis* – the Greek for sense perception) and the kinaesthetic – the movement that 'moves' us. Take a look at the beauty of the facetted tear-shaped Acheulean axe-head from 1.4 million years ago; the achievement of *Homo erectus*. We examine it today as a manufactured tool that conveniently marks the entry into the Middle Stone Age. But – and this returns us the Garner's novel and releasing the woman from behind the rock veil – perhaps we are seeing these objects wrongly or only partially. We are seeing them framed by a narrative of technology rather than poetry; a hominid subject sweating in order to overcome the resistance of an inanimate object. Perhaps it is the rock itself that is speaking and the craftsman or woman giving expression to what it is saying; to what he or she perceives it to be saying about the relationship that comes from the exchange of touches: that the stone has meaning prior to the consciousness of its perceiver; meaning in the very boldness and perfection of its existence. The rock is rock and more than rock; it 'meets its obligation by pure/undoubtable being' – as the poet Denise Levertov wrote of ivy. The tool formed from it is a tool and much, much more than a tool. How else might we explain the burial of what must have been a very highly valued axe-head in red quartz – quartz quarried many miles away from where it was found – interred with what are now the fossilized bones of over twenty-eight individuals identified as *Homo heidelbergensis* excavated in Atapuerca in Spain in the Sima de los Hueso? *Homo heidelbergensis* is thought to be an evolutionary development in Europe of *Homo erectus*. Some paleoanthropologists have dated this burial to 600,000 years ago. That an object so precious should be placed with the dead says far more about what it was than simply being a 'tool'; even though it was probably used as a tool. With such a 'tool' we approach a pure perception that dissolves internal and external, and the closest imaginative arts of pure perception are music (for ears), painting (for the eyes), sculpture (for touch), perfume (for smell) and cooking (for taste). I will return to this in Chapter II when we venture into the world of ice age culture.

Povinelli's work suggests chimpanzees have far weaker 'foresight', and therefore planning and design potential, because they cannot easily generalize on the basis of the particular. Their perceptions are taken up fully by the particular. Nevertheless, imaging and imagining is a more primitive mode of experiencing the world, perhaps experiencing it in more 'accurate' ways; 'accurate' meaning here 'closer' to the ways things are. There is a sense in Povinelli's account of 'physics for monkeys' that in becoming human, in becoming a symbolic species, much is gained that enables the great cycles of axial civilizations to turn, but something too is lost. Our fields of awareness can become too conceptually bound; too circumscribed by rational consciousness. Being becomes a metaphysical question, rather than living. The real is held at a distance. The cognitive scientist Nicholas Humphrey has argued that the exceptional artistic and musical abilities of people with autism may well reflect this more primordial mode of processing the world manifest in chimpanzee behaviour. This is far from saying autistic people are less well developed intellectually. That just isn't the case. We are back with the insight (given to me by a friend) that imagination is the suture for our wounded animality. What chimpanzees and autistic people share is a weak grasp of the other as other; what Raymond Tallis calls 'everyday transcendence'.

For Tallis there is nothing religious as such about his use of the word 'transcendence'. In fact he avows an atheism. Transcendence is the experience and recognition of the world and social beings as other and he associates it with the development and use of the index finger. Chimpanzees in their natural habitat don't point (thought they do gesture). Children learn to point from a very early age (ten months). Autistic people rarely point. Pointing, Tallis notes, is dialogical. Through pointing the hand becomes a relational tool, signalling *to another person*: a social tool for preverbal communication. Such a use of the body manifests not only consciousness of self and agency but also consciousness of another's consciousness, another's mind. In pure sentience everything is consumed immediately and the animal is lost in its sensing. Pointing invites someone else to share in the world opened up before the one who is pointing. It signals, but the sign is an embodied one – not an abstract one like a linguistic sign. It communicates prior to entry into being a 'symbolic species'; though, of course, along with other indexical gestures (the raised eyebrow, the sidelong glance) it is now frequently found alongside and accompanying symbolic communication; heightening emphasis. It performs an interpersonal skill related to teaching and learning. It engages in the difference between minds, and tests the extent to which that difference may be crossed, so that what is present in one mind and absent in another might lead to mutual acknowledgement and recognition. Like Garner's woman behind the rock veil, the transcendent begins with an intuition of what is hidden. Seen in the unseen it handles the invisible.

But with everyday transcendence is there also a mourning for what is lost: the immediate fusion of sensing and sensed? Is this the suture that marks the imagination; the mark of a wounding? In his novel, *The Marriage of Cadmus and Harmony*, the Italian writer Roberto Calasso laments the passing of metamorphosis in ancient Greek literature: 'The Minotaur would be slain. Pasiphae was to die in captivity and shame. Humans could no longer gain access to other forms and return from them.'

LIMINALITY

Ancient languages retrain a trace of older embodied knowledges. Abstract nouns still carry material weight. So, in Sanskrit, *muḥka* is 'face' or 'mouth', but also 'beginning', 'chief' and 'direction'. The emphasis throughout this chapter on the physiology of feet and hands and sensing as the basis for our experience of the world suggests that imagination is and is not a mental state. It is cognitive and can be foundational for what are often called abstract 'second-order' mental representations. But the roots of imagination are deeper-set within forms of memory and embodied knowledge that are older than developed consciousness of being conscious. Like believing and desiring, imagination is a *disposition towards* that is somatic and affective, and belongs to what might be termed 'deep mind' as distinct from ratiocination; belongs, that is, to the older 'reptilian' brain rather than the neocortex. Povinelli draws an interesting (and no doubt controversial) inference from his laboratory results. He accepts that chimpanzees manifest behaviours analogous to human beings, but underlines the dangers of *our* use of cognitive terms to describe these behaviours. We are projecting advanced psychological operations that developed much later. He goes on to observe that higher-order mental states in human beings probably neither accompany nor cause our own behaviour as often we are led to believe. There are more 'ancient' psychological mechanisms, he suggests, and there is growing evidence that this is exactly the case (see Chapter III). Is imagination one of these mechanisms? This returns us to feet and hands that 'know' and acquire knowledge. Imagination operates in and opens the space for sensibility; for making meaningful memory and thought. It treats liminality, produces liminality and is most intense in liminal conditions, because it is itself born of the experience of limens; invisible thresholds like internal and external, the seen and the unseen, crossed and recrossed.

On thresholds (as with sutures) maximal tensions gather. They are not places as such, but rather utopian spaces in the Greek sense of a 'non–place' (*u-topos*). In the past, sacrifices were made to gods and libation offerings made before a boundary was excised into the landscape for a building, for a field, for a city. We live constantly with liminality.

They are often invisible woundings – cuts, dissections, differentiations: from the circumcision rituals so fascinating to anthropologists, to implicit codes of social conduct; from the entrances inviting us into different architectured spaces (a public square, an indoor market, a cathedral, a pub) to the opening lines of a poem or a novel, the opening shots of a film or the first scene of a play. Artists sometimes play with the dense ambiguities and dark paradoxes of thresholds. In Chapter V I'll suggest that Shakespeare does so when it comes to dreaming.

There is a moment in the liminal when the world does not cohere, perception fragments, and a base fear of the meaningless and uncanny arises. In literature the liminal is often entered into and invoked by mist or fog. Think of the opening of Dickens' *Bleak House*: 'London [...] Fog everywhere. Fog up the river, where it flows among green aits and meadows; fog down the river, where it rolls defiled among the tiers of shipping, and the waterside pollutions of a great (and dirty) city. Fog on the Essex Marches, fog on the Kentish heights.' The most terrifying aspect of Susan Hill's *The Woman in Black* is not the malicious ghost luring children to their deaths, it's the house on the island wrapped in mist down the long causeway between the sinking sands. The liminal draws you out from the safe and familiar and transposes you from one world into another. It may be the same world, but once you have crossed a line then the dimensions of the ordinary world fracture, suddenly, irrevocably. With the entrance to a building the line is marked, but between people, the line is unseen – and the tension mounts. Dickens again: 'the dense fog is densest, and the muddy streets are muddiest, near that lead-headed old obstruction, appropriate ornament for the threshold of [...]'. Caught between realism and allegory, the sentence pulls us in a gothic direction. In *Bleak House* this fearful and intimidating threshold is to the Temple Bar. But the threshold we are trying to reconstruct here – which must have been no less fearful, no less intimidating, to those who first experienced it – is when imagination dawns.

In the thirteenth book of the concluding section of Wordsworth's autobiographical poem *The Prelude, or Growth of a Poet's Mind* (1805), the poet visits North Wales, walking to the top of Snowdon with a friend to see the sun rise. In the last lines of the previous book he narrates how 'I seem'd about this period to have sight/Of a new world', but we hear nothing more of this than it was recognized to be 'That whence our dignity originates.' It was a summer's night, warm, with low-hung cloud, thick and sweating moisture that covered a sky 'Half threatening storm or rain'. The two ascend in darkness into the damp fog, Wordsworth in front, seeing nothing until suddenly they are above the cloud level and he views the moon 'Immense above my head, and on the shore/I found myself of a huge sea of mist.' The cloud inversion presents him with a magnificent panorama in which the peaks of other mountains are seen by moonlight and, in the distance, the sea. It's then the distinctive moment occurs:

> and we stood, the mist
> Touching our very feet; and from the shore
> At distance not the third part of a mile
> Was a blue chasm; a fracture in the vapour,
> A deep and gloomy breathing-place thro' which
> Mounted the roar of waters, torrents, streams
> Innumerable, roaring with one voice [...]
> in that breach
> Through which the homeless voice of waters rose,
> That dark deep thoroughfare had Nature lodg'd
> The Soul, the Imagination of the whole.

Mist, darkness, lunar illumination, imagination and a blue chasm, a wound in rock, roaring with innumerable watercourses not seen so much as heard; eerie, unfamiliar, 'homeless voices'. Later, in tranquillity, Wordsworth draws from the experience 'The perfect image of a mighty Mind', hidden and yet 'exalted by an underpresence'.

THE MOMENT

We will not venture into divinity at this time; 'everyday transcendence' will do. And we can admit here that there's a degree of fiction in all imaginative reconstructions drawn from traces, tracks and inferences. But the fictional is not the opposite of the factual; that's another threshold crossed and recrossed in cartographies of the invisible.

Even the word 'degree' hints at calculations that cannot be conducted. We are grubbing now among remains, beachcombing fragments from vanished, forgotten, even unknown kingdoms. Each item retrieved is a reminder of our fragility and transience, like children catching snowflakes from a deep night sky. Only as the flakes melt in our hands we melt into the drifts of prehistory towards a time we will never know. But somewhere between 2.5 and 2 million years ago, somewhere either in Africa or in Eurasia or on the wayfared paths being trod by who knows how many hominids, that distinctive wounding moment Wordsworth describes was experienced by one, by several, by many – who can say? There was an accumulating knowledge of landscapes known through their feet. There was an accumulating knowledge of their bodies known through their hands. Feet and hands are both exploratory; pointing and bipedal, visual orientation each gives direction. Something is coming towards them; they are moving towards it. There is sentience and consciousness that they share with many other animals, but there is something more, ahead of them – hidden and invisible in what they see and hear and touch. Desire and curiosity are stirred. There is possibility, as perception exceeds what is sensed, groping towards what is unsensed yet felt. And there is time, in walking, for the mind to deeply wander. Wandering becomes wondering and a prickling along the skin, a flutter in the stomach, accompanies wonder, as it accompanies awe and fear. Neural advancements deep in the prefrontal cortex, the parietal, occipital and temporal lobes, and the cerebellum have opened a gap, a blue chasm, in consciousness. On the far side of that gap is 'everyday transcendence', concept formation, self-consciousness, agency, even articulation. They are not there yet and there is no 'light switch' illumination. It may take another hundred thousand years or tens of thousands of miles to get there. They pace through their evolution. They live with the sense of the gap that, in the evolution of their brain size, gets wider, deeper. The play in that gap of thousands of liquefying, 'homeless' images hidden in their bodies, in wiring memory paths prior to memory, is haunting. There is a far older yet sensed 'presence'. The 'other' was out there, offering threat or security. It was the unknown and the unavoidable that meant going on or going back. These ancient hominids inherited this from their animal predecessors. In recognizing it as such they would never again look at each other, or the world, in the same way. As in my own moment on that Norfolk night, they stare at something that they cannot see – a black hole opened in consciousness itself. And they are drawn towards it.

Wandering becomes wondering as the imagination opens landscapes for us, in us, to us and into the unknown.

II

Palaeolithic Horizons

et's try and recover that decisive 'moment' again and take the next steps in the development of the human imagination.

The black hole of the inconceivable, the depthlessness of the unpresentable, installs a question, and imagination *as* consciousness *within* consciousness unfolds. It unfolds in a space of the uncertain where a bush might be a bear and an unfamiliar mushroom food, ecstasy or death. It unfolds prior to that plunge into the inconceivable where all the senses are taut-tight and frozen. Something stirs: a need like hunger or thirst, not a desire; for this is as basic as biology. It is a need to understand that roots curiosity in visceral turbulence and heartbeat; where to resolve an issue and understand brings relief; and relief is pleasure. Imagination flowers in something registered, something communicated. But what is communicated in this non-verbalized and primordial address percolating strongly to the surface in the singularity of some encounter?

In the West, in the wake of the subject, we might say 'Me?' – in the accusative. I am addressed. I didn't conceive of this myself. It comes from outside and is conceived in encounter – like an electron that only exists when it collides and initiates a quantum event. I am encountered. The address comes from what is other *as* other in my experience of the environment. The cosmos discloses something of itself; so perhaps 'to me?' in the dative might be better. It is not 'I', though I have been forced to use that pronoun grammatically. 'I' already assumes a centre, a standpoint, a memory not swallowed up in the immediate, a focus of control and agency – and I'm very far from such certainties here. Recall: the Venus with the Horn in that rock shelter deep in the Dordogne. She has no face and no attempt is made at creating a face. In the stunning cave art that has survived, animals *do* have faces, expressive faces: aggressive rhinos (Chauvet, France); bison in their death throes (Niaux, France), gentle grazing reindeer (Font-de-Gaume, France), sly, sleepy horses (Cosquer, France). Elsewhere there are lions, cave bears, owls and occasionally a fish. In part, we identify their species, even their sex, by these faces. But few depictions of a human being have a face that is recognizable as such. Where humans are depicted they are stick-like, walking winter trees with bare, black limbs or bulbous feminine forms with pendulous breasts and luxurious thighs. When the earliest of our kind stared on a sunlit day or a moonlit night into the stillness of a lake or pond, what they saw in their reflection was not an 'I'. They did not experience themselves as 'I'. The carved and painted faces of the animals stare back and ask the one who paints and carves, 'what are you?' As King Lear came to understand when gazing upon 'Poor Tom', human beings are fundamentally 'unaccommodated'. At first, these hominids probably saw nothing at all. Terror cannot see; it feels and freezes.

The feeling of horror brings the self to a certain realization of itself *as* other. This is Nan Shepherd, Scottish novelist and mountaineer, encountering the primitive and unimaginable while walking with a companion one summer in the Cairngorms to Loch Etchachan. This is a corrie lake thousands of feet above sea level, a narrow loch that 'has never, I believe, been sounded. I know its depth, but not in feet':

We waded on into the brightness, and the width of the water increased, as it always does when one is on or in it [...] Then I looked down; and at my feet there open a gulf of brightness so profound that the mind stopped. We were standing on the edge of a shelf that ran some yards into the loch before plunging down to the pit that is the true bottom. And through that inordinate clearness we saw. So limpid was it that every stone was clear [...] I waded slowly back into shallower water. There was nothing that seemed worth saying. My spirit was as naked as my body. It was one of the most defenceless moments of my life [...]

That first glance down had shocked me to a heightened power of myself, in which even fear became a rare exhilaration: not that it ceased to be fear, but fear itself, so impersonal, so keenly apprehended, enlarged rather than constricted the spirit.

I don't think the fact there is a companion and Shepherd uses 'we' is insignificant. There being another person does not prevent her from experiencing a profound vulnerability, a profound alienation that immediately isolates. From 'we looked into each other's eyes' we plunge into an intensely personal recognition that 'My spirit was as naked as my body.' What is real, that which is itself apart from human consciousness and nakedly there, simply imposes itself on her alone. The external is *made* external and sharply, even dangerously, distinct. But its appearance as external liberates 'a heightened power of myself' rather than constricts. The liberation itself is an after-reflection in Wordsworthian 'tranquillity'. At the time of encounter it is ineffable, a 'gulf of brightness' that exposes itself. So, perhaps, the most fundamental avowal the awakening of the imagination installs is 'alive' or 'living'; Shepherd's 'my life'.

Wordsworth saw his 'blue chasm' at a 'distance', but on the edge of a traumatic chasm – and the first experiences of mind as mind must have been traumatic to early hominids because it was disruptively alien – on the edge of overwhelming threat and the appalling possibility of annihilation, what is foremost is 'alive' or 'living', 'defenceless'. Without this experience and what is imagined in and through the experience of the more abstract 'life' cannot be grasped. But with this 'living' comes the equal awareness of the intractability of not being there at all, death, extinction. Without that 'alive' there can be no burials, no respect for *Leibe* (the living body) and no rituals (however meagre) accompanying and commemorating such respect. Living poses itself as an elemental question. And it *is* a question. It is not at all self-evident what life is, because life as life cannot be thought in its immediate appearance. The mind is frozen, for what is encountered is more primordial than thought. With it comes a dynamic physical and psychical awakening recollected in tranquillity.

All this experience predates, and makes possible, that astonishing cultural explosion that marks some important and yet-to-be-explained watershed in human becoming (between 40,000 and 50,000 years ago), when the Middle became the Upper Palaeolithic.

BLOMBOS

To follow this idea up I am driving down the famous Garden Route in the Western Cape (N2), South Africa, and into the remote past. It's early spring and after going over the Sir Lowry Pass, I descend into rich farmland, rolling in green acres of winter wheat following the rains. The land teems with sheep, cattle, olive groves and vineyards, and the air carries the astringent scents of fynbos, wild thyme and eucalyptus. At a turn in the small town of Riversdale, I head for the Indian Ocean and a wide bay that, in August 1486, offered much-needed shelter to Bartolomeu Dias venturing to find a passage to India by circumnavigating the Cape of Good Hope. Sailing, in winter, through the Roaring Forties and the tidal currents where the Atlantic meets the Indian Ocean, the whole enterprise would have been lost without this bay. But our destination is further back in a time that Dias and European culture had no conception of until the twentieth century. Just off the Garden Route is the Blombos National Park, and there are caves on the coast here in which the oldest-known human artefacts were discovered. They date back 70,000 years or so, but the caves, now on a raised beach at the retreat of the last ice age, were occupied much, much earlier.

Prehistoric archaeology is finding South Africa an important place as the cradle of civilizations. A museum of that name in Johannesburg displays early findings of hominid culture, including the skull of *Australopithecus africanus* that came to light in 1924. So much palaeoanthropology has focused on the before and after of the 'out of Africa' event. But down here are the hominid species that did not leave Africa. They colonized it. Down here the archaeologists not only talk of the australopithecine findings, but also of the paranthropus discoveries – *Paranthropus robustus* and *Paranthropus boisei*. Each species offers a fine-grained step towards *Homo sapiens*. And the DNA is genetically more diverse and probably older than anywhere else. It's *Homo sapiens* whose artefacts were unearthed at Blombos, and Blombos is only one of five important archaeological sites at the southern tip of Africa. At a site further along the coast towards Port Elizabeth, Klasies River Main Site, the oldest remains of an anatomically modern human (possibly predating fossils found in Israel) lead some to postulate that the human genome was spawned in this southern part of the African continent. We all may have come from round here.

So what happened in the development of the imagination of hominid species as they travelled down the Great Rift Valley running from northern Jordan down to Mozambique? Paleoanthropologists working in South Africa made public in September 2015 what may be the answer, or an important missing link between the australopithecines and *Homo erectus* as evidenced in the Turkana Boy (1.6 mya) uncovered in Kenya. They unveiled the discovery of *Homo naledi*. And this could be the most important unearthing since Lucy.

Naledi was discovered along with hundreds, maybe thousands, of other fossilized skeletons embedded in the poetic Dinaledi Chambers ('The Chamber of Stars'). In fact, the number of remains and its remote, difficult-to-access location suggest a ritual burial place. If this is so (and there is as much speculation as there is doubt), it would be the oldest burial site in the world. The brain of *Homo naledi* is small and the hand less developed than ours, with its fingers curved for climbing. Its toes are also curved. The body is slight and the shoulders ape-like. Dating becomes vital to see where it might be placed in the evolutionary tree. The first suggestion was around two million years ago, but by August 2016 it was being advanced that the fossils were 912,000 years old, though the genus is older (perhaps two million years old). All these datings are being made on the basis of comparisons with the remains of *Homo erectus*, but currently five different dating techniques are being employed in seven different laboratories around the world to gain greater accuracy.

Descending towards Still Bay, still on the Garden Route, the Indian Ocean appears, but I turn off towards another, smaller coastal town called Jongensfontein. The turn to Blombos is easily unnoticed. It's a wide dirt track to the right. And when noticed, and taken, it's best to have a four-wheel drive. There are ten kilometres to travel on this track through a sand-swept scrub of aloes, ericas and cycads (one of the oldest plants on the planet). The soil is rich red loam – the colour of blood when it rains. Bright red cardinals and bright yellow sunbirds flit from side to side. Once, before the major ice age around 100,000 years ago, this was lush tropical forest stretching from a much more distant coastline, but it is home still to buffalo, eland and bushpig. Today the terrain is dry scrub with stunted trees, richly colourful. But it's the past we are in pursuit of.

The track down to the cave, and it is little more, is even easier to miss: a house just before it, its occupants named, a gate informing you this land is private, wends it way down through the De Hoop Natural Reserve to the coast. It's on foot for a further four kilometres from here. The excavation is still ongoing and unwanted traipsing through a delicate site could bring untold damage and contamination to what is not on the surface. They're digging now to a time before the last major ice age and the very earliest *Homo sapiens* who occupied the site. The path winds through a gully to a ragged shoreline with scraggy sand patches. The remnants of mollusca and crustaceans, millions of years older that anything mammal, litter the place, while waves of copper-green and pewter-grey batter the rocks.

The cave is a mouth in a sightless cliff face staring west across the ocean. From the outside it is a low rock shelter, nothing more, inaccessible except by an extended metal ladder. It's not the impressive series of connected caverns and crystal architraves of Cango, further inland. But it opens up to prehistory inside. Around here it's the only limited protection not hostile to settled life, and not at all like the beaches flocked to down the coast towards Mossel Bay. And this would not be easy living even with the abundance of food, fish and chamois in its vicinity. Life is uncompromising here. Sheltered from the high sun and the penetrating rain, the rock-slit is still prey to the wail of the wind from the south and the west, remorseless oceanic spume and thick sea mist. The continual susurrus of the waves would make hearing the approach of a threat difficult – although, as I said, in the past it was further inland. At present, even on a calm day, breakers two metres high crash below. When the sun sank into the ocean before them, fire would have been necessary, more for protection that light. The beauty is austere: rutted slabs of rock washed orange with ochre and, at night, stars as numerous as the scattered mother-of-pearl oyster and abalone shells creating an incandescent sea, unapproachably remote in the abyssal dark.

Why are we here? Because beyond all the exactitudes of staying alive in this place, time was found for the formation of a cultural life. Imagination becomes a conscious activity; but to take a tangible form, time in the day needs to be found, and the activity or its products commonly regarded as valuable, invaluable. Cultural activity that is somehow essential requires a division of labour. We are here picking up traces in order to explore the way the primitive imagination, operating unseen in the embryonic mind and walking the invisible, took visible form. It is the appearance of imaginative form that interests us in this place, among a people who have left Acheulean tool production far in the past. When the minds of human beings were awakened to a different form of consciousness that separated them from their animal forebears what did they imagine, and why? That is our question. And it is important because in our biologies we still dream the remnants and revenants of their dreams, and their nightmares.

In the vast antiquity of hominid development and differentiation, we can say nothing of the imaginations of early predecessors for nothing of their cultural life remains beyond the firepits and the tools. Only with Neanderthals and early modern human beings is it possible to probe their inner life. And it was dominated by black and red. But the firepits and the tools tell us something – something that is fundamental to we who, throughout modernity, have attempted to separate nature from culture. There was no such distinction, and where the attempt is made to distil the purity of one from the other, the mechanic from the organic, it is the mark of a disturbing barbarism.

The weather may split and wash away granite and gneiss, the wind may gather sand and snow into undulating cones, the sea may swamp the land with salt deposits – but plant life and animal life, in fact all forms of organic life, cultivate. And in cultivating they change the elemental. The exchanges between sea, rock, sun, wind and rain began when our magma planet began to cool 4.567 billion years ago, and we who overhear those exchanges today are fine when all is temperate and terrified when they are torrid. These exchanges eclipse all our conversations about national identity and financial stability. While we might understand the grammar, the laws, of these exchanges, we simply deal, as all animal life deals, with the effects of their rhetorical performance. It is in our dealings that we cultivate and become cultivated. We cultivate as a way of clinging on to life.

The implicit cultures of firepits and tools arose in intimate association with the natural. They were responses to the natural, forced out of the natural by the natural. Firepits and tools are expressions of the biological need to survive – in climates not conducive to hominid sensibilities, in their basic craving for meat to feed their expanding brains and their bipedal anatomies, in a need to thwart the ravenous, predatory dangers that beset them. Nature demanded their cultural development; and in its development hominids and humans changed the nature that produced them. Even when we come to examine pierced teeth and shells and body art, we have to look at decoration and what archaeologists call 'jewellery' differently. Decoration was no leisure pursuit; there were no hours to idle away.

Archaeologists working in the Blombos cave have described it as a 'paint factory' on discovering two abalone shells, bones and stones that they believe formed a 'toolkit' for the production of ochre compounds. Again, their frame for thinking is 'technological'; whereas I prefer 'poetic'. But such compounds were basic, along with charcoal and, later, manganese for the pigments with which they daubed their bodies and the cave walls. The minerals were ground and mixed with animal fats; and ochre can be used as an adhesive paste in such a state. If this 'paint' is right then people down here were involved in symbolic expression 100,000 years ago. The shells date to around 100,000 years – much older than the most ancient piece of decoration found also at Blombos: a piece of incised ochre, dating around 70,000 years ago. There were several collectives of *Homo sapiens* in the area, but the ochre is plentiful here. I pick a polished piece from the beach, washed over aeons by tidal activity. If this was a production site, then was there trading between the collectives? As I have pointed out, there are several early human sites along this coast. Much, much later, in Solutrean deposits (based on distinctive leaf-shaped stone points dating between 27,000 and 17,000 years old) found in the cave of Le Placard (France), a quantity of stone tools were discovered that suggested there was a specialized plant established there for their production.

There are no cave paintings at Blombos. The earliest such paintings so far are thought to be the miniature buffalos and pigs discovered on the wall of a cave in Sulawesi, an island of the east coast of Borneo (dating to over 40,000 years old) and the work in the El Castillo cave in central Cantabria, Spain (dated to 40,800 years old, and raising the question of whether they were executed by Neanderthals). At both sites the most prevalent art form is the stencilled printing of hands. We will return to this.

The incised piece of ochre discovered in the cave I am visiting in Blombos depicts an abstract design. Thirty thousand years later such designs, expressive of degrees of conceptual abstraction, are found evident in many other caves and notched on bone fragments: dots, lines, arcs and grids. We have no idea what they mean, only that they mean – something. And this is where the creative imaginations of the archaeologists themselves are fired. But we are not entering these imaginations. We are staying with the primitive and the early emergence of the symbolic – with imaginative creativity prior (from all the evidence we have) to the image-making. And to get there we have to travel a long way back before Blombos – to sentience itself.

THE ART OF EMBODIMENT

In the closing pages of Marcel Proust's *Time Regained*, the novelist reflects upon the writing of his multi-volume novel and the nature of the imagination. Our senses falsify the world and that's why the memory of impressions can deepen, illuminate and transform our understanding. There is then deviance in all perception, and imagination works its magic as it plays with that deviance. But both this deviance and this play demonstrate that 'for the creation of a work of literature, imagination and sensibility are interchangeable qualities'.

Imagination and sentience are not interchangeable, but there is certainly a close association and the quality of one affects the quality of the other. Attention to sensibility seals every suture between animality and humanity. In the light shed by molecular biology we are understanding the evolution of sensing and its relationship to movement and locomotion. From sensing we arrive at the development of nervous systems, brains and sentience. Intelligence may not be some fluke of evolutionary fate. It might be 'more-or-less inevitable, an emergent property that is wired into the biosphere' (Simon Conway Morris). From our sensing the outside is brought inside through electronic signalling, and this signalling is the basis for our perceptual processes, the nervous system that transmits them and consciousness of being alive.

This relationship between sensing and cognition erases some of the lines that neatly divide hominids and humans from our animal heritage. So Nan Shepherd's experience before the chasm might have analogues in animal sensibilities. Working in the Gombe National Park, Tanzania, the primatologist Jane Goodall observed this remarkable phenomenon:

> In the Kakombe valley is a magnificent waterfall. There is a great roar as the water cascades down through the soft green air from the stream bed above. Over countless aeons the water has worn a perpendicular groove in the sheer rock. Ferns move ceaseless in the wind created by the falling water, and vines hang down on either side. For me it is a magical place, and a spiritual one. And sometimes, as they approach, the chimpanzees display in slow, rhythmic motion along the river-bed. They pick up and throw great rocks and branches. They leap to seize the hanging vines, and swing out over the stream in the spray-drenched wind until it seems the slender stems must snap or be torn from their lofty moorings.
>
> For ten minutes or more they may perform this magnificent 'dance'. Why? Is it not possible that the chimpanzees are responding to some feeling like awe? A feeling generated by the mystery of the water.

Chimpanzees hate getting their feet wet. In an interview Goodall comments: 'It's like wonder. And then they perform a wild "dance". These performances really are like a kind of primitive dance, because they are very rhythmic, very different from normal display.' The display, she records, is performed again in the first great drops before a downpour. Other primatologists have noted similar behaviour in response to rain (de Waal), wind (Bekoff), wildfire (Pruetz and LaDuke) and earthquakes (Harrod). Some, like Goodall herself, raise the question of 'animal religion' and employ 'ritual' to describe such displays. What is significant is the compulsion behind this creative response; the natural compulsion towards cultural expression.

Sensorimotor response becomes animated dance; the impromptu becomes a learned, instinctive form of affective experience. If this is not 'religious' in its tone or formality (and the verdict is still out on this), then it does show something that might be called piety. And 'piety is wisdom', according to the Book of Job. The embodied processing and creative work of the imagination stimulates a fluidity between the unconscious, preconscious and conscious through images laden with feelings, memory fragments, metaphors and analogies. This is its plastic nature – from which the reaching beyond oneself into the world and the making sense in and through that reaching beyond takes place. It *makes sense* of sentience in and through a spectrum of mental states, rooted in the daily physiological fluxes (energy levels, and changes in endocrinal, digestive, respiratory, immune and pulmonary systems). Not that these mental states are determined by our physiological conditions in a logic of cause and effect. The causality is circular, with mental states also triggering the physiological condition. The work of the imagination can change the way we feel about ourselves – it can deepen sickness and foster health! We can add another level here.

ONE STEP FURTHER

In Chapter I, I drew attention to feet as the means through which the world is continually being sensed and the sense of touch that informs memory and fosters imaginative intelligence. With Goodall's observation of primate responses to the elemental we return to feet in a remarkably new way. Dance is the registration of that sensing that takes on emotional colouring and kinetic response to that connectedness with the land. I've already mentioned the Giraffe Dance of the San people, but dance also bonds. Goodall doesn't mention (though it is implied) that the chimpanzee display is a *shared* emotional response. Though perhaps beginning with one animal this response infects others in the group – as one baby crying in a maternity ward sets all the other babies crying. This embodied emotion then reinforces a communal connectedness with everything and everyone around it. The environment becomes *inhabited* through this.

From the biological world the cultural world emerges; and dance as intentional, compelled movement is a crossing and recrossing between the natural and the cultural. It can also be a profoundly imaginative state prior to symbolic representation as such. It's a psychosomatic activity relating empathy to a dancer's 'feeling for' and an observer's 'feeling of' movement. It is often noted that the depictions of the animals in parietal art and cave painting mimic movement, even specific animal behaviours. But what is taking place in this studied understanding of the physical movements and actions of animals in early human creative artwork? What is the imagination enabling here – not as decoration, but actually something much more primordial and powerful? At one level we might suggest an empathetic entering into the minds, bodies and emotions of the animals being hunted. But the chimpanzees of Gomba display a prior empathy – with the environment as such. The pulsing plunge of water falling, registered as noise and rhythm and spectacle, is entered into and imitated among them as noise and rhythm and spectacle. There is an imaginative 'feeling for' and 'reaching for' movement that can subsequently develop into and become dance. Such dancing, however crude, enacts, and in enacting reinforces a bond between emotion and muscle memory, relating both to landscapes. Dancing is an essential experience. The body attunes itself to three-dimensional space binding one to the other. It generates incorporation and togetherness. Expressing shared emotional exuberance, it locks the human into the animal world, and both into the physical, weathered environment.

Early cave artists capture the bonding observed among Goodall's primates. What is called the 'Chinese Horse' at Lascaux has been caught with its tail raised in flight, javelins sticking out from its sides, shitting with fear. Such forms of mimetic binding exercise empathetic resonance, materially and imaginatively. I have more to say about resonance later. As we move, we make 'real *the vast matrix of living tissue that enables it*' (Kimerer LaMothe).

The first imaginative and embodied art seems to have been architecture: the turning of caves and rock shelters into habitats; turning rock into an outer protective skin. There is some evidence of organized living space among hominids. Hearth positioning and discrete dumping areas for empty shells point to what archaeologists call 'spatial patterning'. But dance may have been the second imaginative art, accompanied by music. We have at least one example of an early flute that may, indeed, be Neanderthal in origin, and animal skin stretched over animal bone to form drums. I'm introducing a possible Neanderthal connection here because we know their ancestor was *Homo erectus*, coming out of Africa on the first exodus around two million years ago. The cultural explosion and interest in the major cultural irruption of symbolic behaviour evidenced between 40,000 and 50,000 years ago, lends weight to a story of *Homo sapiens* triumphalism and uniqueness; an old story with its roots in Renaissance humanism. But the cavorting chimpanzees at Gomba raise questions about such cultural interruptions of *Homo sapiens* origin. Corporeal consciousness, imaginative activity and symbolic expression are not at all just characteristics of anatomically modern humans.

If architecture was the first imaginative art and musical dance the second, then these must have been followed closely by another art also profoundly related to embodiment. We have examples of polished shell, teeth, bone and beads crafted from stalactites and obsidian, all pierced for wearing around the neck. They may have carried social significance and been markers of distinction or caste. They certainly accrued symbolic significance. But probably one of the earliest of these arts was body painting. The pieces of ochre found on the floors of caves and shelters occupied by Neanderthals suggest body art was practised even though nothing survives of its character or its use. Camouflage for hunting suggests itself, or even body painting that allowed the wearer to enter the mind and flesh of the animal he or she was pursuing. But the attention to embodiment evident in later imaginative creations perhaps indicates something more.

The hominid body and its evolved sexual dimorphism reduced its covering of hair, and must have revealed new contours and tones of flesh – muscles, breasts, bellies, gonads, the face and eyes. The later geometric markings and the lush curves we find in cave paintings (or incised on ochre or bone) may well have begun as markings upon hominid and human bodies, accentuating these contours and tones. If so, it points to a deepening appreciation of being embodied, and embodied in a distinctive way to other animals. The sensuous and sensual scripting, smearing and fluting of flesh by flesh on flesh, primes a multitude of emotional responses, making the body and its different parts bearers of cultural, imagined and affective values.

We carry our culture in the way we move, so that prewired embodiment primes emotions that compel symbolic activity. Imagination originates then in the body's openness to the world and its movements within it. Body art both requires, heightens and stimulates certain body comportments as the Maori *moko* tattoos on the All Blacks, along with their Aboriginal 'Haka' war dance, dramatizes aggression and primes endocrinal changes. New Zealand legend tells of *ta moko* being crafted in the underworld (Uetonga) by the parents of a princess of that world, Niwareka. She had been married to a warrior who abused her trust and love, and sent her back to the underworld. In deepest regret he sets off to find her and enters the caverns of the underworld only to be ridiculed by her relatives for his appearance. Following his heartfelt apology and before returning him and his wife to the world above, the king of the underworld teaches the warrior the art of *ta moko*. It was an imaginative practice born in caves in the war for survival.

CARNALITY

This attention to what I would call flesh – the body as it is affected by contact and sensibility in, through and beyond form – is evident in the Palaeolithic imagination in several ways. Take those stencils, for example, when ochre-based paint is either blown over the hand and pressed onto the walls of the cave or daubed directly onto a hand that is then pressed on to the walls. It is has been observed recently that many of these hands are female and possibly the marks of the female artists who created the etchings and paintings. And there are even the hands of children among these stencils, suggesting play. Animals love to play. It is something universal in our evolution. And these hand stencils are found in caves located around the globe – Europe, South America, Borneo. What is prominent is the tactile; the touch of stone surfaces is expressive of connection. For Aristotle touch was the primordial sense;

the sense common to all sensing. Usually there are several handprints together, like the crowded scene found in Cueva de las Manos in Santa Cruz, Argentina. There are communities here relating directly to land; the fertility of women in the exaggerated forms of bas-relief and portable art; and the red resin of ochre mixed with water reaching into or out of rock intimating blood lines, menstrual flows and the porous, malleable nature of surfaces. We should never forget that these prints are found deep in the inner workings of caves, rock wombs in the bowels and intestines of the earth. Their production in the shadowed interiority adds a further dimension to the tender sensitivities of touch. There is an immediacy here of elemental presence, the exposed, open palms of human creatures on rock panels and buttresses, and what the American poet Robinson Jeffers describes as 'the mysticism of stone'. The earth, and its intimate connection with all things, is a form of flesh. One form of flesh lives with and alongside another; one living through and upon the other. Primal. Utterly fundamental – from the Latin *fundus*, a farm, a piece of land.

When we examine some of the animals depicted, this same focus upon flesh is evident. Horns and legs are suggested but not detailed. They are often left unfinished and shortened, tapering off into the surface of the wall in stylized ways. It is the roundedness of the body and the heaviness of the head of a bison, a horse or an antelope that is captured and accentuated. The elegant lines, painted or etched, generate mood and capture movement. These bodies display a vitality and dynamic impulse that the shadows cast by spitting torchlight down draughty tunnels would have animated further. Archaeologists like André Leroi-Gourhan have attempted to trace the stylistic development of cave art towards photographic realism and lifelike attitudes. I'm not sure about this. What it more evident in these horses with their arched necks and these muscular bison is a profound sensuality. The same sensuality is found in the bellies and breasts of the carved and modelled women.

The earliest Palaeolithic art (Aurigancian – from around 40,000 years ago) reveals the association between imagination and fear generated by the All Blacks' appearance on the rugby field and their dance. Imagination is deeply rooted in our emotional life as it emerges from and impacts upon biological and physiological processes. So fear is important (along with joy it is one of the most researched affects). The attention to the work of fear renders more complex the relationship I proposed in Chapter I between imagination and wonder. Fear and wonder are not antithetical states; awe and dread are more on a spectrum of affect that moves between degrees of one and degrees of another according to context and culture. The wonder I experienced on that Norfolk night in summer when staring up into a black hole was, in part, an affect evoked by an unfamiliarity with the term itself. Neither a metaphor nor an oxymoron, nevertheless 'black hole' was imaginatively suggestive and when pinpointed to a specific location in the deep space above us brought about a dilation in experience that made me a speck of insignificance in a vast cosmography. The wonder registered by any number of cosmologists exploring the birth and formation of stars in distant galaxies (an estimated 300 billion of them) must have a similar effect. But the experience of awe in such astonishing encounters is related in aesthetics to the sublime. In earlier ages some registered this overwhelming as dread; most famously, the seventeenth-century French mathematician and philosopher Blaise Pascal. Staring up into the sky at night he is 'engulfed in the infinite immensity of spaces of which I am ignorant, and which know me not, I am frightened, and am astonished at being here rather than there; for there is no reason why here rather than there, why now rather than then [...] The eternal silence of these infinite spaces frightens me'. There is an intimate relationship between imagination and fear. The 'I' shrivels and can be engulfed by the pleated abyss of nothingness and infinity.

But the imagination can also be invoked by the fearful. The sun drops rapidly beneath the horizon outside the sea-fluted echoes in the Blombos cave. In the twilight, distance opens a vacuum in which the seagulls fall silent. Only the rock rabbits scurry and forage among the rocks. I will have to leave soon or I will be threading my way up the overgrown path to the car in darkness. The wind turns chill and the shadows thicken. What is feared takes on many phantom forms as imagination plays with sounds and rock shapes, a rustle in the fynbos undergrowth, a spool of sand falling from the cliff face above and behind. In the earliest Palaeolithic cave art the animals most often depicted are predatory, dangerous species like lions, rhinos and bears.

In the cave at Chauvet there are the gouges made by bear claws on one of the walls. Millennia later, by around 20,000 years ago, that changes. The animals represented then are horses, aurochs and bison. And, as the weather begins to improve, deer and ibex predominate.

There might also have been another predator; there are some suggested cases of cannibalism among Neanderthals and anatomically modern humans. One of the unmistakable fears felt as twilight deepens at Blombos is being attacked and killed by one of my fellow creatures. Perhaps this is the culture and context that has shaped my own imagination – the urban legends of the stalker and psychopath activated in the middle of a rural nowhere. Imagination inflames and exaggerates possibilities as the endocrinal system engages with the environment and adrenaline rises. Fear and sexual desire feed further imaginative hungers. The bowels stir. Imagination, *memoria* and the stomach are inextricably related in the thought of St Augustine – as we shall see.

The inhabitants of these rock shelters and caves were much closer to the earth than we are. Their bodies, their memories, their imaginative acts, and the cultures expressing them, were each shaped by the climate as it gave (warm, lush savannahs) and took away (permafrost tundra and incendiary deserts). I am bird and frog, mollusc and mammoth, dolphin and lion – they live in me as evolved DNA and I in them. But early human beings knew and lived that association more intimately. These peoples did not have histories of civilizations that exalted the human above the animal; they did not have the hubris of believing they were a special, even chosen, species. At every moment their superiority was threatened, their vulnerability exposed, and their hopes and desires compromised by austerity. They experienced futures torn open with every turning by the unexpected, and therefore levels of anxiety and fear unknown from the Neolithic settlements onwards; except in warfare. Little could be taken for granted; their security was vestigial: the unknown pressed in on every side. What they struggled to express in their imaginative work was their place in such a world, what this world was and who they might be. The world was not the same for them. There were many dimensions to that one world.

TRANSCORPOREALITY

Entry into the Palaeolithic cave, for the South African rock art specialist David Lewis-Williams, is to become an explorer of the inner reaches of the human mind. Investigations in the cognitive and neurological sciences into altered consciousness interpret what he finds. Caves in their tight, claustrophobic passages, expansive galleries and steep verticalities, mimic the shaman's journey into other worlds. These worlds were three-tiered — heaven, terrestrial life, underworld — and the animals depicted were spirits appearing to the shaman through the membrane of the cave walls. But this is a journey into disembodiment; a spirit world transcending of the corporeal.

Certainly, what we experience in caves distorts sensory perception: the cold can be intense; the smell of damp, old earth is sometimes so strong you can taste it; water surges and drips unseen while shuffling along echoes; the rock is often porous to touch or slippery; and shadows open and close space in a way that disorientates balance. And some of these caves are very long indeed. In La Cullalvera in Spain the paintings and engravings are over one kilometre from the entrance; Niaux in France is 1.3 kilometres in length with a further 600 metres of lateral galleries. Only human beings and bears tunnelled this far into caves; bears using urine to track their way through the darkness so as not to lose their way. Consciousness, even over short distances, is altered and imagination becomes excited by such alterations.

Werner Herzog, the German film director, explores this entry into the cave of forgotten dreams and the journey into the subconscious. But he describes a journey towards a place where the 'I' is absent. Filming a research team given special access to the sealed vaults of Chauvet, his camera plays with the natural bridge of the Pont d'Arc carved by the Ardèche River, tracking through it one way and then another. The Pont d'Arc is a natural door from one world into another, comparable to those Inuit sculptures of windows formed from compacted snow or lintels and thresholds of smoothed boulders that face out, in either direction, upon Arctic skies of cerulean blue. The world passed into or out of is not a spirit world, but another dimension of this one. The cinematic imagination, rather that psychoanalysis or cognitive science, dictates his approach. His films had already explored the pleated realities of nineteenth-century Peru (in *Fitzcarraldo*), the Inca empire of the sixteenth century (in *Aguirre: The Wrath of God*), and the gothic fogs of the Carpathian Mountains (in *Nosferatu: Phantom der Nacht*). Herzog's *Cave of Forgotten Dreams* uses the caves to explore the imagination as it subtends film-making; the place from which cinematic myth-making emerges. It recalls film to its very roots – as an entrance into the cultural subconscious. True film-making, it suggests, offers us a seat in the planetarium of our vast and deep collective minds.

But while Lewis-Williams is insightful as he leads us through the spectrum from wakeful consciousness to daydream, hypnogogic states and hallucinogenic dreaming as we pass through the caverns and galleries of Lascaux; and while Herzog conjures for us the nightmarish beauties that lie beneath the forensic examination of surfaces that have digitalized the inner spaces of Chauvet, probing the depths of film-making itself; I prefer to see the caves more materially as stomachs, and our entry into them as being devoured. The Old English *wamb* is stomach, belly, bowels, heart and womb. I view the Palaeolithic caves and rock shelters as mountainous *wambs*. To enter them is to enter the entrails of sedimentary stone; calcite intestines. Their existence, their exploration, their occupation and their decoration is profoundly feminine and reproductive. In some images one animal is inserted into another – a mammoth overlays a bison, a woman overlays a bison. Bodies are entering and interacting with other bodies, emerging from other bodies. This is what I mean by transcorporeality; it describes how the outside is also the inside. The cave mouths are entrances into the dark and secret intimacies of embodiment, eating and excreting, giving birth and dying. Sex isn't a feature and the carvings of women are not erotic. The mountains are mothers – the entrails of the earth. Interviewed on camera in the 1990s (the film is available on YouTube) an Inuit shaman explains to his interviewer: 'All our customs come from life and turn toward life [...] the Great Woman who rules over all the sea mammals [...] Our greatest fear is that the animals we kill for food and clothes have souls like ours. [What we fear is their] revenge against us for using their bodies.' Among the San, no hunter will allow his shadow to fall across a dead prey. This is just an imaginative connection. Students of these creative outpourings in the caves have been warned: contemporary ethnography should not be used to interpret archaeology. But it's suggestive.

Earlier archaeological interpretations often speak floridly of 'sanctuaries', 'chapels', 'apses', 'altars' and 'shrines'. Tylor (1832–1917) and Fraser (1854–1941) were already employing words like 'animism', 'totemism' and 'sympathetic magic' to explain these ancient images and their powerfully affective qualities. But names stick. Even today some caves are called 'sanctuaries' with depicted 'sorcerers' (Les Trois Frères). Certainly, many were never inhabited. Few were domestic dwellings. But 'sanctuaries' is wrong, like speaking of the religion of these ancient peoples is wrong.

This is a highly contentious field of study, not least because of the difficulty in defining both 'myth' and 'religion' and identifying their relationship. Neanderthal burials, older that Palaeolithic art, offer some teasing glimpses into some sort of *cultus*. There have been attempts to construct some Pangaean mythology as the source of a tree of mythologies spanning the world. A mythology going back to around 60,000 years ago and arising from the worldview of those *Homo sapiens* descendants of the 'African Eve' who migrated across the world. But this is contentious, and other scholars dismiss any suggestion there was a development of religion before the Upper Palaeolithic (beginning around 20,000 BCE).

I'm no expert here. I look at the paintings and rock carvings we have and I would accept Andrew Lang's suggestion from 1882 that imaginatively they expressed 'nascent religion' – a set of sensibilities from which religion (beliefs, myths and ritual practice) emerge more clearly at a later date. The link between imagination and this religious propensity will crop up again when we look at mythic sensibility or mythic resonance (Chapter VI). The mythological digs deep into the biological where the instinctive becomes the intuited and intuitive. What we have in Chauvet is evidence of a mythic sensibility that arises where creation meets not just consciousness but carnal and imaginative responsiveness. The kind of responsiveness displayed by those chimpanzees at Gomba or the baboons I can watch from my *stoep* who often sit still for five to ten minutes watching the lake from the water's edge. Mythic sensibility stirs that in-and-below consciousness which is creative, generative and formative as it engages in an environment that is also creative, generative and formative. In this engagement mutuality, sympathy and empathy engender the sense of 'spirit'.

We cannot embroil this cave art in our debated concepts of the holy, the sacred and the profane, just as when we stand before them we have to find ways to divert words like 'art' and 'decoration' from what they mean today. If, putting to one side older views of religion in terms of propositional beliefs and language-based claims, and viewing religions as concerned with wonder as much as evil, then while there is a wonder here in the shape and size of these forms, I'm not sure about evil. Even the wonder is quietly understated and factual; not something rigorously scrutinized in terms of something fascinatingly dreadful. There is awe and inspirational response, but there is no language that can pin this down; rather there is a foraging for a language. And there is something too visceral here to take on *our* language of transcendence; too visceral also to employ words like the 'numinous' that point towards some essential and universal experience of the ultimately real. It is evident in several such places that people came and wedged bits of shell and bone-flakes into the sensual cavities of the cave walls. These are places invested with blood and fire in the pigments of ochre and manganese. They are sites of profound symbolic investment from a time when symbolism was not an abstraction from the corporeal but pertaining to its very quality. Archaeologists have imagined scenes in which rituals took place by torchlight in vast internal rock-bowls shimmering with crystals from lime deposits, or public ceremonies for which the dark mouth of the cave was a backdrop. These may well have taken place, later.

A convincing case can be made for Lascaux as a place of ceremony, with its great Hall of Bulls opening inwards from the cave mouth. This space could house a whole community at that time (fifty or so people); the bulls themselves are only properly seen stampeding when you stand at the centre of the hall. And undoubtedly there is something very strange, even disturbing, about the skull of a cave bear on a rock plinth surrounded by the skulls of many other cave bears, in Chauvet. But what would these people be worshipping, or placating or exorcizing or conjuring?

The paintings are difficult to understand as 'hunt magic' since all the evidence points to the fact these animals were not their source of food. The paintings at Lascaux have been dated to around 18,500 years old. But 18,000 years earlier, at Chauvet, it is not clear that any such sacral ceremonial was intended, despite the bear skull. Such images flicker with the sepia light of nostalgic projections and the deep breathing of carbon monoxide, always possible in these caves, that can bring on hallucinations. There is something hallucinatory about this art. The anthropologist Lévy-Bruhl has characterized what he terms the 'primitive' mental experience of reality as governed by dreaming.

We don't have a language to articulate the experiences of these hominids and early human beings. But because place mattered, because place was material, because rock and bird and fire and bear and being alive as another species mattered (literally), these sites were most profoundly 'home' – they were intensely valued and *that* made them sacred. There were primordial sites of 'dwelling', and they were lived and inhabited imaginatively. They were places where the world was imagined and experienced as imagined; a world where the boundaries between bodies and realities and times flowed into each other. Images on the same cave walls that seem so similar we now know, through sophisticated dating techniques, were made thousands of years apart. What began, in a much earlier time, as an etching of a horse or a bison, would be retouched with paint, and the painting retouched. Images were scratched and painted on top of other images in palimpsests of imaginings. Time was fluid. In his film, Herzog, like a man imprisoned by an inner alienation, interjects: 'we are locked in history and they were not'. Surfaces too are malleable, species and genera mixed and multiple, and yet in some continuum we can only guess at. And Herzog knows: it is the intensity of their silences that challenge us most deeply.

They confront us with the deep power of the imagination – imagining as such. For we cannot get sidetracked by questions of authorial intention or historical background or cultural context. All this has been constructed for them later. That is not what they present. We have to find other frameworks for our response to their work. They present overwhelmingly powerful corporeal forms without any or little sense of their own bodies. Apart from 'Venus with the Horn', the people who painted and sculpted in these caves lacked a body-imaging ability with respect to themselves – as if they were not conscious of or completely forgetful of their own embodiment. Cave art actually seems to offer us an argument *against* human uniqueness. There is little self-consciousness or introspection evident. These early human beings were conscious and imaginatively conscious *of animals*; and frequently animals they *did not* eat. Their world appears to be one in which they sought identification with the animals; the animal to them was more important than what they might be; the animal was their entry into any deeper meaning, any everyday transcendence. If they imitated them in their dancing, if they represented them in their painting, sculpture and portable 'art', it was because they participated in *their* energies, activities and even world views. The works speak then of a certain alienation or distance from the animal communities to which they felt they belonged. They were not contemplating their place in the natural world but rather finding ways to express their wounded difference within it; for difference is evident in the variety of species depicted. The productive work involved in the making of these images also gave them, as likewise the animals they imaged, a sense of agency. But what made this embodied agency distinctive among these other distinctivenesses, and why?

There is that which is 'preconscious' about their work, because the self-consciousness that is so closely associated with body imaging (it is how we think and feel about ourselves) is apparently absent. In terms of arguments for the different operations of the right and left hemispheres of the brain, the people who worked in these caves for over 20,000 years had more developed right and less developed left hemispheres. They were more empathetic than calculative in their cognitive capacities; more emotionally expressive and less instrumental in their logics. Their conception of consciousness was low-levelled, enhancing a more essential embodiment. Note: this doesn't tell us what the cave paintings and sculptures mean, only how *we* can understand the raw experience they convey and be affected by them. They are expressions of something lost to us – the immediacy of the imagination *lived* in and through the body.

The only other framing for our response to these expressions lies in those twists, turns, tunnels, alcoves and grottoes of the caves themselves; the light, shadow and angle in and from which they are perceived;

and their geographical location (river, sea,
paintings and sculptures are as much about the
they are about flesh, predominantly animal t.
sensibilities to which they attest root imagination .
and sensory.

There's something apophatic or ineffable here, and I do.
terms in a theological or mystical sense, but they are not met.   . ne
fact that they are not metaphors is possibly what gives rises to .ligious'
interpretations of these Palaeolithic works. It is not that we are clueless
about what these images portray – a water bird in flight (from Hohle Fels
cave), a swimming reindeer on a mammoth ivory (from Montastruc). But
what remains apophatic or ineffable is that there is an evident speaking,
call, in and through their very presence, and we don't know either what it
is they're saying or how we are to respond. In our surprise at them we are
rendered speechless. The apophasis or ineffable is *our* experience with
respect to them. There's a horse engraved on a rock surface in the open-
air at Foz Côa, in Portugal, in lines as simple and assured as any by
Matisse or Hockney, and, perhaps, these early human forms did *not* eat
horses. There's a gentle, reverent appreciation of the form and body
somehow at odds with the struggle to survive and levels of accustomed
savagery. For the animals they *did* eat would be clubbed to death,
battered apart and stripped of their skins. Here is a work of strong
empathetic imagination. But it emerges from arms that were frequently
elbow-deep in animal viscera, smashed bone and ravaged flesh. These
forms give themselves to be contemplated because that is how they
arose – as contemplations taking form.

So we can recognize *what* these people imagined, and go some way
towards *how* they imagined, but we cannot answer *why* they imagined *in*
these ways. They speak of loss, not of meaning; but the loss is ours as we
stand before them. On the whole the images themselves seem carefree.
No loss there. And they are not wild imaginings – for they compose an
artistic tradition possibly 30,000 years old. But then do *we* know the
meaning of what *we* imagine? Did they? Meaning folds back, beyond and
beneath, into bodies moving in and out of other bodies and the way that
is and was perceived and lived. We observe a meaningfulness that we
cannot comprehend, only look upon and wonder and affirm its

...aspable) meaningfulness. What we appreciate is the artistry of the making and the power of the imagining.

THE HYBRID IMAGINATION

Transcorporeality, and all it is attempting to understand and describe about the profound relations between the human, the animal and the land, reaches a rich imaginative intensity in those images and sculptures in which the animal and human become fused and expressive of profound kinship. These are imaginary beings, monstrous hybrids: a weird and fabulous level of being human that we have least access to. I have mentioned the bird-man of Lascaux, drawn in a shaft dropping fourteen feet below the Hall of Bulls and remote to most. A bovid whose entrails have been torn away is possibly the rhinoceros that has gored him. He's surprised, it seems, for his penis is erect. But perhaps later than this early narrative depiction is the isolated painting of a strange beast in the cave of Les Trois Frères of a man with the upper body of a horse and the antlers of a stag. Maybe the face too is a stag's, but if it is then the stag face is morphing into that of an owl. Shaman, sorcerer, hunter disguised – who knows? It is small (only a metre high), powerful, and dominates a position high above a wall deep into the cave. The ultimate and terrifying last stage in hallucination on a crawl through a tunnel to get there? So Lewis-Williams believes. Then there's the much earlier bison-man, painted around a pendulous stone dropping from the ceiling of the cave at Chauvet whose main figure is the naked loins of a (faceless) woman.

But the most impressive of these melds of human and animal, and by far the oldest, is the sculpture of the 'Lion-Man'. The Lion-Man stands 29.6 cm tall, is 5.6 cm wide and 5.9 cm thick. It is possibly the oldest figurative art ever discovered at 32,000–40,000 years old and was one of the prized and most acclaimed displays at the British Museum's Ice Age Art exhibition in the spring and summer of 2013. The difficulty that is communicated to us as we examine this sculpture from various angles and the pictures of its reconstruction (because it was found in fragments and to date is still not fully pieced together), lies not so much in its antiquity, but in its sheer visceral presence. We have some insight into how it was carved with a flint knife. How it would have taken in excess of 400 hours' labour to fashion. We have created notions of the possible social organization that would enable its creation in a hunter-gatherer community. But none of these details explain its presence *for us, today*: the way it installs the uncanny in its strange, free-standing isolation. Again, adjectives like 'sacred' or 'shamanistic', and nouns like 'talisman', simply open wormholes of suggestion, star gates into unknown universes. Its utter physicality bears us towards a complex otherness that speaks. It is not the otherness of a transcending spiritual realm. It is exactly the opposite. It is the otherness of a deep embodiment of feeling and mind, the wielding of stone, the scrapping of bone and the grappling with what is seen only in the imagination. Whatever is 'holy' here issues from a tight and intimate web of physical relations between the animal (the lion's head, the mammoth's tusk), the mineral (flint handheld tools themselves shaped, discovered in other petrified materials, the rock shelter), the cosmic (the daylight needed to carve the figure, the darkness that housed the figure, the torches that made it appear in the darkness of the cave) and the embodied consciousness. One further difficulty: this metaphor in bone may not be a human creation if the modern human is *Homo sapiens sapiens*. If the more recent C14 dating (never particularly accurate) of 40,000 years holds, then possibly we are looking at a figure carved by an earlier species of *Homo sapiens* settled in the Swabian Alps in Germany (Cro-Magnon), but equally possible is that it is a product of Neanderthal culture. We are 35,000 years away from the jackal-headed Egyptian deity, Anubis; and we have no Rosetta stone that might enable us to access what it is saying.

Interpretation is itself imaginative engagement and, since their discovery, these painted and sculptured caves and rock shelters have generated plenty of imaginative speculation. The speculations say more about modern perceptions than ancient practices and thought processes. The fact there are so few of these figures, along with the fact that so few human forms figure in the paintings and sculpture, is indicative of a perceived difference and distinction. It has been suggested these Palaeolithic artists demonstrate human superiority over the animal hoards – with hands as the figure for this hegemony: the hands that brought these creatures into an order they were imposing upon creation through hunting, butchering, consuming and stripping these animals of all things useful for human survival. I am very far from sure about this, and that was not Herzog's experience when entering the caves either. Perhaps the depictions of docile deer and horse indicate a guilt, a loss of innocence in the very establishment of human ascendency. But I doubt it. The human remains that we have show they lived with painful fractures and ravaging muscular and joint diseases. They lived a very fragile difference from the animals they portrayed. They weren't hunted but they weren't invulnerable either – climate and hunger ruled them as it ruled everything. Perhaps the Lion-Man is a memory of when the distinction and difference was less pronounced; though it is interesting, surprising and suggestive that it is the heads of these shift-shapers that remain animal, not the bodies. The heads are expressive of animal intelligence, animal imaginings. Entertain the penetrating gaze of the owl's eyes in the Sorcerer of Les Trois Frères, and you'll see what I mean.

Their world was one, but not in the way we think of oneness now. André Leroi-Gourhan may be right about detected stylistic stages, but he is wrong to believe the aim was photographic realism. The bloated, yet frequently perfect forms with their foreshortened legs and the twisted perspective of their faces, feet and antlers were not trying to be 'realistic' (whatever that might be). Size varies from enormous bulls to tiny mammoths. There is little if any sense of foreground and background that normally organize objects with respect to the body-centred spatiality of the observer. They dance in friezes across the walls, they float above the ceilings of the caves and, in some places, they were carved into the floors. This is not 'realism', as the levitating people, animals and musical instruments in a Chagall painting is not 'realism' – nor was it ever meant to be. It is not out-of-body mysticism either, or sympathetic magic. These forms are not lodged in a recognizable world. There are no mountains, lakes, rivers or forests that locate them on the land. But there is no conception of transcendence: no skies, no moon, no sun, no stars, no sense of day and night. This is the world devoured, painted often by spraying the pigments, red, black, yellow out of the mouth and on to the walls to be smeared into form with tree bark or leaf. 'Devour' here is not simply what meats these artists ate. The evidence is unclear as to which of the animals depicted were eaten. Fish were surely eaten in quantities as these caves were by fresh water or the sea, though there are very few fish depicted. By 'devour' here I mean internalized, recognized as part of them, as the cave itself was. That meant the dead were never dead, but they lived on in a different way, in a different internalized dimension. And the dead here include the animals as the shaman's comments I cited earlier indicate. The past was never past; and the future was unimaginable. In the present the passage from one body into another was the way things were and remain. As they knew: they ate and clothed themselves through the bodies of the creatures they killed. Either they drew them to give their remembered form material presence. Or drew them that the form might fix them for a kill in a present moment of a future hunt. In these places time and the world were ingested, and it was this that made them sacred, treasured; places of intimate and grave belonging. The caves, to repeat a word I used earlier, are *wambs*.

CONCLUSION

I am not convinced there were other worlds (above or below) for these hominids and early human beings; spiritual, diaphanous worlds with ectoplasmic souls and rock walls as veils. But there were dimensions of this world that they perceived and experienced that we still do know in some sense in dreams and apprehensions. What is apprehended is a deep belonging that arrests all isolation and alienation; a participation. But in what are we participating? What subtends imaginative, precognitive response? We may never be able to answer those questions, but that is why these paintings, etchings and sculptures retain a power over us that is more than just aesthetic. The experience is much too raw – images torn from the unknown, carved and daubed and scratched in semi-darkness for a past, and of a past, we can't retrieve. And yet we have perhaps similar experiences – invoked when a distant bell stirs on a still evening, as moonlight falls on a stretch of snow edging distant hills, and we are awoken in the early hours by the cry of what might be a fox, or an owl, or a wildcat, or a baby. And then imagination flares as intelligence seeks to grasp what is occurring and why the impact of that occurrence is so startling. It flares in an interstice between sentience and sense evoking cognition prior to anything being cognized. It is not an operation under our control and neither are the resonant worlds it conjures. The I, ego, self, person arrives much later.

When we are facing the creations of Palaeolithic people the question they seem to raise to the surface is: 'This is a ... ', 'That is a ... ', but what am I through whom these figures pass and come to have form distinct from their actual presence outside the cave? I am reminded of the story early in the Book of Genesis where all the animals assemble before Adam to be named, but among them none is found like himself. There's an acceptance, a recognition, a disappointment, and then Yahweh, his Creator, draws him into a deep sleep and a deep dreaming. We are never told whether he awakes, only that from his body Eve is formed; and he knows himself differently. There may well have been men – later – with birds on sticks (Lascaux) and a hypersensitivity that gave them command over something they all experienced as a profoundly textured belonging. But all we have been exploring is prior to institutions, their powers, dominions and authorities. It is prior to the organization and disciplining of knowledges and fears. And it points to an aspect of the imagination that nothing can subjugate – its freedom. It is not an untrammelled freedom. It is pliable and weaves according to cultures, circumstances, languages and personalities – but it nevertheless remains unpredictably alive.

Herzog's intuition is right – this Palaeolithic imagining is the stuff of cinema and cinematography, because it's the stuff of dreams. It's what directors see and cameramen shape: the closing sequence of *Dr Caligari's Cabinet* (1920), as Friedrich, who has been investigating the abduction of his fiancée, is wrestled into a straightjacket in the asylum and the camera focuses on Caligari's face with 'Now I know how to cure him'; the '*accablante mélancholie*' of a winter landscape with the mists rising from sodden land and a black tarn in Jean Epstein's *Fall of the House of Usher* (1928); the gothic crypt with its sound of falling water and close-ups of rats and wasps eating corpses where the vampire wives awaken in Bela Lugosi's *Dracula* (1931). Film explores the further reaches of our imagining, desiring and believing as we move seamlessly between dream, memory, feelings and perception.

I have stayed too long at the 'paint factory'. It is now just a black mouth in a scaled cliff exposed to the white tides. Dusk has fallen into night. But over the high shoulder of land to the north a moon that is almost full is rising – a huge, alien light too close for comfort. Over the weekend, they tell me, it will turn blood-red. But its startling presence clears my mind, steels my nerve and disciplines the imagination as I start my ascent through the veld to the car. Not yet seven, and my senses are on fire with the cold sea-wind on my back. As the roaring of the tide recedes the air is full of the scratching of cicadas in the dry trees to right and left. A swiftly darting shadow suggests bat flight has begun. The fat stars are becoming visible. This is the primal stuff out of which myth emerges. It is not yet myth as it is not yet story. But it is not silent; it is speaking of *something*.

PART TWO

ARCHITECTURES

III

Imagination and Mental Life

awake in a strange hotel room in Manchester after a one-day conference and a heavy meal that went on too late. It's the twilight before dawn, but I have an early train to catch so I fight against sinking back into the hypnogogic. Besides, I had dreamed of one of my middle brothers, who died two years earlier after twenty-five years of suffering with a degenerative and genetic illness. In the dream my brother, full of amusement and health, greeted me from some vehicle he was in charge of. He had driven trucks for a living when he left the army. The recognition that it was really him came slowly because his face was slightly tanned and glowed, his smile wide, his eyes bright and focused. He had put on a healthy amount of weight and he looked really happy; happy to see me and happy to register my surprise at seeing him so buoyant and flourishing. So I sat in bed while a thin grey dawn broke over central Manchester and thought about him. We had grown up in Manchester.

But the predawn brings with it memories of this location between Piccadilly Station and the university. I don't know the hotel, and the rooms are so small it is only possible to be in them overnight. They are not habitations. No one could live in this room, however clean and comfortable. I do know the area; the area before the hotel was built here. When I was fourteen I knew it well. It was a sad area of red-brick mills flaking and rusting in the post-industrial decline. Neither Margaret Thatcher, nor the Tories, had found votes here then. It was not yet deemed to be an area for development inviting the investment of tax-avoiding entrepreneurs. And being gay was not at all chic; it didn't come with a 'pink pound' and a desire for loft apartments in former Victorian mills. It was a dank, built-up environment, in shadow even in sunlight, abutting the red-light district. Only at this time the mills were home to a multiplicity of small-time retailers hawking small-time trinkets.

I had a friend, Charlie, who worked here in just such a wholesaler's outlet. He was fifteen (you could leave school at that age then). He had animal energies: whippet thin, face of a fox, pigeon-chested. He was moon pale through chronic undernourishment and asthma. Charlie was the postwar equivalent in every detail to the Victorian urchin; another Joe in another Tom-all-Alone's. His father worked at the Salford dog track (now the site of a casino and housing estate), and three nights a week Charlie had a second job ensuring there was enough scent on the mechanical hare to draw the hounds. On the other nights there was stock car racing. I often worked with him, rubbing something clear and pungent from a green bottle into balding fur wrapped round a contraption that zipped round the track faster, it was hoped, than the dogs chasing it. Charlie's day job was in the warehouse, sorting the stock for these retailers. He would pocket several items – watches, pens and lighters mainly – and I would walk down the side street of the warehouse, meeting him at a back door with a duffle bag, and ferreting the goods away. He probably fenced them.

The dream of loss and jubilation and the memory of grey rain falling from a grey sky and running down sour red bricks smelling of sour boiled cabbage mix as I shower and shave in a highly constricted space. Space not place. I have to leave the hotel quickly, minus breakfast, to catch my train to Oxford. But images dreamed and remembered continue to play as the train moves through the Cheshire countryside and down towards Birmingham. Bereavement and guilt weave themselves into the landscape and the weather. I sit with a book I'm reading on the origins of world mythology, reading a paragraph about Phoenician creation myths and Siberian shamans, dozing without actually sleeping as the carriage rocks, reading another paragraph about Jungian archetypes, vaguely planning things I need to do when I get back home, scrolling through a few emails. Around Wolverhampton I surrender to the impossibility of doing any work. I put my headphones in and listen to the soundtrack from Baz Luhrmann's *The Great Gatsby*. I let images from the film surface into daydreams and questions that don't reach articulation but are allowed to linger, morph and drift in any way they will as the train moves on.

It is important to understand what we are doing here, burrowing through the drift of one of my mornings. We are trying to grasp two things. The first is the structure of experience from within which imagining emerges. The second is the character of the imagination itself as a dynamic force field, for good and evil, shaping and firing that experience. In this part of the book we are constructing the mental architecture that supports and generates imaginative activity. Why is it important we understand these things? Because there has been a long history of dismissing the activity of the imagination as make-believe or fantasy, and so many of its products as entertainment, illusions, delusions and leisure-time diversions. We will meet any number of significant thinkers, philosophers and artists in this study for whom 'the imaginations of their hearts' was a byword for evil. And it can be, as we will see. Even when imagination was on the ascendant in the eighteenth century, Samuel Johnson could speak of its 'dangerous prevalence' and its vain 'fumes'. But first, in order to recognize the power of the imagination and what it makes possible, we need to understand how deep it actually goes. There's power in the things we sense.

To get at the complexity of human experience and the imagination's participation in that complexity, we have to start by recognizing that there are images before there are names. Most great poetry is trying to name that unnameable; it pries the edges of words. But, think of all those times you can picture someone and can't remember his or her name. As any film director knows, the way something is imaged, lit, set to music and framed has effect and is affective; dialogue between characters and the voice-over amplify the effect/affect, but language is not primary. This is the way we live as myth-makers and dreamers of dreams deeper than our discourses. Words are only the tips of things. Consciousness alters continually as the chemistry of our bodies colours with the input of what is sensed. To separate out acts of perception, memory, imagination and conceptual reflection is to distort the way they continually interact and affect each other. For the most part, these different forms of consciousness seamlessly shift from one type to another, one mode of reference (autobiography) to another (remembering a film through sonic clues), one mode of mental life to another. And much of this occurs beneath intentionality and reflexive awareness. It requires no prompting or monitoring unless we wish to concentrate and focus our attention for a time. There are processes in place which organize perceptions, memories, imagination and even actions in a subpersonal and unconscious manner. Furthermore, while the consciousness is ours, only in isolation from others is it most ours. And even in isolation it never entirely belongs to us: wind, temperature, light, objects in a structured space all impact, all effect. Time of day also impacts: as we lose conscious focus (towards bedtime), regain conscious focus (in the time it takes to fully awaken) or find concentration difficult (when blood sugars are low in the afternoon). Even when fully alert, in company, other people drift in and out our consciousness, their embodied consciousness crossing ours more like phantoms than shadows. We are back with the transcorporeality of the everyday that was fundamental to the imagination of early peoples.

I'm crossing Midsummer Common in Cambridge, returning from a fruitless expedition to buy a picture frame for my son and his partner. It's heading towards Bonfire Night, a slate-grey day, and the chestnuts lining Victoria Road are stripped bare. It's a time of year that reminds me of all the plague victims buried beneath the common centuries ago. I imagine rickety carts piled high with corpses pulled late at night by men in beaked leather masks towards large open pits where other men stood with immense shovels next to mountains of lime. The images have been spooled from Ken Russell's film *The Devils* (1971). A young woman walks along the path towards me. We are the only two people around. She's an Adele lookalike in a tailored camel coat, the collar turned up. She's talking to someone on her mobile, chatting and oblivious to the dead beneath her feet or to me on the same path. At the very moment we cross she says into her phone, 'I just feel as though my life hasn't really begun.' Then we both pass on, and I carry her aimless longing with me for days, months, years.

Vignettes of the ordinary. How can we understand this play of mind and mood, and imagination's work within it? Walking over long distances lives this best; when I run I'm plugged into a playlist that turns everything into a rhythm. As Nan Shepherd understood, 'Walking [...], hour after hour, the senses keyed, one walks the flesh transparent.' Walking unlocks memories, half-forgotten things and fantasies just as it opens lungs, discharges hormones, circulates blood and releases gastric juices. Walking long distances or over difficult terrain drives one down towards a state before somnambulism. The journeying is not so much into oneself as into the dilution of oneself. And sometimes it is neither memories nor fantasies we engage – it is pain, loss, humiliation, shames that we only half-recognized or half-experienced when we first encountered them.

I recall a man telling me of his sponsored walk on one of the longer routes of the El Camino, over the Pyrenees to Santiago de Compostela. He was an ex-marine and had undertaken the walk as a test of his stamina, but early one morning he lost his way while ascending steeply to a plateau in darkness and driving rain. Then he was confronted and assaulted by his father. His father had been dead for decades, but the image of him suddenly overwhelmed his ability to walk. 'I don't know where it came from', he told me. And then he narrated how an anger boiled up with him against his father. He started shouting out loud, demanding of this powerful image before him why he had never touched him, never held him, never kissed him. He could find no memory whatsoever of any physical affection his father had shown towards him. All his father had presented to him, a military man himself, was distance and a stern, stoic front. And at some point on the ascent, to his utter surprise, the ex-marine just sat by the side of the track in the rain and wept uncontrollably, his whole body racked by the sobbing. 'I have spent so much of my life wanting him to be proud of me. I have made choices I live with now dictated by my need to win his approval.' The unspoken question – this was a brief acquaintance and we have not met since – was, 'Who am I really?'

Sometimes, like Nan Shepherd on the edge of the abyss in Loch Etchachan in the Cairngorms, we are woken up sharply into the realization we have been sleepwalking through life for decades. It is this volcanic interaction of lived experience, memory and imagination that we are exploring in this part of the book.

If we can call it a domain, then the imagination is mercurial. When it gets expressed in any number of symbolic forms it bubbles up and permeates that expression. But its roots lie deep in the unnameable and the smoky place of cracked crazy mirrors and semi-remembered half-forms. It is the source at individual and institutional levels, personal and social, of all our utopian hopes and dystopian fears. That's what makes it radical. Like the mantel of the earth itself, a rock core floating on vast plasma lakes of molten metals, symbolic expression can vent or mask its phenomenal power. The imagination is the volcanic magma bubbling beneath our earth-bound sociality. Culture, society, polity and governance in all their shape-shifting institutional forms emerge from this magma. Our histories, as time bent, fissured, fractured and melded, are subordinated to the titanic pressures of the imagination. The social itself is imaginary.

It begins with sentience, as we saw; sentience that is always inadequately expressed because it is inadequately available for expression. But we can plunge deeper into the biological and the physiological to see how imagination is entwined with our flesh. We can sketch the structures of experiencing, the architecture of sensibility and *making sense* in which imagination plays its vital, life-bringing part. In doing so, certain characteristics of imagination come into greater focus. Pivotal here is the part played by emotion in embodiment and intelligence.

A DEEP MIND ODYSSEY

Minds can only reside in vats stimulated by computers in Cartesian thought experiments. Even in the science fiction of *The Matrix* (1999) living bodies are required to generate the pixels enjoyed. The film is as much about saving the body as it is about overthrowing the system of illusions (and the machines that create them) that colonize and use those bodies as sources of energy. Minds are spread throughout living, sentient bodies and the biochemical and molecular processes that maintain them. Their location is neither in the brain nor the central nervous system, though both systems play vital, regulative functions in the operation of minds. As such, mind is continually spiralling through a circular causality: responding as the body changes and exchanges in relation to the environment and then, in turn, changing the body's chemistry through those responses. It is as changeable as the 'the mood-language of weather' (Alexandra Harris); it determines the weather within us.

Let's return to that early morning in Manchester and add further layers. The hotel is unfamiliar. The grey, predawn light is cold and my waking abrupt. It has not been a restful sleep. I should have left the conference dinner much earlier. The food, though good, was eaten after the day's long proceedings. I'd chosen steak and my digestion was working hard through the night to break it down. The conversation was stimulating, conducted in many different directions and across many levels with people I either hadn't met before or knew well and hadn't seen in many years. Snippets of conversation and response had played through several bouts of sleeplessness. I'd drunk too much wine and not enough water so when I awoke my mouth was dry. And the central heating and lack of ventilation had narrowed my nasal passages. My stomach rumbled as I lay back, feeling somehow guilty for my dead brother, though he was radiant in the dream. But the guilt was written into me in association with hospital beds and *my* visiting him fit and well while *he* lay there staring and helpless and pitiful beyond anything I could say or allow myself to feel. Why was it that I remained fit and well and he lay there? Why had that damaged chain of DNA bypassed me but hit two of my brothers? And I felt guilty also for being there in Manchester in a spot I once knew well, though totally changed now. Whatever happened to Charlie? Why was it I danced into university and onwards, and he remained, wheezing and sickly – doing what? I have no memory of how our friendship ended (or began). The accumulating guilt only aggravated my indigestion, and dredged up not only memories but also an anger at myself. However cramped the shower, the water sloughed off an early emotional drift towards self-pity. And my body ached irrationally for both caffeine and sleep.

I could go on, but won't. We can already recognize that what we think, imagine, believe and remember is profoundly emotional and attuned to any number of bodily sensations in the gut, lungs, blood and bones; sensations changing continually with internal and external circumstances. Our mental life is just that – living. And living is a continual reading, scripting and *making sense* of the world. But that needs more unpacking by descending into how and why humans make sense from sentience.

DESCENT TO THE BIOTIC

At no point in its evolving history did the human species fall down from the stars. A number of ancient myths seem to suggest that. In the Sumerian account of the creation of humanity from around 5000 BCE, we begin with godlike beings working on an earth created through primal forces and ruled by Anu, the god of the gods. The work was long and hard and so the gods (Enki and Ninki) created humankind as slaves to do the work for them. Where Anu came from is uncertain. Much later (eighth century BCE) the Greek poet Hesiod described how this mating of the gods brought about a titanic struggle in which Prometheus (with Athena) created the first human being out of mud and stole fire from heaven to give the figure life. For Prometheus it entailed an eternal sacrifice of himself since Zeus punished him; a sacrifice recreated and reinterpreted in the tall cloaked figure at the beginning of Ridley Scott's film *Prometheus* (2012). The figure is left abandoned by an alien spacecraft on a barren rock plateau, swallows some noxious concoction that initiates a process of disintegration, and collapses into water falling into a deep pool beyond the plateau's edge. As his body breaks down so it generates the chains of polypeptides, proteins and amino acids necessary for life as we know it. In the Jewish, Christian and Islamic account of the origins of humankind we have Adam formed from the dust of the earth. He too is godlike, in his own complex way – being in the image and likeness of the God who created him. Whatever that means.

All these accounts offer a beginning for the history of human acts. There could be no history, no story, if a teller of stories didn't begin somewhere. That doesn't make the teller right, but giving an account is a *making sense* of the fact we're here and we have done things beyond surviving and reproducing ourselves – like build cities and institute ways of governing ourselves, for better or worse. Accounts need beginnings. Making sense attempts to answer the questions of how and why, and any such answers call upon imagination and the development of mythological thinking.

I'll follow up on the myth side in Chapter VI; for the moment we will stay with mental life, how it arose and what that means for our understanding of the imagination. For the building blocks of life may indeed have come from outer space. They came from somewhere, and there is something prescient in those ancient myths that speak of human beings moulded from mud. There is no evidence for or against life anywhere else in this universe or in any of the quilting, bubbling, inflating multiverses either. But if there were life anywhere else then, like here, it would have to come from a metamorphosis in which molten rock becomes amoeba; where prebiotic clay becomes self-replicating cellular membranes.

The formation of those membranes is key. 'Origins of Life' scientists tell us life itself comes down to a semi-porous membrane seven millionths of a millimetre thick. This membrane works to maintain its own boundary while openly negotiating everything around it – in a continuous exchange of matter and energy. So this self-producing cell for some biologists is 'intelligent'. 'The self-producing [...] organization of biological life already implies cognition, and this incipient mind finds sentient expression in the self-organizing dynamics of action, perception, and emotion, as well as in the self-moving flow of time-consciousness' (Evan Thompson, 2007). This is controversial of course, but if correct it has some far-reaching implications for our exploration of the imagination: all living things produce, participate in, maintain and further deep mindfulness.

We are back with what I called in Chapter II 'transcorporeality', where 'body' is the maintenance of a semi-porous boundary between inside (autonomy) and outside (other bodies with which it is in exchange and which, in turn, modify its behaviour). The multicellular nervous system operates within and maintains itself as such with respect to the other systems of the body (the immune, respiratory, endocrine and digestive systems, for example). And that body is continually interacting with other bodies (human, animal, vegetable, mineral). In this way discrete bodies work with all the other discrete bodies composing ecological, geological, meteorological, planetary, solar and even interstellar systems.

Making sense becomes elemental and primordial for all living things. It's not just human beings who are so engaged. All cellular life is involved in making sense of its environment. It reads, it selects and it is propelled towards this and repelled by that. It doesn't have consciousness at this level but it has agency. And all cellular life does this through sensing. In and through sensing it cultivates a world that gives it its best chances for survival and flourishing.

We might model this on a weekend trip to the superstore to buy what is necessary for a week's work to be done and the household to be fed. I'm always amazed how once or sometimes twice a week a family of four or five can get through a trolley crammed high with groceries. We enter the vast emporium stocked with tens of thousands of different products. We pass the coffee shop because we're in a rush. We pass the babywear because the kids are grown up now. We pass any number of sections because we don't need fruit bowls, children's toys, garden tools, bath sheets or a plasma screen. And we walk carefully down aisles containing foodstuffs we are interested in: rice (not basmati but risotto), tinned tomatoes (chopped not plum), bread (walnut, unsliced, not rye), beer (what's on offer?), etc.

Making sense in this context is exchanging the money we have earned for the supplies we need to maintain a daily sustenance such that future monies can be earned and the next generation grow to become money-earners in their turn. This is circular causality governed by what grabs our attention (olives not shampoo). But our activities in the aisles are not without impact on the layout of the store and what it stocks. If no one went to the coffee shop then we would visit one weekend to find the coffee shop replaced by a dry-cleaners. If customer perambulations around the floor indicated they went to the bakery before going anywhere else, then we would visit one weekend to find the bakery had been moved closer to the entrance and the saucepans banished to a remote corner. Mindfulness, the mutual operations of intelligence, emerges not as something separate from the material but as deeply related to it. It has evolved (and evolved in us rapaciously) because it fosters survival. We are caught up in an exchange of intelligences, evidenced in intentional directedness towards this rather than that, the selection of this rather than that, in which sense is continually being made, modified, thwarted and remade. We are a part (a single shopper) in a whole (the world of shopping), but both bodies and intelligence emerge in the relationships that govern the operations of part and whole, the circular causality.

A creative and generative *making sense* is found at the level of the single cell and this is levelled up when it comes to complex multicellular bodies. Foundational to living, this *making sense* marks a deep continuity between life and mind. It also makes all living interdependent, adaptive and transcorporeal. Social relations too are part of a survival strategy. We adapt, and that generates a 'smart' environment. In our superstore analogy, our choices (aggregated up with the choices of other people) inform the shop's layout and stock. They make the shop an intelligent, responsive setting for intelligent, responsive shoppers – who may go elsewhere if they cannot obtain what it is they need conveniently.

THE BIOLOGY OF THE IMAGINATION

Important things follow this sortie into the biological for our ongoing exploration of the imagination. Two in particular. The first concerns everyday transcendence. Our current models of transcendence have arisen from dualisms of body and soul, and the spatialization of up and down rooted in the 'metaphors we live by' (George Lakoff and Mark Johnson). They are also based on the ego as control centre; an ego without a body like a brain in a vat. But transcendence in this biological model is related to the inside/outside nature of being a body at all, and the porousness of that membrane. Philosophical reflection proceeds this way: I am not a tree, so when I gaze upon the tree, the tree exceeds the directed intention of my particular gaze. In other words: the tree is out there and independent of me. Such 'transcendence' is 'everyday' – in the sense Tallis gives it and we encountered in Chapter I. This everyday transcendence is essential to being part of the world as an individual. But with this biology we can understand that that reaching forward to what is outside of us, that stretching towards a fulfilment of a desire, need, hunger, is written into all organic things. Every cell that composes us – trillions – not just some isolated ego, is negotiating its involvement in the totality of what is out there, continually. Whatever the ego is, whatever self emerges in and through these negotiations, it is not anything substantial or stable. It is caught up in an ongoing process of taking inside what is outside and putting outside what is inside; crossing and recrossing a highly permeable boundary between other bodies.

Imagination is shot through with all these crossings beyond ourselves towards that which satisfies a deeper emotional, somatic and chemical compulsion. And as it does that it constructs (with memory) all the stories we tell about ourselves and give us a sense of who we are.

The second important consequence of this biological sketch concerns the relationship between nature and culture. Basically they are co-evolving, co-adaptive and co-constituting; each a part of a dynamic system in which the inside is changed by the outside and vice versa. It is not that the boundaries between nature and culture are dissolved (though we have to begin by understanding the complexity of what we mean by 'nature' and 'culture') so much as recognizing how the boundaries are porous (like those membranes); one continually intertwining with and impacting upon the other in terms of both limits and possibilities. This is circular causation again. The co-evolving of natural and cultural activities brings about hybrid forms and behaviours. What distinguishes them is time: the adaptation involved in evolution is time-thick, while the adaptation involved in culture is time-thin. The speeds of change are variegated. But in short: what preoccupies our imaginations may be plastic and malleable, but with continuing activation they hardwire the kinds of embodied people we become. We are – past, present and future – what we imagine.

Our mental life (and imagination as key to mental life) is just that: living. All aspects of cognition, including imagination, are living. Imagination operates in and through and alongside sensing, sensibility and making sense of what we feel, experience, respond to and refuse to respond to in our environments. It is fundamentally adaptive, and it from this that it draws its creativity and plastic nature. Imagination is not only deeply mindful, it's work in us is as vital as feeding and breathing; it is a hunger and a human need. It needs feeding. In Chapter V we will see what happens when it is not fed. In Chapter VIII we will see what happens when it is not fed properly. It is because imagination is so vital and keyed into our ability to survive that it is so very powerful – for better or for worse. It emerges as a form of mental life from the evolution of our physical existence.

ELEMENTAL PASSIONS

Sensing and making sense is not sentience. No one is saying a single cell feels, perceives or experiences. To feel, perceive or experience, sentience is required. Sentience is sometimes referred to by neuroscientists as 'core' or 'primal' consciousness. It is an awareness arising not in the brain, but the brainstem (where the nervous system and the brain connect). It is associated with all the mid-brain processes that regulate our bodily life without us giving a second thought to them; processes that generate the deep awareness of our being embodied and our being alive. It is from this backdrop of primal awareness, like the white noise hissing between distinct radio stations, that consciousness emerges. The neuroscientist, Antonio Damasio, calls it the 'feeling of self' and in so doing associates it with affectivity and emotional processing at inaccessible depths of mind. All our sensory experience is underwritten and pervaded by this sentience. At this level, the skin is our multicellular equivalent of a unicell's membrane – the porous boundary of our organized embodiment; that place where the inside continually touches the outside; the '"press" in any impression' (Sara Ahmed).

We are emotional beings prior to being human beings; that's the animal within us. Among the affect theorists and cognitive scientists there is much discussion about any difference there might be between an affect and an emotion like fear or joy, anger or shame. The debates turn upon 'appraisal' – that is, when a judgement is made about a feeling, naming it 'fear' or 'joy', etc. There is discussion too about whether emotions can be discrete or whether they mix, match and interweave: joy can bring apprehension; anger can generate animated excitement, for example. But the moment when an affect becomes an emotion is difficult to assess. Naming an affect can amplify its power, but naming can also work the other way to invoke an affect. Call a person a 'victim' and their world changes. Our affective experience of the world is richer and thicker than our words, but our words can invoke the richness and thickness of affective experience. And emotions can certainly mix and morph one into another.

It is because we are emotional, affective creatures prior to being human beings – and because being embodied in highly specific and differentiated ways continually impacts our emotional and affective ways of being in and experiencing the world – that sensory deprivation is the worst of all tortures. What can happen here shows the strong association of imagination with sentience and affect. In his book *Hallucinations*, Oliver Sacks tells us that 'Total visual deprivation is not necessary to produce hallucinations – visual monotony can have much the same effect. Thus sailors have long reported seeing things [...] when they spent days gazing at a becalmed sea. It is similar for travellers riding across a featureless desert or polar explorers in a vast, unvarying landscape.' Anyone deprived of a varied sensory input is susceptible to hallucinations. But when this human response to sensory 'monotony' is coupled with being confined and alone the imagination becomes psychotic.

I'm not talking about the solitary confinement of the war hero Steve McQueen plays in *The Great Escape* – shut up in a concrete bunker with a window looking out on the parade ground outside, and a baseball he can bounce and catch to while away the time. I'm talking about solitary confinement in a concrete bunker without light, where sounds coming from outside are deliberately muffled, and the body is naked. As Sacks shows us, in such total deprivation the brain doesn't stop working. Interviews with inmates who have experienced the 'hole' bring to light the way the brain compensates for sensory deprivation by continuing 'to see'. It produces hallucinations from memories of stored sensations that prisoners attest to be 'as real as' perceptions and experiences. The internal model of the world that the brain has been building up since the day we were born gets projected into the deprivation to compensate for it. Periodically, we will return to this.

Half of all suicides in detention centres are related to solitary confinement because of the incipient sense of going mad that such isolation triggers. The psychological evidence is overwhelming. In Dan Edge's 2014 Frontline documentary *Solitary Nation*, the mental health of the prisoners decline as their attempts to attract attention and make contact with the world become more desperate. They secrete small blades in their mouths before being incarcerated, or push faeces under the door of their cells, or smear the floor and walls with it or with their blood, or they run into walls to fall back concussed. The inmates in Edge's documentary were not in 'holes' totally depriving them of sensation, nevertheless '[a]ffects are propulsive – pushing bodies into the world [...] bodies are anticipating things, compelled to form relationships with the world' (Donovan Schaeffer). This world is denied to these inmates; the world that we and all organic life are compelled to engage with – as we saw with the single cell.

Bodies feel, that is their nature, and feeling is 'propulsive'. Though there is some evidence that other animals can dream, and they certainly have memories, between affect, its appraisal and articulation for human beings there is a *formed* response. 'Formed', that is, rather than a reflexive wail, snarl or flight; rather than a reflexive facial expression, a muscular spasm or a sigh. The formed response can be a gesture (of dismissal), a sound (Oh! Ah!) or an image. These formations (probably early precursors to symbolic forms) announce an intentional propulsion prior to agency, prior to the will of a commanding ego. Expression, in dance, say, or music, or film, or literature or designed construction, can make these underlying formations vivid, amplifying and providing them with richer, thicker self-conscious and self-determining articulations. These propulsive intentions have no single aim or directedness. As in play, they have no instrumental end other than to display themselves.

THE X FACTOR

To better grasp what I'm suggesting here let's tune into the winner of *The X Factor* in 2012, a young singer called James Arthur. The winning song was a remix and cover of Shontelle's 'Impossible'. There are still online arguments over whose version is best. But for the purpose of providing a concrete example of what can seem abstract and complex, all I want to point to is the affective propulsion that's beneath language and agency and closer to animal responsiveness, while still being formed in a distinctly human manner. What I want to show by doing this is the way imagination is totally engaged with that 'propulsion'.

Shontelle's song is sad. It's about the break-up of an intimate relationship. Its emotion forms a surface water for the lyrics, especially in the chorus:

> Tell them all I know now,
> Shout it from the rooftops,
> Write it on the skyline:
> All we had is gone now,
> Tell them I was happy
> And my heart is broken,

All my scars are open.
Tell what I hoped would be
Impossible.

There are moments when Shontelle is angry, regretful, even hurt. But in her version the song climaxes musically on the second reiteration of the chorus, modulated in a similar way to the first iteration and the final one full of resignation. So the climax gets muted. The singing is beautifully in tune, the words clearly enunciated: angel innocence gets chewed over by bad choice of bloke.

James Arthur, like many of the contestants on *The X Factor*, came to the competition untrained and untutored. He had a complex biography that continued to haunt him after he won the competition. His second hit in 2013 was entitled 'Recovery'. He didn't look like a pop star. The photograph for the cover of the song shows him standing side on, his head hanging almost in shame, his gaze on the floor. His right arm, bared, is flung across his chest and clutches his left shoulder. His left arm, semi-bared, is tucked into his pocket. The heavy tattooing on the arms makes them look tortured, and the whole image is in black and white. It's an awkward, almost twisted pose, expressive of complex emotional tensions. All this finds expression in the way he takes up the song. It is blisteringly emotional.

It begins with a series of soft moans, as Arthur seems to go down into himself and into the opening reminiscence of the first verse. The words are sung quietly, soulfully and carefully. But in the second verse the breathing begins to rasp, breaking up the lines of the lyrics. From this same modulation and tonality he enters the chorus for the first time. There's sadness; there's regret – as with Shontelle's version – but it's still tuneful. It's in the second set of lyrics where something else emerges. Here an anger erupts, which is accompanied by him hitting his chest on 'empty promises [...] I know, I know.' It feeds into a much more vigorous reiteration of the chorus accompanied by jerky movements and a painful vulnerability, expressed with the eyes. 'And my scars are open.' He then pulls back to a quiet reiteration of the song's opening reminiscence – 'I remember years ago [...] ' – finding space from a present trauma in a past recollection. This is where Shontelle ends the song. But as Arthur sings this reiteration of the opening his breathing becomes unregulated, the lines of the lyrics break, and their articulation is half-formed. He turns his face away from the camera, burying it into his chest, and he comes to a stop, pauses, then launches into a third iteration of the chorus. The notes, shouted, invoke the disturbing as he carves into himself – 'All we had is gone now! Tell them I was happy! And my heart is broken.' The lyrics break off. Arthur just wails and howls that brokenness while a backing chorus repeats 'Impossible. Impossible.' When he picks up their words, 'Impossible' is dark with sunken depths of despair.

Throughout the performance, it is not the song that rivets; the lyrics tell a pretty average story, the music cleverly plays with pitch, high notes to low and back to high again. What holds the viewer is Arthur's overwhelming emotional pain, controlled, performed, but continually emerging from and returning to levels of inarticulate hurt. The pain is both visceral and immediate. Its rawness cuts through all the mediations of music and language, staging and production, camera angles and filming, and television itself. The feeling comes from a vast and complex domain of affect beneath self, producing formations through propulsions of its own. These formations lie in unconscious gestures, raucous notes, broken breathing and half-images beneath and behind the words. These are instinctive reflexes. The formed affective propulsions are inseparable from the energies expelled in expressive delivery. The song is not one of these propulsive formations; it is a symbolic form. But Arthur makes that form the vehicle *for* the affective formations. It becomes the means whereby Arthur can enter into the imaginative world of the lyrics; identifying himself with them in such a way that we are forced to hear an elemental passion that is prior to language. It leaves us breathing, but breathless; and not a little frightened for him. The suture between animal and human breaks apart. The open wound bleeds.

The imagination, as a dynamic process of affects in the body's immersion in the world, emerges in this coming-to-form that is prior to and beneath all public communication. It propels us into public communication. The French social theorist Cornelius Castoriadis likens the imagination's power, its shape-shifting and amorphousness, to volcanic magma. But it's more like the swarming or murmuration of starlings in Britain on winter mornings and at winter sunsets. The birds awake and simmer with movement as the first light appears or as the last light fades. The simmering becomes waves of turbulent motion before, suddenly, they take to the sky, thousands upon thousands of them rising together and then turning, spiralling, twisting in great acrobatic curves of shadow, keening and calling. Each bird is a single element, pulsing with energy, caught up in collective patterns, vectored by the wind but unpredictable, spontaneous and motile in its formations. Imagining is not just engaging pictures in our head; in part because imagining is not just a visualizing activity. The engagement is profoundly affective and somatic. The elements that emerge in the process might include an image, a colour, a gesture, a sound, a rhythm, a line, a texture, a touch, a scent, a tone, the snatch of a song, a resonance or the filament of a memory all wheeling with electrochemical transmissions, firing releases of hormones impacting behaviour, propelling and propelled. All these elements are prior to (but constituent of) symbolic representation, and conscious thought; they are propulsive formations before they are forms.

There are many other singers whose performances, particularly live performances, have this same elemental quality. The history of blues music is studded with them. Every one of these performances enables us to appreciate how costly such physiological and psychological processing must be; how much energy has to be pulled into the processing from across the body, the brain and the nervous system. Like a man or a woman in a competitive sport, Arthur's triumph must have pumped his body with adrenaline that took hours to calm and for which he must have paid as it subsided with an enormous hunger and emptiness.

ATMOSPHERES

Imaginative processing and experiencing involves every part of the brain or the brainstem. There's an activation of the prefrontal cortex where consciousness becomes cognition, the parietal cortex that effects movements and the limbic anterior cingulate where affect is managed and stored. There's not one single peptide released: endorphin receptors are jammed, ketamine, epinephrine and serotonin circulate, awakening response rates and inhibiting or stimulating the secretion of acetylcholine that impacts the visceral motor systems (those gut sensations).

The steroids kick in: oestrogen, testosterone. Imagination propels and primes response and reaction: sweating, churning in the stomach, quickening of the heartbeat. It is a whole body experience, a swelling orchestration of myriad material elements, taking to the sky like those starlings, and leading to anywhere or nowhere. It is not a chaotic process, but it isn't ordered according to a predictive cause–effect rationale – and most ratiocination is cause–effect-based. But there is a shaping, a patterning, a formation prior to articulate form itself.

If this process can refigure the way we experience the past, and mould the way we experience the present, then it can only deeply impact our responses towards the future. Time has never been linear; that's an illusion of ego-focused instrumental rationality with highly valuable, utilitarian consequences. Time is granular and polychromatic, as writers from Augustine to Proust, sensitive to the verbal tenses of human experience, have always known. It is this processing – biological, physiological, environmental, psychic – that renders us so susceptible to the atmospheric. Here in swirls of invisible pressure beneath discernment we become the barometers of impress and affect, and conjurers of vaporous formations. The flow of variable lights and shades, warmth and chill, and the material textures around us evoke intimations, intuitions and hushed suggestions. Place takes on density. Ions in the bloodstream buzz electrically, senses hum, attuning themselves to nuance and unfelt modulations: a still room on a summer morning; a copse in the fold of a hill on a late afternoon in autumn when the leaves underfoot are damp; the wasteland of an industrial estate in the early hours; a stretch of dark fenland fringed with the flayed trunks of birch and ash in winter – each complex composition of circumstance affords a different atmosphere. British painters like Ravilious and Grimshaw have captured the longing and alienation these atmospheres evoke; poets too. Sometimes the waves of feeling are as allusive as those neutrinos physicists tell us about that pass through everything, none ever being captured. Sometimes these waves come with muscular power.

It is out of these atmospherics, the pressings and impressions, that myths and stories are generated – like Grendel's mother shape-shifting through the murky wetland or the scratching that seems to come from behind the wainscoting in the House of Usher. Barely registered, these are murmurings along the flesh. 'How little resistance we have to these longings that come with evening: the vague yearnings for the place we haven't come to yet, or the place that we have left without hope of return', the Scottish poet, Peter Davidson, writes. Here in swirls of invisible pressure beneath discernment we live the histories we have never known and fragments of recall: 'I just feel as though my life hasn't really begun.'

The pull of the lyrical that tries to capture and conjure these atmospherics is seductive. Imagination *is* seductive. The murmuration of those elements into transfixing quasi-forms is a chemical cocktail plugged into hungers, desires and needs aeons old. Their potency is a *pas de deux*; as vivacious as it is dangerous. Some presses and impressions of the atmospheric bristle and fissure: you are not alone in that silent room or beneath the branches of that ancient copse or behind the warehouse of that industrial estate. Grendel's mother doesn't come out of nowhere, because the imagination is already stippled with dark ambiguities. Joy can throb with anxiety and exhilaration with fear. Destructive things can emerge creatively in twists of hate, anger, threat and betrayal that are as vicious as they are visceral – vicious to the extent that they *are* visceral. Poppies may grow now where corpses lay in clay pits strewn with body parts and landmine litter. But these atrocities were imagined by someone, planned by someone, executed by someone who is or was also a barometer of affect. Even you and I. Few of us know what we are capable of *in extremis*. There are demons and they don't always emerge like Grendel's mother with nightfall. We will encounter them later.

NEAR-DEATH EXPERIENCES

Arguably, the most detailed neurological work on the imagination has been conducted with respect to sleep/dreaming (we will engage with this in Chapter IV) and the analysis of near-death experiences (NDEs). Why NDEs? Because, sometimes, they are accompanied by vivid experiences of being out of the body and even passing through tunnels towards a welcoming light. It is as if the imagination becomes most active during metabolic crisis. In a study published in the British medical journal *The Lancet* in December 2003 the cases of 344 consecutive cardiac patients who were successfully resuscitated after cardiac arrest in ten Dutch hospitals were examined: 18 per cent of the cases alleged having NDEs, with 12 per cent offering a very similar 'core experience'. The phenomenon has been reported across all ages and across the globe.

In part, the article in *The Lancet* reflects a growing number of recorded NDEs due to advanced medicine enabling people whose metabolism goes into crisis, for various reasons, to be rescued from the brink of death. The wealth of accounts available have inspired a number of recent novels and films that have made experiences of the afterlife central to their plots. They provide us with insight into the secular imagination since neither Alice Sebold's *Living Bones* (film released in 2009), nor Gayle Forman's *If I Stay* (film released in 2014), nor Clint Eastwood's film *Hereafter* (2010) – to name some of the more famous examples – are explicitly associated with any religion. But these novels and films use some of the details found in the firsthand accounts themselves: in a collision with an oncoming car, the body tingles, life flashes past, a black space (often tunnel-shaped) opens; eventually a light is detected along with an encouragement to move towards it, for the light holds the answer to everything; it emanates a overwhelming sense of peace before a demand kicks in to return down the tunnel and to the body.

Many have taken such experiences as evidence of an afterlife, but the neurological investigations that the article in *The Lancet* first published, and the subsequent explorations it helped to encourage, seek to 'explain' the interlacing images as brain events. In pursuing these researches into non-conscious activity the work of the imagination as a preconscious operation is foregrounded. Memory, emotion and sensorimotor processes are all evident in which the whole of the brain, particularly the deep midbrain, is involved. They generate the architecture and even narrative structure for the experience. As with all perception (and our dreaming), the linearity of the experience masks the 'gaps', and ensures continuity when no continuity is present. The different senses operate at different speeds – sight is much slower than hearing because its processing is more complex – and there's a full half-second between any perceptual experience of seeing and seeing itself. Imagination like morning mist ground-covers. It fills the gaps. It does this continually, making our experiences coherent; making them *make* sense, become meaningful.

We *create* the stories we live by in our heads and through our bodies, and we do it continually.

We are returned to the testimonies of those inmates deprived of sensory input by being putting in dark 'holes' and the way the brain simulates perceptions and experiences when it encounters metabolic crisis in sensory deprivation. We know something of how this happens in different parts of the brain and how it is stored in various forms of memory. To neurological accounts of NDEs has to be added the physiological effects of the sickness, or cardiac failure, or being stabbed, or being catapulted through the windscreen of a car; the events that trigger the crisis. Enough said: much goes on neurologically and physiologically in a NDE – and nearly all, if not all of it, in a blackout following the loss of consciousness. This does not stop the imagination from working. But with no external inputs, the NDE experience is thrown back upon what is stored in the memory.

The aftershocks of the NDE nevertheless have very real consequences. The experiences frequently effect major changes in the lives of those who experience them, like the atheist Oxford professor of logic, Alfred J. Ayer. When later questioned by one of Ayer's former undergraduates who became a medical doctor, Ayer reported: 'I saw a Divine Being. I'm afraid I'm going to have to revise all my various books and opinions.' Imaginative engagement can then affect future perceptions and behaviour in the way dreams can leave an after-effect that shapes one's mood through the morning. Like the dream of my brother with which I opened this chapter.

GRACE NOTES

Tomorrow is, of course and always, another day. That morning on which I woke up in a one-night hotel in Manchester is well in the past. The experience, though, isn't. The memory isn't either. And yet what I am increasingly appreciating, even in that small sliver of time, is how little I am able to grasp its nuances, tones and textures. It is laced with lacunae where more meaning hides; intimations of otherness, impossibility and elsewhere. We are many-layered and we can only perceive what we have evolved to perceive. We edit our realities continually; or rather they are edited for us by operations in the deep mind. We will never intellectually grasp these operations as they are lived corporeally. But scintillas of something more flash like lightning in what seems a clear opal sky. Maybe this is inspiration – breathings that bubble beneath consciousness and burst energetically within our imaginations into fabulous forms. To move with these movements is living profoundly within our skins. It is not irrational – it feeds rationality and rationality is dependent upon it; though rationality can forget that, with serious, unbalancing consequences in which the emissary of rational thought becomes the master (Iain McGilchrist). But that which evokes intoxicating 'poetic magic' (C. P. Cavafy) can also evoke feral fury.

IV

Imagination and Memory

The relationship between imagination and memory has a long history. Both are rooted in sensing and the processing of sensation, and at certain points in history imagination was confused with memory. The confusion arose early. In Greek mythology Memory (Mnemosyne) is the mother of the creative imagination – the nine Muses. For nine nights Zeus copulated with Mnemosyne and each night produced a Muse – Erato, Euterpe, Terpsichore, Polyhymnia, Clio, Calliope, Melpomene, Thalia and Urania. The work of the Muses was to inspire the creative imaginations of poets, dramatists, historians, liturgists, dancers, musicians and scientists (astronomers). Among the British empiricists (Hobbes, Locke, Hume and Godwin) memory and imagination were viewed as synonymous. Where the mind was a *tabula rasa* recording experience, memory became the passive imprint of that experience and imagination the act of its retrieval. But this was too neat an approach to the relationship between them, and couldn't account for all those unintended distortions that can occur in that retrieval. What about all those ancient worries about possession, madness and mendacity that gathered about the Greek *phantasmata* or the Latin *imaginatio*? So what is the relationship between imagination and memory? Exploring that question, we will run headlong into those ancient and perennial worries, and recognize there is a great deal of substance to them.

DISTORTIONS

There's a disturbing but significant story about the events of 9/11 told by Rob DeSalle and Ian Tattersall, curators of the American Museum of Natural History in New York.

> At one recent museum event, one of us was asked, 'Where were you on 9/11/01?' He replied: 'I was in my office at the AMNH [American Museum of Natural History] that overlooks Central Park. I heard sirens and noticed jet fighters flying over the park. I remember it was a nice clear day out of my window.' It turns out that these 'recollections' were inaccurate on many fronts. For one thing, his office at that time didn't look out over Central Park. The actual office had windows, but they faced the interior of the museum. In fact, the building that he remembered being in on that fateful morning hadn't even been built in 2001.

They conclude the story with the comment: 'Why this quirk of our memories should be so, biologically speaking, is still a subject of great interest to scientists.' What this account reveals, though neither scientist goes into it, is an adamantine *link* between memory and imagination; but they are certainly not the same. Coyly, they don't reveal which of them conjured this memory. In a sense it doesn't matter. What matters is the conjuring itself.

In the past it was often said that memory unified all the fragments and filaments of consciousness, and the wholeness it offered made up the self, you, me, our identity. But things are much more complicated than that. Peering into the blank stare of someone you have lived with, loved and known well, it is very distressing to watch their mind unravel. It is incredibly hard to relate to the person who no longer recognizes you. Alzheimer's, Huntingdon's, viral encephalitis – whatever the cause, their inability to remember is unsettling to you who remember them. They unsettle *your* self-affirmation by their inability to affirm what you recall; their inability to share. And yet they themselves remain unaffected. As nursing staff tell you: *they* find it strange, but not disturbing. The link between selfhood and memory is not so neatly in alignment. Whichever of the curators it was whose memory of 9/11 lied, he reveals the way the mind is affected by trauma (and a longing to identify with a national situation). As the British psychologist, Frederic C. Bartlett, observed in the early 1930s: 'Remembering is not the re-excitation of innumerable fixed, lifeless, and fragmentary traces. It is an imaginative reconstruction.' Memory is a building site, not a building. We are planted in sand, hoping it's home. This raises questions.

We know that the brain will do anything to make the world appear stable, and make us comfortable with living in the order it generates for us. So if memory is key to our sense of ourselves – because it sums up all that has happened to make us who we have become – then to what extent is that self, that you, that me, that identity, a figment of our fantasies? It is one thing to be informed by quantum physicists that 'Our senses are adapted to our scale [...] [they] allow us to see, to smell, to touch, to taste, and to hear [...] the reality within which we live' (Christopher Galford). But this reality is not the whole picture. It is quite another to ask 'How real are we?' That question has existential bite and it's why memory is of great interest to neuroscientists: it gives us access to the way we process and create the world and our selves imaginatively.

MNEMOSYNE'S ALCHEMIST

Winter in Annaba, North Africa. Colder than you might think: intense blue sky refracted through the frost on the hotel windows. This is not Naples or Alicanti. This is Algeria, where temperatures overnight can drop to −4°C and rise to 27°C by noon. Though ringed by the Edough Massif, the eastern extension of the Atlas mountains, there's a presence of vast desert openness everywhere, for the Massif stretches out into the Sahara. The openness drains the energy from the light until, at night, the cosmos is disclosed with fat stars from unimaginable galactic distances. Too cold for sandals, the sand infiltrates trainers and socks and pockets between the toes as I walk down the tight stone *allés* of cafes smelling of coffee, cardamom and mint, during the midday call to prayer.

I'm making for the ruins of the ancient city of Hippo Regius, one of the key cities of the Numidian kings who took control of its once Phoenician peoples. It's a city that has frequently been caught up in ancient rivalries because of its harbour and strategic position on the Mediterranean. Conquered by the Romans in the second Punic war it became, eventually, a vassal province second only to Carthage, further along the coast. What remains of the old city – that fell to the Vandals and then to the Byzantine empire and then to the Muslims and then to the French – lies on raised land above the port. It's ensconced by the complex weave of modern Annaba. It's a disappointing trip: there's just a couple of paved streets, Roman columns or the stubs of such columns, the walls of a villa, and what might be a shrine on a piece of flat scrubland fringed with wild olive trees and dominated by a modern basilica dedicated to St Augustine. The site is a well-kept piece of devastation, a memory of ruins, slowly weathering into forgetfulness.

It's Augustine I've come for – to pay homage. Although what Augustine has to say about the imagination is largely negative. Credited with being the first to use the Latin *imaginatio*, he uses the word sparsely because, as he pointed out in a letter written around 389 CE to his old friend Nebridius, the exercise of the imagination generates illusions (*falsas*) and is evil (*malo*). He prefers the word 'cogitate' because it brings together (*cogenda*) and it gathers (*colligenda*) and both words are 'related as *ago* (I do) and *agito* (I agitate) or *facio* (I make) to *factito* (I make frequently)'. The translation 'agitate' can seem too passive; *agito* is an active, more a living, foraging pursuit.

It's clear that imagination reminds Augustine of his youthful enrapture with the myths of the Manichees – a Christian Gnostic sect who held to a cosmic struggle between dark forces and light, and a priestly hierarchy in which the illuminated (*electi*) were served by the 'hearers' (*auditors*). In his *Confessions*, written in Hippo Regius probably in the last years of the fourth century CE when he took over from the former bishop, Eraclius, he recalls how the Manichees fed him 'a diet of the sun and moon' and 'splendid hallucinations'. In the monastic garden attached to the basilica, he conjured those times in which imagination deceived him. The word he uses for this deception is *phantasmata*, and *phantasmata* possess the power to dangerously mislead.

For Augustine, the power of Persian fire myths, propagated by the prophet Mani, acted like a spell, entrapping converts in an enchanted world. He compares these myths to the food offered by the sorceress

Circe to Odysseus' crew; a food that turned them into pigs. Addressing God, Augustine writes: 'I took them to be you, I ate [...] You were not those empty fictions (*figmenta inania*), and I derived no nourishment from them but was left more exhausted than before (*exhauriebar magis*).' This was not the food of angels (the Christian Eucharist), but the diet of demons. The verb *exhaurire* has vampiric qualities – it drains, it dries up, it empties. And while *magis* is a little adverb meaning 'more', in this context it attracts the verbal resonances of *magi*; those Persian magicians and astrologers. Like many in his time and later, Augustine was also drawn to the seductions of astrology. These *phantasmata* and *figmenta* that we picture to ourselves (*imaginamur*) stir up forces deeper and more dangerous than anything one can dream or even 'the fables of the masters of literature and poets'. The emptiness they create and foster are 'deceptive traps', demonic *decipula* (devices, snares).

Just to the south of Annaba lie the desert wastes filled, in the early Christian imagination, with all the temptations of Satan. Had Christ not begun his ministry by being sent into the wilderness for forty days and forty nights to do battle with Satan? So, in imitation of Christ, eremitic monks like St Anthony went off into the wilderness, to do battle likewise in dominions where the jackals roamed, the vipers slithered and the spirits howled. This was a land of the uncreated and the undead: the place of mirages and psychotic disturbance in the baking fierceness of the sun and the stalking shadows of the moon. Augustine, like the Greek poet Cavafy, had no need for such journeys:

> The Laestrygonians and the Cyclopes,
> the fierce Poseidon you'll not encounter,
> unless you carry them along within your soul.

Augustine sat in the cool of his walled monastic garden recognizing that these chthonic forces were inside him. Late at night, episcopal duties done, he sat in the *scriptorium* in the smoky glow of oil lamps, and dictated to a small coterie of secretaries a journey he made deep into his soul, beyond and behind the *phantasmata* and the *figmenta* of the imagination. And there he discovered memory (*memoria*); and not only memory. For wandering through the most remote and inaccessible hollows and 'vast halls' of *memoria*, he also discovered God: 'you were more inward than my most inward part and higher than the highest element within me (*interior intimo meo et superior summo meo*)'.

Drawing upon Plato, Augustine explored the immensities of *memoria*, which, in the same letter to Nebridius cited earlier, he believed *could* be exercised independently of images conjured by *imaginatio*. But that employment of memory independent of the imagination seemed not at all possible in practice. In conversation the patristic scholar, Carol Harrison, suggested that for Augustine there is a good and bad way of recollecting. The latter is based on *phantasmata* and the former founded upon *cogitatio*. Certainly, *Confessions* is far from being a pure work of memory. As Peter Brown observes, '*Confessions* is not a book of reminiscences'. It's the reframing of some biographical events in a certain way for a certain end. Exactly what that end is has been the subject of shelves of commentaries; but any reminiscence is always act of reframing. The once-idealized Monica, his mother, now becomes a mundane and sometimes foolish woman; the time spent with his friends on an estate in northern Italy (at Cassiciacum) is a return to the innocence of Eden; the dispatch of his partner for up to thirteen years is described in a single sentence – though a sentence weighted with pain; likewise the death of his only son; and on a whole decade that led to him becoming the bishop of Hippo Regius, he is silent. On the other hand, there are gardens and orchards everywhere – Augustine's defence perhaps against the desert wasteland and the noise of civic greed at his door.

No, the idea that you can have memory without imagination does not work, and it causes Augustine a number of existential problems. But what he does recognize is that *memoria* is sunk deep into the precognitive; in its storerooms there are the vestiges of things far older than himself. And despite the storeroom imagery, Augustine didn't conceive *memoria* as a passive receptacle that could operate all the more efficiently if given the right technical disciplining. Memory did not have the stability of an architectured space. Though *this* was memory as he had learned about it through his training in rhetoric, his reading of manuals like *Ad Herennium* and the recommendations of Quintilian and Cicero. In the ancient world, memory systems were conceived, constructed and advocated as necessary for would-be orators who needed to memorize their speeches. In ages in which oral culture predominated, mnemonic practices were handed down from the fourth or fifth centuries BCE. Elaborate spatial architectures were devised that, when visualized, could call to mind things stored away in memory. But this is exactly where Augustine was original; he recognized that the operations of memory were active, profoundly preconscious and always under construction. They were not some kind of filing cabinet.

So Augustine employs the spatial metaphors, but not the architectures. He drew his spatial metaphors from places he knew – caverns within caves, a Numidian palace, a Roman fortress and the broad plains of Campania governed by his friend Paulinus of Nola. But his understanding of *memoria* is dynamic, working within and upon all the various kinetic levels of mindfulness that composed the agency of the soul (*anima*). Its scope was abyssal, galvanizing the plasticity of image-making processes and captivating perception itself as an oscillation between what was within and what was without. In this activity the ego who perceived was like the ambient flame above the smoking lamp in his study – bright, fragile and burning life from a source not its own: 'This power of memory is great, very great, my God. It is a vast and infinite profundity. Who has plumbed its bottom? This power is that of my mind and is a natural endowment, but I myself cannot grasp the totality of what I am.' In the intimacies of himself he is lost in the intimacies of the divine, and the world is turned inside-out. This is the alchemy Augustine performs for Mnemosyne:

> There [in the vast hall of my memory] sky, land, and sea are available to me together with all the sensations I have been able to experience in them, except for those which I have forgotten. There also I meet myself and recall what I am, what I have done, and when and where and how I was affected when I did it. There is everything that I remember, whether I experienced it directly or believed the word of others. Out of the same abundance in store, I combine with past events images of various things, whether experienced directly or believed on the basis of what I have experienced; and on this basis I reason about future actions and events and hopes, and again think of all those things in the present.

'I shall do this', I say to myself within that vast recess of my mind which is full of many, rich images (*imaginibus*), and this act or that follows. 'O that this or that were so'. 'May God avert this or that'. I say these words to myself and, as I speak, there are present images of everything I am speaking of, drawn out of the same treasure-house of memory. I would never say anything like that if these images were not present (*praesto sunt imagines*).

I don't know when entertaining magicians first used the phrase 'Hey praesto!' before revealing what their magic had performed, but this is Augustine's 'Hey praesto!' moment – better translated as 'and while I am speaking, *praesto*! – the images of all the things that I speak about are there.' Replacing the magical enchantments of Mani is more powerful magic – just as in the Book of Exodus Moses performs a more powerful spell-casting than all the enchanters of the Pharaoh's court. And in and through this magic a more powerful understanding of the imagination than the vapid deceptions of *phantasmata* and *figmenta* appears. An 'inner eye' is opened that the invisible might be made palpable for 'mortal sight' (Milton) and 'inward vision' (Augustine). There is a sensing available and operative *through* sensing, and it's spiritual and embodied.

THE WORLD REIMAGINED

Augustine would declare the reality of the soul, and with his account of *memoria* he is content with the ego as a piece of fiction. But he can only be content – it has to be recognized – because the Creator to whom Augustine addresses himself holds the one in possession of that soul existentially secure. God maintains the reality of Augustine's sense of self. We will return to that later in the chapter when God's presence is not quite so in evidence. For now let's explore what happens to the world when it is reimagined in accordance with that 'inner eye', that 'inward vision'.

We can make a distinction between the imagined worlds of literature, poetry and film, and the world reimagined theologically; between what Spenser is doing in *The Faerie Queen* or Tolkien in *Lord of the Rings* or

Eisenstein in *Alexander Nevsky*, and what Augustine is doing as a
Christian theologian. We can say the world reimagined by a Christian
theologian is hedged in by biblical authority and ecclesial pronounce-
ments, and built on the sure foundations of revelation. Spenser, Tolkien
and Eisenstein would not wish and could not make such claims for
their imagined worlds. Nevertheless, though the distinction is one
available to rational analysis, it is a distinction that is not lived as such.
The imagination cannot make such a distinction; the imagination cares
nothing for legitimating truth claims. Augustine reimagines the world
through *memoria*, or rather he makes a vast internalization of the world
by digesting it: 'memory is, as it were, the stomach of the mind'.
We return to those Palaeolithic caves and to the Anglo-Saxon *wambs*.
While seemingly absurd as a metaphor for mental processes, Augustine is
aware the stomach is not 'wholly inapposite'. What is the process
of 'rumination' (*ruminando*) in the one is 'recollection' (*recordando*) in
the other. What drives both processes is 'appetite'. The world is
consumed both through and as sensations turned into images. It is not
that the world outside ceases to exist, but the membrane separating them
(as with all membranes) is thin and porous. According to Augustine's
thinking, I am drawn to the ocean because the ocean is also inside me; I
am drawn to the swirl of the constellations because that same cosmic
swirl is within me. His exploration and appreciation of the world that
memory has internalized gives way to awe, wonder and an ascent that is
also, simultaneously, a plunging towards that which is bottomless.
The imagined emerges from the sublime expansiveness within, through
the internalization of the sublime expansiveness without.
An unimaginable vastness is presented, both inside and outside, in
which that tiny filament of 'I' is immersed; that self, itself, also a product
of the imagination.

We're back with the persistent sovereignty of that 'I' or eye – the one
who is perceiving and internalizing. And Augustine's existential
insecurity is, at times, palpable; in his proximity to plenitude he is very
close, far too close perhaps, to nothingness – the nothingness from which
all things were created in his theology.

The self that he meets, creates and recalls in his *Confessions* is an
imagined, though certainly not idealized, *persona* stripped back and

made fragile by yearning for the unimaginable. He is at once a marvel and a wretch. *He* is what his imagination *is* in the play of *memoria*. But he frets that he doesn't know 'how these images are created', how sense impressions can be stored when the objects sensed 'have no entry to the memory'. So he indulges in mind games, conjuring the image of the sun (*nomino imaginen solis*), but in his conjuring what he is bringing to mind is 'not the image of its image, but the image itself'. And that worries him because it brings the actual sun too close for comfort; he wants 'the image of its image' – its Platonic form. Suddenly he detonates all those architectural spaces, all those storehouses, halls and palace rooms in his head, asking: 'Surely memory is present to itself through itself, and not through its images?' Memory surely operates, he thinks, beneath and beyond image, and he finds this reassuring because he's still not comfortable with image-generation from sensations of the world and the deceptions that are all too possible. As an ex-professor of rhetoric, he knows too well 'the long, twisting lanes of speech' that the persuasive use of images can create. As a man with nocturnal emissions he knows that the 'illusory image within the soul has such force upon my flesh that false dreams have an effect on me when I sleep'.

Fifteen to twenty years later he will probe this idea more theologically than psychologically. In *De Trinitate* he will conceive that the sheer self-presence of memory opens into an understanding of God the Father, the active source and generator of the Son as His Word and Logos, as His offspring and self-image. It is the Trinitarian mind of God that guarantees a relationship between truth, memory and image-making in us. It also guarantees psychological integrity; for is not Christ the self-image of the Father and we the image of His image? Such theological thinking, beyond and beneath psychological reasoning, will help Augustine to come to terms with the way imagination is fundamental to active understanding and communication as they operate at levels both human and divine.

But here in the *Confessions* this theological conception is still inchoate. When he grapples with it he creates an awkward sentence in an awkward Latin: 'Surely memory is present to itself through itself [*sibi adest*], and not through its images?' The awkwardness centres on that '*sibi adest*' (to be towards itself through itself). Nevertheless, upon the weight of this little phrase pivots that which is divine about *memoria*. This is the narrow edge where the mind of this man sheers off into the mind of God. This is the point where being in the present becomes being in the presence of; and it is from and because of this point that the world, the *cosmos* and all that is created can be reimagined.

In *De Trinitate*, this operation upon the imagination as the 'inward vision' is the illuminating work of the Word of God within us; only available by grace and only realizable in participating in God's love that fashions our being made in God's image. Our imagination is enflamed by this love; inspired by this grace. Grace is key. There is no direct link between the human imagination and being made in the image of God, as there will be later with the Romantics. Only our learning that we are loved forges this association. The temporal structure of the world and our experiences of it – 'I combine with past events [...] all those things in the present [...] and on this basis I reason about future actions and events and hopes' – are dissolved by divine illumination into the eternal *praesto*. All those objects of the world, absent though imaged in memory, return as present only in the presence of God's grace. But all images (the imagination and, indeed, memory) will pass away when we see God face to face. For now the visible is permeated with the invisible just as Augustine's past still lives on in the present. Only as such can generative memory and active imagination aid redemption, for Augustine; he sees his own history and the world in which he lives, by grace.

We are a long way from the confidence placed in the imagination later by Wordsworth and Coleridge. All that changes in cultural history at this point is the tenor of Augustine's assertion to Nebridius around 389 CE that memory can be exercised without the images produced by the imagination. The tenor of his observations on the imagination remains anxious but not fear-ridden; imagination can be a gift of our being created in the image of the divine. And *that* secures the truth, always open to correction and judgement, of the self who is confessing. To push towards a more positive appreciation of the imagination will take around another 1,300 years. For much of his writing career, Shakespeare too shared Augustine's misgivings.

CEREBRAL CARTOGRAPHIES

We will pick up this historical trajectory, and Shakespeare, later in the chapter. For now we need to understand something more about the workings of memory and imagination from a more material perspective because we need to understand why today's neuroscientists are so interested in the workings of memory, the distortions of the imagination and its relationship to the question of who we are. We will start to see the power of the imagination as it treats the immersive power of the past. Augustine's theology secures the flickering flame of the self, the soul, which might otherwise be engulfed by such an immersion. Contemporary science is exploring that immersion without its theological anchoring and recognizing the multiple and overlapping forms of memory that impact the imagination. For memories, as traces of the past, lie everywhere. We live with the thick accumulations of those pasts recorded in all the materiality of how we have evolved and continue to evolve. To restrict the use of the memory to cognitive recollection, to a mental act, is radically to underestimate its power of over us. Different forms of memorial are written into us at levels from the genetic to the muscular. They are individual and they are collective. They are also written into the landscapes within which we live. Their internal and external cartographies and the relationships between them are complex. Our knowledge is still inchoate.

Externally, each of us lives in places sculptured by the past; not just by human plans and projects, acts and events, or historical peoples, but also by the weather and the oscillations of our planet through the solar system, rotating and tilting on its axis. There are mountains here, rivers and lakes; there are valleys there, plains and tundra. Glacial movements, volcanic eruptions, the slide of tectonic plates, the rise and fall of sea levels – each have written upon the habitats we live in and modify. The earth has a past that it remembers and it has shaped what we remember. It is as much the Norfolk landscape I recalled in opening this book – and history's tracery upon the village of Walsingham – as it was a memory of the five friends and the skyscape we observed. When we drill down into an ice core or excavate the ruins of some ancient monument, we discover something of the way pasts shape and frame everything animate and inanimate. Ashes, bones, pollens, feathers, roots and blood lie beneath wherever we walk today. The land bears a memory as the universe itself bears a memory. Astronomers observe and record incidents that happened at the frontiers of the universe 13.8 billion years ago: stars that have died; galaxies that have evolved; and black holes that have collided.

Internally, as scientists moved from the introspections of psychology to the experimental forensics of molecular biology, memory was discovered not just in distinct locations of our brain – with short-term memory in the frontal lobe and long-term memory in the temporal lobe – but also in complex distributive networks. Patients with amnesia still remember how to ride a bike, return a tennis ball and fear snakes, because beneath the processing of perception and the calculations of cognition, memory was found in the unconscious. In the oldest parts of the reptilian brain memory is coded into the sensory and motor systems. This form of memory is called 'non-declarative' because its operations are silent and automatic. In a sense this gives credence to Augustine's desire for memory without imagery, but there's nothing creative about it. Through practice, habit, conditioning, sensitizing (usually related to fear and threat), priming and emotional learning, certain synaptic connections are strengthened. Ionized molecules rush down neuronal channels like hoards of holidaymakers heading for the sea on a very hot day, and they congregate at synaptic gaps where the channels end. They congregate so that they might get transmitted across synaptic gaps between one neuronal channel and another. Then they leap the gap, like those same holidaymakers jumping into the oncoming waves, towards post-synaptic receptor cells on the membrane of neuronal channels that communicate with various parts of the anatomy. Any memory 'storage' is involved in this channel-and-groove cutting across the brain through the activation in and across these synapses. All of this comprises the body's reflexive remembered knowledge, and memory as a mental activity emerges from the processing. 'Storage' may suggest a fixed location in the brain, but while there are certain areas that are key to the processing of memory (like the hippocampus and the medial temporal lobe more generally) a number of brain regions come together and contribute distinct aspects that form what is represented in the memory. The memory of a friend and the memory of a traumatic incident are stored as changes in the strengthening of synapses in different places and at different depths of the non-conscious and the conscious. As such, long-term memory changes the structure of nerve cells; it involves protein conversions switched on or off by genes that mould the architecture of the brain. Geneticists in Israel working with the families of German Holocaust survivors have observed the impact of trauma genetically upon the bodies and behaviours of second- and third-generation kin.

The same carved out and distributive networks that laid down the memory are activated again in retrieving it. But memory retrievals are not stable. Moods, cue-inducing contexts and additional information can 'resculpt previous existing representations' (Larry Squire and Eric Kandel) and modify their content. Even forgetting can alter memories; for memory constructs and reconstructs coherence out of whatever fragments are called forth. Imagination creatively forges connections to *make* coherence. This kind of conscious remembering is called 'declarative' because it exhibits itself in the mind, but the neuronal changes happen before any information impacts on the memory system in the media temporal lobe.

Non-declarative and declarative memory each has its own logic and neural system, but there are points of intersection. In the activity of the mediating temporal lobe, memory and imagination work together to the point of fusion, and confusion. Children are particularly adept at producing 'false memories' accompanied by high levels of detail, strong affective content and physiological effects (smiling, crying, increased heart rate, etc.) that convince cognitive scientists watching video playbacks. They are not intentionally lying; they are persuaded of the reality of these past events.

Just as optical illusions play tricks with perception, so the deep mind plays tricks with memories. We saw this with the two New York curators thinking back to their experience of 9/11. The associative power of memory is co-opted for the associative power of imagination, and this issues into unintended distortions. Coleridge, following in the steps of the British empiricists, will determine fancy to be 'no other than a mode of Memory'. On this basis he begins to develop his famous distinctions: memory represents, imagination presents; memory reproduces (at least intentionally), imagination produces; and memory is retroactive while imagination projects (seeing the present in a new way).

Following in the wake of the nineteenth-century German philosopher Ludwig Feuerbach, Freud delved into what the imagination projects, and in projecting displaces. The burden of Feuerbach's most famous thesis, *The Essence of Christianity* (1841), was that God was the imaginative projection of a human ideal. We made him in *our* image. While recognizing the power of the imagination, Feuerbach didn't recognize that projection works both ways: on its object and on its subject. If it creates God as an object in its own image, then it also creates the subject who is imagining – and then all horizons disappear with the subject too dissolving into its own fantasies. Nietzsche and then Freud did recognize this. Augustine, we can recall, needed theology to secure his own existence.

We don't need to get overly technical physiologically. The main point is that both memory and imagination draw, in their different retroactive and projective ways, from stores encoded in neuronal tracks laid down by experience, and from emotions operating beneath and through conscious cognition. Each emerges from a dynamic system in which time is bent by their *gravitas*. Whatever memory represents is always shaped by present interests and future expectation; whatever imagination fabricates is pulled up from what has already been learned even if it is not consciously remembered, and 'is rapacious to escape the laws of human transience', as the poet Jane Hirschfield observes. Imagination cooperates with some of the same non-declarative memory mechanisms like sensitization and priming, for example.

PRIMING

Writers testify to the way one word can trigger a sentence, a paragraph, a line, a poem. One pencil line or brush stroke, one colour or texture, primes what then might take on form as the resonances in that line, stroke, colour or texture are drawn out, pursued and plumbed. One note can prime for a musical phrase, and then a composition as rich and profound as Samuel Barber's *Adagio for Strings* in B flat minor or Albinoni's *Adagio for Strings* in G minor can emerge. We can appreciate this priming in the opening of James Agee's well-known lyric:

110

Sure on this shining night
Of star made shadows round,
Kindness must watch for me
This side the ground.

From the qualities of calm and quiet experienced on a summer's evening there emerges a sense of secure duration, cosmic and personal, that begins from the sibilance and open vowel of that first word – 'Sure'. Then from that word, its sound and felt texture, the rest of the poem flows. The seventeenth-century Japanese poet, Bashō, advised his students: 'if one syllable stops the tongue, look at it hard'. The point is: the syllable is alive. It darts like a young salmon upstream, carving a way forward through mental and emotional resistance. Sibilance serpents and circulates throughout Agee's lyric, coming to rest at the conclusion of the sentence on 'ground', a word primed by the rhyme two lines earlier of 'round'. From the word 'sure' not only are thought and feeling brought together, but a tone and a rhythm are generated. The iambic metre, the short fourth line, the 'o's, open 'a's and 'u's muting the staccato 'i's, curve the grammar and modulate the meaning. Syntax is a way we order our perception of the world so when the syntax of lines two and four is being stretched awkwardly, then the stability of the world wobbles despite the predominance of strong and simple monosyllables. As with Coleridge's 'Frost at Midnight' there is a 'secret ministry/Unhelped by any wind' such that 'its motion in this hush of nature/Gives it dim sympathies with me who live.' And this ministry opens poetic perception.

Priming provokes and propels. Even my own composition of that last paragraph was primed by the mention of Samuel Barber in the previous paragraph. Barber composed a stunningly beautiful setting for Agee's poem. As Hirschfield writes: 'During writing, in the moment when an idea [or word] arrives, the eyes of ordinary seeing close down and the poem rushes forward into the world on some mysterious inner impulsion that underlies seeing, underlies hearing, underlies words as they exist in ordinary language [...] All writers recognize this surge of striking: in its energies the objects of the world are made new, alchemized by their passage through the imaginal, musical, world-foraging and word-forging mind.' The Greeks called this work *poiesis* – a dynamic and creative crafting. It was not an ability poets possessed, for the Greeks, it was that by which they *were* possessed. *Poiesis* was a following, a being led, by a creative power cosmic in its activity. The poet deeply understands that language has never lost its onomatopoeic resonance with reality. Words are saturated with feeling and sound and, as such, grasp and grope for other words, feeling and sounds. What starts as priming can end up with form-finding – excavating inner reaches in order to give expression to what the priming invokes. That's why creative endeavours stir us, quicken us, change us at some remote molecular level; priming our own inner reaches in ways we glimpse but cannot grasp: they put us in touch with something more elemental than the autobiography of the artists through whom such a creativity is shaped.

The imaginative activity provoked by priming *makes* present. It rides the present; and in this it defies or occludes the absences involved in memory. We can listen and become absorbed by another's reminiscences – although whether we are absorbed in the storytelling more than what is being remembered is difficult to say – but we cannot participate in them, because we do not share those reminiscences. But imagination solicits participation. Memory requires a conscious belief – self-belief that it happened as you remembered it; the belief of others in accepting its testimony. But imagination requires the 'suspension of disbelief' (Coleridge) that another believing might become possible – 'poetic faith'. We read a good novel and we disappear into it, not conscious of the act of reading, forgetful of the complex translation processes involved in turning written signs into mental symbols, and mental symbols into what the ancients called *imagines agentes* (living images).

MADNESS AND DISPOSSESSION

The provocations of priming can entice us into creative activity such that we become absorbed and lose our self-consciousness. Any number of artists have attested to the self-forgetting that occurs within the creative act of crafting. There is a suspension in that absorption from the localities of time and space, and this suspension is then communicated, passed on, and enactively imitated by the reader, the listener, the observer. When the American painter Mark Rothko finished a canvas he would sit in front of it for hours in contemplation at what had emerged; as if he himself was astonished at its production. He sat enfolded into the primitive depths of his own colours. Stand before one of those great canvases today and you feel the same hypnotic power. You are drawn into the vibrancies and movements, moods and proclivities of colour on the edge of certain delineations that might, but don't, become form. I had to leave the Rothko Chapel in Houston because the bruised darknesses of Rothko's late paintings upset my inner sense of balance. I was losing myself in the huge febrile nothingness they created.

It is with this self-forgetfulness that we return to the fragility of the self that Augustine sensed before the immensities of *memoria*; we return to those unimaginable depths that the surface ego has to deny, control or ignore if we are to create the stabilities of our social, political and economic worlds. There are people whose capacity for laying down new memories is impaired by disease and lesions, and yet they still retain the 'proto-self' (the basis for the 'core self') that can continue to operate on undeclared memory well below 'conscious self'. There is something about the way Antonio Damasio describes this proto-self, locating it deep at the back of the neck where the brain stem intersects with the spinal cord, that associates it with the work of the imagination. We'll see this connection again in Chapter V. For now, Damasio relates the proto-self to what he describes as 'wordless storytelling':

> Telling stories, in the sense of registering what happens in the form of brain maps, is probably a brain obsession and probably begins relatively early both in terms of evolution and in terms of the complexity of the neural structures required to create narratives. Telling stories precedes language, since it is, in fact, a condition for language [...] The story contained in the images of core consciousness is not by some clever homunculus. Nor is the story really told by *you* as a self because the core of *you* is only born as the story is told, *within the story itself.*

And this suggests to me that imagination is prior to memory; earlier in evolution as brain maps merge into images, and images connect by association into primordial stories in which *you* and *I* as proto selves emerge. Imagination is certainly, on this neurological model, beneath ratiocination – affirming one of the key signatures of the Romantic theory of knowledge.

If this is right, and imagination furnishes our earliest and most primordial sense of ourselves (prior to self-consciousness), then this might explain why imagination also has the power to dispossess us, returning us to something far more primitive and animal. It is this power to dispossess that so worried the ancients and made them wary of imagination. And the fear of such dispossession and being led astray forged the history of imagination as a concept in the West.

In the sixteenth century, Sir Philip Sidney recognized the power of the imagination as a 'fury' – although he called 'imagination' after the Latin humanist word *inventio*. The poet is 'lifted up with the vigour of his own invention' and 'doth grow in effect another nature, in making things better than nature bringeth forth [...] Nature never set forth the earth in so rich a tapestry as divers poets have done [...] Her world is brazen, the poets only deliver a golden.' Make no mistake, as with Augustine the theological still grounds this operation of poetic invention, but it is less overt. The poet betters nature by returning it to its prelapsarian form: paradise without snakes or mosquitos. But Sidney is coy, or Protestant, about divine empowerment. Unlike Milton, he won't leap to an association between poetic inspiration and the providential guidance of the Holy Spirit.

This is not a study in the history of the imagination. I'm only noting here the slowly emerging understanding of the human mind that enables memory and imagination to be recognized as dynamic, affective and embodied systems. The difficult passage of the 'imagination' – from late antiquity, through the mediaeval period, the Protestant Reformation and well into early Enlightenment thinking – was based in the perceived corruption of fundamental human desires by an imagination which, as with Augustine, was understood as a mode of memory. As we saw, the early writings of Coleridge still recognized imagination and fancy as acts of remembering – until, that is, he encountered Wordsworth (autumn 1795) and his notion of 'recollection'.

The advent of Romanticism changed the fortunes of 'imagination' and its relationship to memory. As Coleridge narrates and explores in his memorial to its birth, *Biographia Literaria*, distinctions awoke between fancy and imagination as a deeper self-examination of his own and Wordsworth's poetic practice began. 'Kubla Khan' (autumn 1797) and 'Rime of the Ancient Mariner' (winter 1797–8) have nothing to do with declarative memory, and whatever is being drawn upon as 'experience' in these poems is very loosely and unconsciously tied to the 'personal'. Eventually, and famously, he rejects the empiricist's mind as passive and architectured according to distinct faculties, and plunges into a mental life where differences are a matter of flows, folds, powers and intensities.

The dispossession of self that imagination enacts is not its erasure, but rather its total absorption in the imaginative act as it engages with being immersed. But what is it immersed in? In one of his notebooks, in a jotting written in September 1807, Coleridge describes the imagination as a 'Laboratory, in which Thought elaborates Essence and Existence'. 'Essence' here is understood as the individuality of a thing – 'the innermost principle of the possibility of anything'. As such, for Coleridge, imagination brings about an immersion that is at once an improvised, experimental and playful engagement with what is sensed, instinctively and intuitively about the intense particularity of being in the world. The engagement is with what lies beneath the conscious self whose 'stories' are composed out of memories (true, false, modified); and what lies beneath the rational judging installed by the conscious self. 'Essences' are felt rather than seen, groped for rather than seized upon, apprehended rather than comprehended, because they are 'seen by the mind in moments of strong excitement'. It is this dispossession that Keats later called 'negative capability'. In and of itself this 'capability' is neither aesthetic nor ethical. It might become the condition for the production of either great poetry or enormous empathy, but it does not necessarily lead to either of them. It is, though, transformative.

MERCURIAL TEMPERAMENTS

We can examine the tensions of imaginative engagement in this immersion and dispossession by turning to *A Midsummer Night's Dream*. Shakespeare employs the word 'imagination' more frequently in this play than anywhere else in his work. It is a play, I suggest, that explores the work of the imagination figured as the moon; though I will say more about that lunar association in Chapter V, on dreaming.

Following the fairy mayhem released upon the Athenian lovers in the wake of the quarrel between Oberon and Titania, Theseus the Duke coldly concludes:

> Lovers and madmen have such seething brains,
> Such shaping fantasies, that apprehend
> More than cool reason ever comprehends.
> The lunatic, the lover, and the poet,
> Are of imagination all compact.

It's a speech that appears to place his own marriage with Hippolyta very firmly in the realm of *realpolitik* – and that's often how it has been read. I think it says more about Theseus himself, and so it has something of a self-reflective monologue about it. His marriage cannot take place until the old moon has waned and the new moon arises – though we are not told why. But the play's events unfold because of this in the last phases of a dawdling full moon; and the wedding takes place when the moon's mercurial influence is least effective. Here in Act 4 is Shakespeare's first use of the word 'imagination' in the play, and we see that Augustine's fears of *phantasmata* are back. Theseus will drive home the distinction between 'cool reason' and the imagination's lunar 'pact' with lovers, madmen and poets twice more in the same imperious tones:

> And, as imagination bodies forth
> The forms of things unknown, the poet's pen
> Turns them to shapes, and gives to airy nothing
> A local habitation and a name.
> Such tricks hath strong imagination.

But Theseus is not as solidly rational and self-disciplined as he would like us, and Hippolyta, to believe. For all his stern upholding of the 'Athenian law' with respect to Hermia and her father's wishes, when Oberon confronts Titania early in the play the fairy lists the number of women with whom Theseus has been unfaithful. And we start to see Theseus's self-possession unravel at the performance of *Pyramus and Thisbe* on his wedding night. As the court watches what would indeed seem 'lunatic', and 'the silliest stuff' that Hippolyta has heard, Theseus falls under its poetic magic:

Theseus: The best in this kind are but shadows, and the worst are no worse, if imagination amend them.

Hippolyta: It must be your imagination then, and not theirs.

Theseus: If we imagine no worse of them than they of themselves, they may pass for excellent men. Here come two noble beasts in, a man and a lion.

With that last remark Theseus is on the brink of descending into the spiralling surrealisms of his own midsummer night's dream. He is drawn to the edge by the idea that imagination might 'amend'; the 'beasts' that attend him are simultaneously both men and not men. The 'man' is in fact dressed as the moon. Hippolyta, the Amazonian, is of stronger stuff than Theseus. As 'thought police' she is more effective. Theseus's temperament is deeply mercurial and lunar. Hippolyta may be luckier than 'Perigounia, who he ravished' or 'fair Aegles', Ariadne or Antiopa, but Theseus's consistency is like the moon's, and like Mercutio in *Romeo and Juliet* (a play that may have immediately preceded *Dream*) he is aware of it, and the dangers it poses.

What is at stake for both Augustine and Theseus is self-assurance, self-control and the power of the imagination to unstitch it. 'I have become for myself a soil which is a cause of difficulty and much sweat', Augustine announces. The metaphor is an acknowledgement of Jehovah's pronouncement to Adam: from dust you came and to dust you shall return. This is the panic that arises from opening the closeted power of the imagination. But, at the same time, imagination promises a healing, as we have seen in Augustine and Theseus's recognition that it can 'amend'; that is, mend the world in a sense we noted earlier in Sir Philip Sidney. By reconciling oneself with the imagination, not fearing but being 'compact' with it, then in the dispossession of the self lies the possibility of becoming a lover and a poet.

From Coleridge onwards, it is exactly this 'dispossession' that gets championed as the ethical core of imaginative and aesthetic experience. In the shift from Enlightenment epistemology to Romantic psychology that Coleridge's introspections articulate, the internal complexities of the self might bring madness but they also present the possibility of *theosis*: a self-emptying that expanded the self beyond its own interests towards a universal empathy. For Coleridge, Leigh Hunt, William Hazlitt and John Keats, Shakespeare was the exemplum above all others of the plastic powers of the imagination. In fact, the impact of *A Midsummer Night's Dream* and Theseus's speech in particular for the changing fortunes of 'imagination' in the eighteenth century, from Thomas Addison to Adam Smith and Edmund Burke, is well attested. In his Notebook for October–November 1811, Coleridge sums up what Shakespeare enabled them to appreciate about the dispossession in imaginative engagement: 'Sh[akespeare] became all things, yet for ever remaining himself.' And with this new understanding of imagination's power, its relationship to memory came more into focus: the aggregating and associative facilities of fancy could 'halo' memory (Keats) and receive sensations, but 'the worth and dignity of poetic Imagination, of the fusing power, that fixing unfixes and while it melts and bedims the Image, still leaves in the Soul its living meaning' (Coleridge). And this is transformative.

There is none of Sidney's coyness or Protestant reticence here. The imaginative artist is a creator in the image of God. As Coleridge observes in a letter to Joseph Cottle in March 1815: 'The Immortal Finite is the contracted Shadow of the Eternal Infinite.' Not all Romantics would go this far. Keats, for example, did not divinize the poetic intuitions of the imagination. He was too experienced in the blood and bandages of his early apothecary training to develop a metaphysics or theology for such sensibilities. 'Negative Capability', as described in that famous letter to his brothers George and Tom of 21 December 1817,

is, when a man is capable of being in uncertainties, mysteries, doubts, without any irritable reaching after fact and reason – Coleridge, for instance, would let go by a fine isolated verisimilitude caught from the penetralium of mystery, from being incapable of remaining content with half-knowledge.

This pursued through volumes would perhaps take us no further than this, that with a great poet the sense of Beauty overcomes every other consideration, or rather obliterates all consideration.

Later, in a letter to his friend Richard Woodhouse, he goes further in sentences that echo down to Oscar Wilde composing *Dorian Gray*: the poet 'no has self – it is everything and nothing – It has no character.' As I said: in and of itself this 'capability' is neither aesthetic nor ethical.

IN THE ZONE

The neuroanatomist Raymond Tallis, whose phrase 'everyday transcendence' we met in earlier chapters, cites Keats's understanding of 'negative capability' and 'half-knowledge' as characterizing the experience of 'wonder'. Here the self is free from its egocentrism and open in being overwhelmed by that which amazes (in the rich Teutonic etymology of that word). Despite a history of associating 'wonder' with religious awe, Tallis, as a self-proclaimed 'atheist', doesn't view 'wonder' as in any way religious. And it need not be. The American psychologist Mihaly Csikszentmihalyi characterizes this 'dispossession' of the self as being in 'the flow' and the flow is strong with the 'psychic energies' of joy and well-being. Both these accounts of 'negative capability' emphasize its positive nature. But Keats like Theseus, to my mind, knows too well the hidden pathologies of engaging the imagination; pathologies that can work upon traumatic or disturbing memories and invoke dark demons; promoting dark, self-destructive actions.

Keats's obliteration of 'all consideration' is disturbingly beyond good and evil. It shares characteristics with what some in professional sport call the 'zone' and those who run long distances describe as going 'beyond the wall'. You hit the 'wall' around twenty miles into a marathon with the experience of excruciating pain, a total lack of energy, a loss of focus and confidence, and the intense ease with which giving up suggests itself. Whatever the tactics and the pace, both disappear into a great silence in your head. How you get through the wall is not something you think or determine. It's something that pertains deeper than mind and physiology. You *become* rhythm, balance and breathing. There is no experience as such. You *are* the track. 'Beyond the wall' is running that continues because it has surrendered all consideration to a single rhythm. And the pace can ride an adrenaline rush because 'beyond the wall' is beyond risk calculation; it's either finish or collapse.

The zone is fed by secretions of stress hormones like adrenaline and norepinephrine. It is a state that is often of a short duration and non-voluntary. It is a paradoxical state: a *sense* of control rather than being in control, low anxiety, high alertness, energized while being totally calm. Mind and body seem to be in unparalleled association. Such a state can lead to surprising wins where the other competitors are forgotten and one is racing against oneself. Entry into the zone pushes beyond left-hemisphere knowledge to right-hemisphere instinct, and it absolutely rests upon a disciplined body that has laid down profound somatic memories. While there may be some 'recognizance' (Keats) associated with will and determination, entry into the zone requires a reactionary response that discipline over long periods of time makes possible.

The most primitive of somatic responses *precede* even non-declarative memory. They are automatic and instinctive – responses of pulse rate, hormonal secretion, blood flows, heartbeat and breathing that are unconscious adjustments to the environment taking place at speeds far quicker than thought can assess. To enter the 'zone' is to allow the body to take over and live the environment on autopilot. Pain or physical discomfort is not registered. One enters one's body more deeply; eased into it such that there is a new level of relaxation and composure. The takeover by the body rests upon breathing – that is, the control of oxygen to the brain and through the brain to the blood, the glands releasing chemicals into the bloodstream, the viscera, muscles and skin. You dig deeper to find that ultimate rhythm, such that, even though moving more quickly, the heartbeat and pulse rate is slower and the new rhythm is struck beyond the normal rhythms that the sports person is familiar with. The self is obliterated.

Keats enjoyed boxing, although he was no professional sportsman, and Coleridge and Wordsworth worked on poetry on long and very arduous walks. The experience of beauty that 'obliterates all consideration' (Keats), empowers the imagination, and forges an agency at one with its action, has psychosomatic parallels with entry into the 'zone'. Beyond the ordinary fragilities of self-importance there is a deeper forgetfulness that both Coleridge and Keats are attuned to; a letting-go such that questions of 'where am I?' and 'who am I?' can just receive no answers. The self remains at some core level, but an absorption takes place that is without experiential coordinates. Nothing might be experienced as such in this dispossession; for the judgement involved in emotional experiences is suspended – at least for Keats. Coleridge's soul in 'living meaning' might accord with some understanding of the 'mystical', but the mystical does not characterize Keats's imaginative condition. What Keats describes as 'negative capability' or 'That distance of recognizance bereave[d]' or the 'feel of not to feel', is a dark paradox.

Coleridge, who was not without his own appreciation of the paradoxes of 'creative faith', could affirm a direct relation between the ethics of self-surrender and aesthetics, guaranteed by a belief that God was both *in* all things and *above* all things. The self-emptying creates the space for inspiration. In doing so, Coleridge can also affirm that the transformation involved in engaging imaginatively at this level (for author or reader) has a divinizing and salvific goal. It must do, because the paradoxes that circulate around 'I am alive' are resolved when the 'sacred river' is traced back to its source in the absolute 'I AM', God. It's not just that primary imagination is 'a repetition in the finite mind of the eternal act of creation in the infinite I AM', as he stated in Thesis VI of the first volume of the *Biographia Literaria*. Rather, a person participates in the divine: '*sum quia in Deo sum*' (I am because I am in God). Augustine (who drew some of his thinking, slanting it towards Christian orthodoxy, from the people Coleridge had also read) would agree. But the principle of '*sum quia in Deo sum*' makes Coleridge's self-dispossession no less existentially worrisome, though a whole lot safer.

Keats has no such theological reassurance. He knows the power of the imagination drops him into 'caverns measureless to man/Down to a sunless sea', but he cannot call the river 'sacred'. Maybe he's more honest: names at this point fall silent. What does 'sacred' mean, or 'God' for that matter? Still the paradoxical rhythm of emptying/filling holds, even if he doesn't baptize it as such, and imagination takes up the pulse of that rhythm. It also exposes the poet to certain nameless and unimaginable desolations. The destitution Keats feared all his life was as much psychological as material. Writing was both the means of keeping him sane and driving him mad. He probed the psychology of the imagination as if it were an exposed nerve in a broken tooth. Its power was unhooked from the *penetralium* of Neoplatonic metaphysics and Judeo-Christian theology. The radical dispossession it brought could be as creative as destructive.

CLIMATES OF FEELING

The dispossessive lurch of the imagination plunges beneath the entanglements of consciousness and self-consciousness; beneath biographies and memories (true, false or modified); beneath the normative judgements of good and evil. But towards what? I suggest a primordial nakedness that uses representations (words, colour, form, genre, sound) to carve an access to something sensed that is more fundamental: a primordial immersion in the environment that senses and generates ecologies of feeling; the climatic tones and textures of sensibilities within the sensed; vibrancies in the grain of the material and embodied. Any ethics lies in the appreciation of tone; a tone that carries moral feeling. It doesn't consist so much in the erasure of Augustine's *amor sui*, but in the expanded empathy that self-forgetfulness can afford. It is broadly an empathy for what, after Keats, might be called 'a poetry of the earth'. Not the 'earth' I think of in English Cotswold prettiness or Pope's Twickenham garden. It has Shakespearean weight, 'earthlier' – flesh, mud, blood and oxygen; the smell of grass and the chill of moonlight. The empathy embraces so much more than other human beings. It's staked into place as well as people; soil turned over and the saltiness of sea air. It's an empathy with the transient and mutable, intimate with death and slow to slide too quickly to anything disembodied.

In James Breslin's biography of the American abstract expressionist Mark Rothko, we are told that the artist rounded on one interviewer, telling him:

> You might get one thing straight. I'm not an abstractionist [...] I'm not interested in the relationship of color to form or anything else. I'm interested only in expressing basic human emotions – tragedy,

ecstasy, doom, and so on. And the fact that a lot of people break down and cry when confronted with my pictures shows that I can communicate those basic human emotions. The people who weep before my pictures are having the same religious experience I had when I painted them. And if you, as you say, are moved only by their color relationship, then you miss the point.

The fact that he uses the word 'religious' to describe these strong experiences is interesting – for he was not a conventionally religious man, despite his Jewish background and his early education in a *Chedar* in Lithuania. But the word emerges from somewhere to depict what is felt, in some sense, at the 'event horizon' of the imagined and the unimaginable. It's an expansive word, dilating the affective textures of 'experience' – like empathy to the nth degree. And 'pantheism' goes nowhere near defining this.

Situating the imagination within an architecture of the human (and the divine) mind preoccupied Coleridge. Wordsworth, despite playing with fancy and imagination in his Preface to the *Lyrical Ballads*, did not share Coleridge's Kantian and Schellingian proclivities. It's not just that the whole Enlightenment project of mapping the mind and ordering the faculties was wrong – the brain and the mind just doesn't operate in that hierarchical, modular fashion, as we have been seeing. But much more important for Coleridge was the understanding that the poetic began at the point of dispossession when the architecture begins to wobble and glitches appear in the rationalized surfaces. 'Beyond the wall' the Enlightenment mind dissolves altogether and when it returns, if it returns, its 'pleasure domes' are recognized for what they are – beautiful tremulous pictures of fragile human experience at the edge of the unthinkable.

But the architectures of the mind may not return from such wobbling in the same coherent way. Here lies the danger in empathy gained through the dispossession of individuality when it is no longer suspended within a relationship to the divine. Identifications with bears and bushes might simply voice an indulgence in self-delusion. But the imaginative rhythm of emptying and filling might submit to bipolar disorder. Not that self-doubt and depression did not assail a saint like Augustine, but the depths to which these plunge towards the 'sunless sea' is terrifying. The ancient anxiety about the imagination, whose history is evident right up to the eighteenth century, is not without its wisdom. In that 'negative capability' the space for the morbid can be exceedingly large. On the other hand, God is no easy answer – as Donne and Bunyan and Cowper and Hopkins all attest. Keats, having come through an intense period of grief following the death of his brother, and self-doubt in the face of his own addiction to opium and flowering consumption, twists the threads of a 'darkling' paradox:

> Ay, in the very temple of Delight
> Veil'd Melancholy has her Sovran shrine.

Darkness falls quickly in Annaba, and with it the barometer. There will be another frost tonight. Shadows shroud the fragments of Hippo Regius. The kiosk entrance is locked and the wire perimeter fence secured. A graveyard emptiness takes hold of dead stone that can no longer speak. A dog howls in a nearby tenement, and in the Church of St Augustine, built on the ruins of a temple to Saturn, I light a candle beneath a milk-faced Madonna and Child for a man whose remains are entombed nearby. They're in a glass case beneath a white marble effigy of the black saint reposing in death. I light the candle for a man who never allowed himself to be a poet while yet understanding in his *De Trinitate* that creation was God's own poem and, sublimely, 'A word is knowledge together with love.' He was a man whose soul was saturated with Virgil; whose high-flying thoughts and soaring, sonorous phrasing shaped centuries of Western civilization. He was a man so equivocal about the imagination while being so practised in it – for the theologian is a dreaming thing. In Keats's *Hyperion*, Mnemosyne, the last of the eclipsed Titans, raises her arms 'as one who prophesied' and Apollo is painfully transfused with a new divinity that will leave her ancient powers far behind.

V

Imagination and Dreams

id Shakespeare know about dream incubation? Did he know from his school-day learning of those citizens of ancient and late classical civilization, like the Roman orator Aelius Aristides, who, ritually prepared, slept among the serpents of Asclepius? Did he know of those who spent dark nights in the scented temples of the god of healing praying the divinity would take possession of their bodies through their dreams, treat their physical and psychological dilemmas and knit up the unravelling sleeves of care? For there is something about the imaginative conception and performance of *A Midsummer Night's Dream* that is close to dream incubation.

The moon, as I said, figures imagination throughout the play. As a celestial body it is the author of contradictions: of tempest and tranquillity, passion and coldness, restlessness and supine detachment. It links the celestial to the terrestrial, meteorological and the aquatic such that its operations, like the imagination, are cosmic. Beneath the moon all the earthly dramas – the fairies', the artisans', Theseus's, the lovers' and the courtly revels – are provided with a cosmological context and an ironic gaze. The transcendent is drawn into the immanent and the immanent gives recognition of the power and influence of everyday transcendence. The external is drawn down into the depths of the internal and the internal gives expression to the external. And so the celestial descends into the psychological. The moon's detachment is shared with the audience (and the play's director). Like the imagination, it affects a withdrawal to a distance from which observation and reflection can be made. In this way its contemplative detachment figures Keats's 'negative capability', while its phosphorescent reflection of the sun brings to sublunar objects a luminosity that both evokes and obscures. Ruminations on things sublunar engage the unconscious or the preconscious; the *Dream* opens up an exploration of the close relationship between imagining and dreaming.

In English we may speak of 'having' a dream, but in several other languages a dream is 'seen'. 'In ancient Egypt, for example, there were two hieroglyphic figures for dream, *resut* and *qed*', the sleep scientist Kelly Bulkeley informs us. The hieroglyphic for *resut* was an open eye; a sign used also for visual perception. We pick up again Augustine's 'inward vision'. At the end of the Shakespeare's play Puck steps forward:

> If we shadows have offended,
> Think on this, and all is mended,
> That you have but slumber'd here
> While these visions did appear.
> And this weak and idle theme,
> No more yielding but a dream.

The language of these lines echo words with a moon-bending significance employed throughout the play. 'Mended' we will come to, having already noted Theseus's suggestion that imagination can make 'amends' in Chapter IV. The word 'offended' is an echo of the Prologue of the artisan's play. Bottom, particularly, has been worried throughout rehearsals of 'offending'. Puck appears to be informing us that the dream/ *Dream* is now over; the perfect tense of the verb 'have [...] slumber'd' indicates a time that has only just passed. The echoing envelops the play in a conclusion. But echoes have no determined end – they travel on indefinitely. '[V]isions' draws attention to the play's hallucinogenic quality and 'shadows', while used to describe fairies and elves, is also used to describe players who strut across the stage. That final line – 'No more yielding but a dream' – betrays the oneiric, witty distortions of the irony at play in what is, textually, an epilogue. Weigh the trochaic subtleties of that 'yielding'. As a noun, 'yield' is the return on an investment, an outlay. So *then* Puck means 'of no more value than a dream'. As a verb 'yield' means to surrender, capitulate as St Paul in the Geneva Bible speaks of 'yielding your body' (Romans 6.13). So *then* Puck means something about surrendering oneself to the power of dreaming – and the play as incubating such a surrender. At this point Puck may be informing the audience how the play should be received – without the hissing of the 'serpent's tongue' – but, while seemingly stepping outside the dramaturgy, he remains in character as Puck.

So the play may not be over. What Puck may well be doing is enlarging the space of the dream so it embraces the world of the audience. He takes up the trochaic rhythm and rhyming couplets of Oberon's blessing and the fairy songs. It is the chant of a fairy spell as the trochaic is the hypnotic basis for the witches' cursing in Macbeth. Magic has always been word-magic, image-magic, as it has also always been number-magic, metre-magic and music-magic. Here at the end is not an end, but another kind of beginning. Puck's epilogue casts a spell beyond the play and beyond the stage, binding the world in its charm – like the 'little western flower' that maidens call 'love-in-idleness' that we have learned about earlier. The 'idle theme' continues.

That last word of the play, 'dream', preceded by that present active participle 'yielding', gives way to that saturated liminal space between ending and beginning again; the space between the closure of the performance and the opening of the applause or hiss. That moment when imagination ceases and a new imagining has yet to begin is, in a sense, what this play explores: the saturation of that space, its poise between worlds seen and unseen. It is in that space that Bottom discovers there's no bottom to his dreaming and (significantly) wants to put it to music. That moment when the last word of the play is sounded and the applause has yet to ring is a fold in time; a caesura in space; when the breath is held. The nature of living is made more expansive and the real more ambivalent. The aesthetic, the psychological and the physiological come together in ways unclear, but suggestive. Just as a poetic thought once read or heard stirs the blood of the one who reads or hears it; 'words are also deeds' (Ludwig Wittgenstein).

Shakespeare's *Dream* allows us to strike out here into the mystery not just of imaginative creativity, but also creation. As the drama unfolds, we encounter complex, relational sympathies, empathies and antipathies between court and forest, the city and the cosmos. And in striking out into the mystery 'spirit' as that which animates both mind and matter, human creativity and creation comes to the fore with language as its hinge. There is something magical not just about the fairies, but also how language can conjure, and how that conjuring can change how things are seen, how circumstances unfold. Like the blessing at the end of the *Dream*, words can have force – enacting and bringing into effect, that which they speak: like a promise or a vow or a dedication. Words can affect changes in life, dramatic changes. Not words on their own, but words as prosthetic extensions of the speaker's psychic and physiological labouring-to-act: intellectual expressions wedded to gesture, sound, breath, muscular contraction and secretions in the throat. To use Puck's language, there is nothing 'seeming' about the changes that such enacted words make possible. And this force that enlivens draws poetic and dramatic language into the provenance of ritual and liturgy; symbolic languages of gesture perhaps, or dance, with costumes and music, each form affecting the way we people *live* in being immersed in the performance.

The fairies perform a liturgy, blessing the water and the marriage bed. These are quasi-folkish sacraments, perhaps not out of place in the pagan Athenian world, but in imitation of Christian rites solemnized by Shakespeare's contemporary priests. These rites are still performed at a baptism, at a wedding and at the blessing of a house today. To employ an Anglo-Saxon word, they hallow and in hallowing exorcise (memories the house still might hold, for example). And this crossing and recrossing of the world of the play into the world of the audience – that Puck's epilogue performs – is all the more evocative when we consider that *Dream* was probably written for and first enacted, like the artisan's play, on the occasion of a marriage. Only it was not the marriage of Theseus and Hippolyta, but that of Elizabeth Carey and Thomas, son of Henry, Lord Berkeley, at his home in Blackfriars on evening of 19 February 1596. The play within the play is concluded with a liturgy that concludes a liturgy. And who can say where Puck's 'seeming' starts and finishes? On an historical level there is a difference; on an imaginative level there is not. Have Elizabeth and Thomas awoken from a dream, like Hermia and

Lysander, like Helena and Demetrius, or are they still in the dream and have watched their dream unfold as those in lucid dreams know they are dreaming and dream still? The end of the play for Theseus and the court is a retreat towards dreaming: 'Lovers to bed; 'tis almost fairy time.' It is as if the drama in the fairy kingdom is just about to begin (again).

On my interpretation, *Dream* is Shakespeare's deep reflection on the power of the imagination, its somatic and affective presence in sleep and dreaming, its generative power in poetry and performance, its psychological associations with love, desire, belief formation and belief transformation. This aspect of imagination's involvement with belief formation and belief transformation is key. It changes the way we see things – which is what dreaming delivers – and in this way it can bring about a 'mending', a healing of the dissonant relations in a daylight world. Like Aelius Aristides, we are transported to the temples of Asclepius.

THE DREAMING THING

Shakespeare is not the only literary figure who associates imagination with deep dreaming. '*Longtemps, je me suis couché de bonne heure* [For a long time I used to go to bed early]', is the opening line of one of great classics of world literature: Marcel Proust's *Remembrance of Things Past*. Like the 'Sure' that opens James Agee's poem that we looked at in Chapter III, the evocations of '*Longtemps*' prime the vast unfolding of the work. The word stretches out towards an indefinite duration where time will be regained (*Le temps retrouvé* is the title of the last volume) or 'amended'. The sentence it surmounts returns us abruptly to a specific past and an early hour that is, in fact, dusk and time for bed. We have arrived at this chapter through examining memory's relationship to the imagination in the last, and much could be said and has already been said about 'involuntary memory' and its impact upon transforming autobiography into Proust's fiction. But the relationship between dream and imagination is also important for Proust.

New Year's Day in Paris, 1908: Proust receives a gift from Geneviève Straus, the young widow of the composer, Georges Bizet, whose son, Jacques, Proust knew from school. She had already remarried by the time

Proust, then fifteen, first met her, but she remained an important friend and correspondent. The gift comprises five slim, leather-tooled notebooks. As Mme Straus knew, Proust was masochistically churning his ambitions of becoming a great writer, having already published several smaller pieces. Sometime in the early part of the new year he opens one of the notebooks and records a dream – it's a dream from which the entire shape of *Remembrance of Things Past* would emerge; a dream that informs the very reason why the young Marcel went to bed early on that evening at Combray when downstairs his family (and particularly his mother) were entertaining a neighbour, Charles Swann.

In the dream he recorded his mother, who had died two-and-a-half years earlier, appearing to both him and his brother Robert, wracked by pain and pleading that her sons no longer prolong her agonies by making her undergo an operation. Throughout her life, Marcel's hypochondria had always forced her own complaints and ailments into the background. He was too ill to travel with her back to Paris for what would be her final days alive. Now the shade returns, powerfully – like the shade of Patroclus returning to Achilles and upbraiding him for being asleep while his slain corpse remained unburied. Later, in the same notebook for the same year, the shade appears again. This time Marcel is rapidly following a crowd of people along a cliff, at sunset. Not quite recognizing any of them, he overtakes them and then:

> here is Mamma, but she remains indifferent to my life, she says good morning to me, I feel I shall not see her again for months. Would she understand my book? No. Yet the power of the spirit does not depend on the body. Robert says I should find out her address in case I am called for her death, but I do not know the district or the name of the person who is looking after her.

Proust regularly noted down his dreams. They gave him access to realms within himself he barely understood and felt it was necessary to understand – for his imaginative art. He was a man obsessed by his own secrets, or rather the secrets beneath the more open secrets he lived with: guilt about the treatment of his mother, rivalries with his brother, his homosexuality, anxieties about his feverish libido, his temptations to indolence, in turn his masochism, sadism and voyeurism, and, always, the fragility of his health. The pathological depths in Proust would have kept Freud and Jung awake at nights. But a searing intelligence salt-burned through layers of self-delusion and with it came an honesty as cleansing as it was ironic. No less than Sir Philip Sidney, Proust was engaged in the redemption of physical reality through the imagination – though the last volume profoundly ironizes the redemption the earlier novels perform. He ferreted among his motivations, observations and cross-examinations of friends and acquaintances to provide psychologies for the characters he created and their paradoxical behaviours – caught as he and all of them were between the bourgeois walk along Swann's way and the aristocratic walk *du côté de Guermantes*. Dreams gave him entrance to two things, he observed in his final novel: desire and time. 'If I had always taken so great an interest in dreams, was this not because, making up for the lack of duration by their potency, they help us better to understand the subjective element in, for instance, love [...] And it was perhaps also because of the extraordinary effects which it achieves with Time that the dream had fascinated me.' Dreaming, he concludes, was his 'second muse'; his 'nocturnal muse'.

Dreams, and reflections upon their 'potency', punctuate *Remembrance of Things Past*. They form part of Proust's examination of the imagination's profound relationship to sensation, because dreams amplify sensation. He wasn't equipped with the psychobiology that Freud was mapping, but he knew his nocturnal visitations were just as revelatory as his involuntary memories and just as galvanizing in creative endeavour. Swann dreams, Elstir dreams, Saint-Loup dreams, Bergotte has nightmares and Marcel dreams. Marcel dreams of women who are remote and enticing, and they act as a refrain throughout the epic from his dream as a child in *Swann's Way*, to his dream as a mature adult when his perverse relationship to Albertine (aka Alfred) begins (when she moves in) and ends (when she dies).

Dreams have always betrayed human frailty; that we are thistledown in the currents of gods and circumstance. Even in the wake of psychoanalysis there are many today, usually of a religious temperament, who find in dreams omens and prophecies, warnings and commendations. Some have even seen in dreaming the origins of religion or religious experience. The ancients knew of angelic conversations and whispered oracles that came with sleep. They also knew of demons and *jinns*, *incubbi* and *succubi* ready to interpolate dreams and possess the soul of the dreamer. The plot of probably the earliest piece of literature, *The Epic of Gilgamesh*, turns twice upon prophetic dreams. The Bible narrates several dreams – from Pharaoh's and Nebuchadnezzar's dreams of warning to the angelic visitations in Joseph's sleep while the Christ child is threatened. On the whole, dreams as omens share a single characteristic – they are responses to fear, ruin, devastation and the eclipse of hope. When we shift beneath the dream scenarios, we encounter the descent of darkness from which sleeping shields and delivers us. The action that follows such ominous dreams has all the intensity of flight or the panic of coming up for air. The association of sickness, guilt and death all circling the figure of the mother in Proust's dream, triggers a fathoming excavation of memory and artifice that covers around 3,500 pages in most editions of *The Remembrance of Things Past*. There is something here we will need to return to, but the point for now is: dreaming, like imagination, didn't begin as a mode of human diversion or escape from the tensions of the everyday. It is a finely tuned mechanism for our advancement and survival.

In literature from Homer and Plato to Virgil, the somnambulant one passes through gates of horn or ivory that discern the truth or falsity of what is being dreamed. As Virgil describes them in Book VI of the *Aeneid*:

> Two gates the silent house of Sleep adorn;
> Of polish'd ivory this, that of transparent horn:
> True visions thro' transparent horn arise;
> Thro' polish'd ivory pass deluding lies.

Dreams have a transparency in the ancient world because their occurrence takes place in borderlands between this world and a more fundamental, embracing reality. Though internally received they have an external agency, and human beings are opened to that external agency, for good or ill, by the passivity of sleep. The gift granted – if the vision was true – was to see clearly, to see as the gods see; to be a seer like Balaam, the son of Beor, the Midian prophet on the shore of the Gulf of Aqaba who 'lifted up his eyes and saw' and said of himself that he was one 'whose eyes are open' (Numbers 24). Which suggests that in our everyday seeing our eyes are dimmed and not 'lifted up'; that we can only see *as*. In true vision we are liberated from the illusions of seeing *as*.

This openness to being shown beyond what can be seen *as* doesn't question human agency, but it does circumscribe it. For Homer and down to Virgil, our lives are hidden within flows of cosmic energies as the wheel of fortune spins in the hands of playful divinities. Neurology may have deeply internalized these dynamics, making them function as processes through which the day's stimuli are digested; psychology may have probed the inner censorships that are relaxed as memory and imagination condenses and displaces under the pressure of the unconscious and their subliminal drives – but the ancient and mediaeval worlds still live with and within us.

Awake (and there are levels of wakefulness), we can admit that the unconscious operation of moods and well-being are governed and integrated, for the most part, by a sense of ourselves as agents with willpower and self-control. But in dreams, such willpower and control evaporates; we are like Theseus – far more mercurial. In sleep there's a drop in the release of the inhibitory neurotransmitter GABA so erotic energies find expression in ways we wouldn't admit to in waking life. For all the policing of his sexual abstinence and the chastening of desires, Augustine despaired of the erotic scenes enjoyed in his dreams. His nocturnal emissions were evidence of a delight he couldn't allow himself to celebrate – though enjoyment was the closest thing to worship in his scale of emotional values. He prayed for God to cleanse him of his secret, hidden sin. While forced to admit, on biblical grounds, that dreams could be vehicles for divine communications, Augustine was as wary of dreams as he was of imagination; both were far too close to fantasy and self-indulgence. Keats, on the other hand, surrendered himself to dreaming, recognized man (*sic*) as a 'dreaming thing'. He welcomed the oneiric liminality. Once, on a walking tour of Scotland, he gazed upon the island of Ailsa Craig in the Firth of Clyde. This isolated peak of blue honed granite became a metaphor for poetic consciousness '[e]ver as if just rising from a sleep'.

In Chapter IV we descended with Mnemosyne into the caverns of the imagination. That same descent leads us to our dreaming, and not just as individuals. We enter our collective dreaming. The ancient omens that appeared in dreams might involve the destiny of the subject to whom they were presented, and individuals noted their private dreams – but providence wasn't privatized. The visions had collective consequence – for that dreamer's relations with others, for that nation, for that religion, for a future about to unfurl. Since at least Freud (though in fact there were books investigating the neurology of dreams before Freud) dreaming has become the private domain of bourgeois individuals in three-storey houses, working out their neuroses cathected from wishes repressed in the daylight hours. But, in the light of evolution, in dreaming we descend into the human condition itself, and the condition of being one mode (successful at the moment) of the genus *Homo*. Dreaming will lead us to metamorphoses – where what is human and what is animal blur once more; where the distinction itself is questioned. In a sense we are back in Plato's cave, captives in dreams to illuminated shadows, only not cast now on a rock screen, but conjured holographically in sleep and three dimensions. Unlike Plato's prisoners we are not instructed as to the meaning of these images by wise but fascist philosopher kings who have climbed up through the tunnels and understood the manipulations in their ascent to the light. No. We are participants in scenarios rich with emotional affect and tonal moods that we have no means of fully grasping in their dramatic immediacy and evanescence. They are *in* us and, in ways that slip through our conscious control, they define us. The domain of dreaming maintains its power because it doesn't offer any representational distance, like novelistic fiction. Dreaming has the quality of being present, like hallucinations. There can be moments when we can tell ourselves in the dream that we are dreaming. There can be moments of self-consciousness within the dreamstate. But even such self-consciousness has to submit to the total immersion in the reality-effect of dreaming. Escape is sometimes possible, sometimes sought, through an electric jolt of fear or pleasure that brings us to other surfaces of reality, other perceptions that we have learned, most of us, to trust. Dreams introduce us to states of altered consciousness, and in doing so they provide access to the very stuff with which imagination works.

AND IT WAS NIGHT

This is one of those short, dramatic statements that punctuate the Gospel of John — like 'Jesus wept'. The diurnal darkness is weighted here with cosmic associations and the ominous threat of a primeval chaos. The stage is being set in this 'night' — that deepens into Gethsemane and the darkness that fell over the whole earth while Jesus hung upon the Roman cross — for a recapitulation of creation from the torrid vacuua of formlessness. This is the 'night' lived primitively in which the circadian rhythm of our biological need to sleep participates. It has been suggested that the need to sleep — and sleep when most human beings do sleep — arose from the demand on animals to lie low in the darkness to avoid predatory threats and the stalking nightmares of imminent, ever-present death. The bush may indeed *be* a bear or an *eorō-draca* (an earth-dragon) or a *wyrm* (serpent) or Grendel. While the wassailed thanes slept in the mead hall of Heriot and the fire grew heavy with ash, outside the fiend prowled:

> But the evil one ambushed old and young
> death-shadow dark, and dogged them still,
> lured, or lurked in the livelong night
> of misty moorlands: men may say not
> where the haunts of these Hell-Runes be (*Beowulf*)

Should we return to the Anglo-Saxon tongue here, not as a text but as an oral performance, we would feel the blood-clotting of the imagery in the stuttering of the syntax and the hoarse, guttural music of horror displaced and condensed by the imagination as it experiences its 'night terrors'. With every line-end, endstopping and caesura, paralysis is possible — only the alliterative bounce of consonants keeps the howling of the vowels at bay and the narrative from unravelling in panic. Word, or rather wording, becomes (because it is) kinaesthetic. Nightmares could well be at the origin of imagination (Christoph Türcke).

Alfred Hitchcock is a master of dreamlike distortions that the audience (as the camera-eye) not only observe but also participate in. Nightmares and dreams play important roles in his films and TV programmes.

In *Spellbound* (1945) it's the dream of a murder by an amnesiac, Edwardes, who is falsely accused of the crime; in *Vertigo* (1959), it's Madeleine's false dream and Scottie's psychedelic nightmare that further the intrigue and the plot. Interpreting these dreams is an act of detection. Much of the fascination lies in the denial that the dreamworld is separate from and inferior to the reality of the waking world. In the ending of both *Spellbound* and *Vertigo* we are returned to the assurances of normal life in a world that is supposedly awake. But while we privilege the world of wakefulness (it pays the bills and puts food on the 3D table) how much time in this waking world is our consciousness actually as alert, attentive and focused such that it is entirely distinct from dreamstates?

Neuroscience tells us that over half of our wakeful life is not focused on any task in hand. Our minds continually wander, and the more unhappy we are the more they wander. Awake we daydream, we project future possibilities in hopes and desires, we 'enter' the lives of other people, trying to understand their motives and attune ourselves to their feelings, we entertain images of ourselves and images of how other people might see us, and for stretches of time we run on a default consciousness or autopilot. And these mental events are only the beginning, because we are constantly telling stories to each other, listening to stories, reading stories, hearing stories, watching TV programmes, downloading and streaming. How 'awake' is such quotidian consciousness? In other words, and sharpening the question, what is the relation between the work of the imagination that sources our dreamscapes (when we are, on the whole, deprived of sensory inputs) and the work of the imagination that both 'propels' us into waking life and permeates much of what we believe is 'real'? What is at stake in such a question is the very structuring and restructuring of sense perception that constitutes the texture of our experience and sense of agency.

CINEMA AND IMAGINATION

Cinema (and TV) gives access to the nuances of imaginative reception, engagement, activation, the formation of experience and the role played by consciousness. Our dreaming has cinematic qualities – both treat mental images and spliced-together narratives. Both call upon and call forth memories. This is why dream and remembrance (or its loss) are often used thematically by film-makers to reflect upon the realities cinema creates and the psychologies of viewing them. Dreaming, in particular, was used as a metaphor in film theory from the early explorations into cinematic experience.

We have explored already how imagination operates across the unconscious, preconscious and conscious mind. And, as we also saw, body mapping and the stories the body tells of itself are deep-mind activities implicated in feedback loops with the systems that regulate our physiological condition. But the extent to which we have access to such 'maps' is unclear. We know of certain meditative states that push beyond imaging or representational thought, and beyond even experience itself. These meditative states have been likened to the forgetting that occurs in deep sleep when consciousness *can still be measured* (by scanning) in very slow oscillations of gamma and delta waves – but *there is no registration* of consciousness because the self is absent (unconscious). But all the indications are that imagination arrives very early in consciousness, dragging with it elements of the unconscious and the preconscious. With it there is a blurring of what is interior (as memory, affect and mood) and what is exterior (as the actions and furnishings of the world), and cinema mimics these processes of production, identification and disassociation.

Freud never engaged cinema in his writings, but if dreamwork is the perceptual representation of dreamthought, its dramatization, then imagination, dreaming, memory and to a great extent film, all 'speak' the same language. The work of each also problematizes the sovereignty of the spectator. A French woman summed up for German film theorist Siegfried Kracauer the visceral and subconscious effects of cinemas: 'In the theatre I am always I, but in the cinema I dissolve into all things and being.' The moviegoer exercises something of what we saw with pre-cinematic Keats and negative capability – although it is the director's imagination that is most exercised. Kracauer teases out the relationship in what he calls *The Redemption of Physical Reality* in dreaming and cinematography. The spectator is caught between self-absorption in the 'trance-like immersion' in successive shots and the self-abandonment that arises from stirrings that came from beyond the image. These two contrary streams meet in 'cataracts of indistinct fantasies and inchoate thoughts' and they 'bear the imprint of the bodily sensations from which they issue'.

The immediacy of the immersion is the stimulation of the imagination by what is not perceived directly. In dreams, the sense of the outside world is greatly minimized: dream perception is simulated. In cinema, while the spectator perceives what is projected, the film itself is a simulation of the world viewed through a camera lens. And this results in a surrender of self-control to a flow of consciousness that is in part voyeuristic and in part self-projected identification.

More than thirty years later I can register the shock when watching Michael Radford's *1984* (in 1984) when we see the starved rat approaching Winston's face *from* Winston's perspective. The film turned on me, and I reacted instantly by extracting myself from the immersion and withdrawing into a solid sense of sitting with a row of others in a local cinema. Radford broke the continuity by using another camera angle to withdraw us from the scene. Hitchcock had a way of refusing you that option because the action was so quick and so improbable it's upon you before you realize – like the knife of the murderer plunged through the shower curtain. There's no displacement. This is Freudian 'condensation'. In the penultimate scene of *Spellbound* it's a revolver, turned upon the murderer, and fired on you point blank. With the only flash of colour in the black and white film just for emphasis! Hitchcock is playing with us again. The final scene of Gregory Peck's embrace of Ingrid Bergman at the entrance to a dark gate leading to a train is an act of massive Freudian displacement. If we go away from this film feeling happy at its resolution, then, as with so many of Shakespeare's tragedies, we have been deeply deceived by the sense of an ending. We are still asleep.

What is important for our exploration here is the way cinema employs the power of the visual to organize the other senses; in this it both mimics and enacts the work of the imagination and dreaming. When I watch, a distance separates subject and object. But dream and cinematic immersion dissolves that distance. Tests by the neuroscientists on participants experiencing virtual reality have shown that the same areas of the brain that integrate various sense data from across the body become highly active. These areas are directly involved in the visual imagination and in mental imagery. It is not stretching it to suppose cinematic simulations can stimulate the same activity. In both virtual reality and cinema what is perceived is stimulated by simulation.

It is the same areas of the brain that are activated in REM (rapid eye movement) dreaming where spikes of electrical energy can be higher than in the waking state. There are moments when you might be aware 'I am dreaming', but those psychologists and neuroscientists interested in what is called 'lucid dreaming' want to distinguish between the dreaming subject and the dream ego who witnesses and even controls the dreamwork, while knowing what is being experienced is being dreamed. These switches between seeing yourself and being yourself is a facility at the centre of empathy and social awareness. Cinematic participation provides insight into these alternating forms of consciousness, especially when cinema becomes self-reflexive and the camera-eye turns back upon the audience and disturbs the sense of any distinction between imagination and a world independent of the mind. But then, as we have already come to recognize, it is only a world seen *as* and seen partially.

It's important to understand that seeing *as* does not mean the world is virtual, though a number of post-modern thinkers argue that. In the 1990s, the American neuroscientist Rodolfo Llinás, proposed that waking life was only an extension of dreaming life governed by sensory inputs. Consciousness, he claimed, was not something generated by sensory inputs but complex and continuous relays of communication between the thalamus and the cortex. When we dream this activity pulls in images from memory and emotion but lacks the constraints of sensorimotor stimulation; when we're awake this dreaming becomes perception because of this sensorimotor stimulation. Thus we continually create virtual models of the world. But this is not what I intend by seeing *as*. We perceive the world imaginatively, that's all I'm claiming. This can give the events in waking life a dreamlike déjà vu as *what* we experience in the waking world is shaped by *how* we experience it. Nevertheless, there is a distinction between being asleep and being awake.

Cinema can model a relation between dreaming and waking, showing the circular operations of one upon the other. What do I mean by that? Imaginative productions in dreams can effect imaginative productions in waking life (as Proust the author recognized) and imaginative productions in waking life can effect imaginative productions within dreams (as Marcel the character describes in his account of falling asleep in the opening book of *Remembrance of Things Past*). What is continuous here across the dreaming and the waking states, and active throughout the circular causality, is not dreaming, but imagining. Films, like imagination, operate in the borderlands between waking and dreaming, showing us how one state is not opposed to the other.

EDWARDES' DREAM AND FREUD

There is an interesting and significant difference between the manner in which the dreams are presented by Hitchcock in the 1945 *Spellbound* and the 1959 *Vertigo*. The difference shows an important change in the understanding of sleep and dreaming which opens a question about the therapeutic nature of the imagination. We have already appreciated how the work of the imagination has evolved as a response to our changing environmental and physiological condition. But to appreciate now how that work is implicated in our well-being as a whole is to recognize how it can also be implicated in our mental and physical disorders, personally and collectively.

The action in *Spellbound* centres on a clinic for psychotherapy. The dream, its interpretation and form of psychoanalysis in the film are directly related to Freud, particularly his analysis of guilt and anxiety complexes. Film theorists at this time were increasingly drawn to parallels between film and psychoanalysis, viewing the dimming of lights in the auditorium and relaxing back into the soft cinema seating as priming a regression to the infantile state. (They must have had different seating back then.) From post-production interviews it's evident that Hitchcock was aware of these discussions. Freud is named in *Spellbound* and Edwardes' dream is disclosed under analysis by a Freud lookalike. It is a dreamscript composed of symbolic figures and objects that need to be decoded, and are decoded successfully as the plot is resolved. Certain dreamsets were designed by Salvador Dali. Dreams present a language of the unconscious; its images become symptoms for what was *not* being disclosed and censored. They were a foreign, hieroglyphic language, and not everything recalled by a patient was relevant to the interpretation of the dream.

So interpretation became selective, homing in on sites of 'condensation' and 'displacement'. Condensation is where any number of impressions and emotions are compressed into a single image or symbol. Freud spoke of the dream having a 'navel, the spot where it reaches down into the unknown'. In *Spellbound* a distorted wheel in the dream turns out to be the barrel of a revolver, for example. Displacement is the effect of censoring the contents of what is wished for or feared. For Freud fear is 'more primitive, more original, more instinctual than the pleasure principle'. The displacement is recognized in the way images and figures acts as substitutes, sometime even contradictions, of the unconscious propulsion. It can be mimicked in cinematography, as we saw in *1984*, by cutting from one angle or scene to another. In *Spellbound*, a man with no visible face turns out to be the true murderer, but he makes only one appearance in a complex series of disjointed scenes. Condensation and displacement are the axioms for interpreting latent dream content. Lacan mapped condensation and displacement on to the linguistic functions of metaphor and metonymy, and film theorists whooped with delight. But we needn't go there. Neither Freud nor Lacan examined films themselves, though they both recognized that imaginative literature was in some sense also dreamwork.

From the earliest awakenings of psychoanalysis Freud saw a direct relation between dreaming and the creative imagination, given that in both cases representational images were organized and narratives were composed. In the first edition of *The Interpretation of Dreams* (1900) he drew upon both *Oedipus Rex* and *Hamlet* to develop his theory of the layered human mind. This was regularly followed by interpretations of short stories (Wilhelm Jensen's *Gradiva* in 1907), Shakespeare's *Merchant of Venice* and *King Lear* (in 'The Theme of the Three Caskets', 1931) and Dostoevsky's *The Brothers Karamazov* (1927). 'Man, as we know, makes use of his imaginative activity in order to satisfy the wishes that reality does not satisfy', he tell us. His psychoanalytical approach was, then, both to the imaginative work *and* its reception. So *King Lear* has an 'overpowering effect' because through engaging with Shakespeare's play we come to terms with 'the three inevitable relations that a man has with a woman – the woman who bears him, the woman who is his mate, and the woman who destroys him'. The Goddess of Love turns out to also be the Goddess of Death.

What Freud brings to our exploration of the imagination, through his analysis of dreams, is a therapeutic operation beyond the questionable ethics of 'negative capability'. If Aristotle recognizes the cathartic effects of tragic drama, then the subsequent work on dreaming and imagination has shown how these states are both part of everyday human functioning. Dreams are important in the processing and consolidation of the day's memories. They also enable problem solving and the strengthening of repeated practices like a tennis serve or a skiing move. But they are *key* to processing emotions. Fear, anxiety and anger are the most regular negative emotions that dreams present. And, maybe surprisingly, 'friendliness' comes out number one. Even so, negative emotions (usually processed early in the sleep cycle) outweigh positive emotions (usually present in dreams just before waking) two to one. Whether they also act to regulate sexual and/or aggressive drives, as Freud thought, is debatable. What has been proved is that sleep and dreaming deprivation is the hallmark of depressives, who cannot recall their dreams because they demand cognitive control and are threatened by its loss. Sleep and dreaming deprivation have been linked to diabetes, obesity and the regulation of hormones and moods that effect self-esteem and social relationships. Could some of our world health issues be related to those whose imaginative powers are unexercised?

SCOTTIE'S NIGHTMARE AND SLEEP SCIENCE

Scottie's nightmare in Hitchcock's *Vertigo* is very different from Edwardes' dream. It's an inventive mix of cartoon and hallucination, a montage of a bouquet of flowers and suggestive memories that culminate in an open grave into which Scottie falls, plunging into a psychosis. He is awake within the dream and the dream triggers a state of mind that lands him in a mental hospital for an unspecified length of time.

The change in the way the dreams are presented by Hitchcock between 1945 and 1959 parallels a dramatic change in the way sleep and dreaming was understood following the discovery at the University of Chicago of phases of REM occurring in sleep and associated with dreaming. Attaching electrodes to students' brains as they slept revealed regular cyclic changes occurring in sleep. A new approach to psychology was opened, and new functions of sleep and dreaming began to emerge that impact upon imagination. In fact, this new approach made us aware that dreaming *is* the imagination in sleep mode; for now the brain was known to be active throughout the night. The new psychology made the 'unconscious' (and Freud) unfashionable. It spoke of the 'preconscious', the 'subconscious' and the 'non-conscious'. Today, following moves in embodied cognition and emotional intelligence, the 'cognitive unconscious' and its operations on our conscious lives are back on the agenda. But the relationship between dreaming and the unconscious is still under-researched. But that's not the direction of my plot-line, and it need not concern us too much.

With REM, a broad threefold understanding of existence was announced: awake, sleep and dreaming. Four stages of sleep were mapped, each identified by electrical waves. Stage 1 is transitional and often accompanied by hypnogogic sensory or auditory events of sights or sounds that are not really there. The transition is brief and shows a slowing down of the brainwaves from gamma alertness. In stage 2 sleep (about half of normal sleep is stage 2) there are responses to external and internal stimuli and the waves are slower again (alpha and theta). At stage 3 the waves are high and slow (delta) moving into the slow-wave sleep of stage 4. This is our deepest, dreamless sleep, and about twenty per cent of our sleeping as a whole. With REM the brain is firing again in stage 1 mode. When your immersion in the dream colonizes your consciousness and closes down your motor systems, and the electrochemical activity is mapped, then 'REM sleep and the waking state are virtually indistinguishable' (Kelly Bulkeley).

We go through several such cycles each night, spending around twenty-five per cent of sleep in a dreamstate. This is where the imaging occurs, though the source of our image-making lies deeper within the brain. The operational structures for REM have been traced back to the brain stem. So if imagination has a locatable origin, then it's here; activated by the neurotransmitter, acetylcholine, that communicates very quickly between nerve cells. Acetylcholine is one of the key neurotransmitters that associates dreaming and imagination. It is in this same physiological region that body mapping emerges, essential for our profound and proto sense of self. So the 'proto-self' is then primitive; a product of the evolution of the mammalian brain. Despite fMRI scanning, 'maps' and 'images' are metaphors. So all we have at this origin of imaginative power is *subsequent* (though examinable) behaviours, and personal records of remembered dreamstates.

Scottie's dream – which doesn't form the coherent, if rather surreal, narrative that Edwardes' does – is opaque. There are no encoded messages whereby the crime can be solved. The beautiful Madeleine doesn't appear in the dream. As Scottie slowly detects what has happened when he finds the woman who was acting the part of Madeleine, the only connection between the dream and what follows is a ruby necklace. The necklace isn't a symbol of anything. If the dream expresses anything it is Scottie's own state of mind. It reveals his fear of dying; the death he has already experienced before meeting Madeleine when a police officer died trying to help him following a rooftop chase. Scottie lived on; but his self-esteem died. And the woman (Suzie) who plays Madeleine in the actual crime is sacrificed to his version of the real when she falls to her death from a tower, like Madeleine, because Scottie had forced her to live out his psychosis. Redemption, if that is what is it is, comes at a price. The grave Scottie stares into at the end of his nightmare is the dark unyielding space we all stare into as the film ends, with an old nun standing behind him saying, 'I heard a noise'.

IMAGINATION AND HALLUCINATION

The depiction of Scottie's nightmare reveals that by the late 1950s something of the mystique of dreaming dissipates. Experimentation in sleep labs, monitoring by EEG (electroencephalogram), diagnostic findings hitched to burgeoning developments in neuroscience, and spectral analysis scoring the language of sleep and dreaming – all bear little of Freud's liberal schooling (in classical literature, Shakespeare and Goethe). The academic papers published in dedicated scientific journals detailing projects and investigations into non-normative sleep behaviour – sleepwalking murders, cases of unconscious self-harming, sleep sex, late-night cooking episodes or adventures in cars – still hold their mysteries (for what is going on in the heads and hearts of those who commit such acts and can't recall or have very little recall of doing them?). But they add little to the study of the relationship between dreaming and imagination. While their work advances our understanding of the relationship between sleep and health, few medical researchers cross into the realms of literature, film and the creative imagination; perhaps because they mainly view dreaming as a form of mental hallucination.

Defining dreams as hallucinations maintains a firm distinction between being awake and being asleep, facts and fantasies. But there are notable neurologists, like Oliver Sacks, who view the distinction as illusory. They point to the differences between dreams and hallucinations that bear upon the metamorphic creativity of the imagination. Hallucinations, for them, are delusional states; while dreams are *not* false or pseudo-perceptions. Certainly, activations of the brain in hallucinations are often the same as activations in those areas in dreams. But the experiences are different. The data have to be interpreted.

As Oliver Sacks describes:

> Hallucinations often seem to have the creativity of the imagination, dreams, or fantasy – or the vivid detail and externality of perception. But hallucination is none of these, though it may share some neurophysiological mechanism with each. Hallucination is a unique and special category of consciousness and mental life.

Hallucinations insist upon their independent reality and they are not easily refused. 'It takes a strong (and sceptical) person to resist such hallucinations and to refuse them either credence or obedience, especially if they have a revelatory or epiphanic quality.'

From the early Romantics onwards, imagination has been characterized by its spontaneity and freedom, but what is imagined by a writer or a musician or a dancer is an internal operation that, only in being given form, becomes external. And giving that form requires certain controls over what the body does (particularly as a musician or a dancer) and what the intellect supports. What is imagined is not an object externally perceived, nor is it beyond the control of the one hallucinating. Nevertheless, hallucinations cannot, as Sacks suggests, bypass the imagination. In Chapter IV, we saw that imagination compensates.

There I cited cases where sensory deprivation is compensated for by hallucinations. We might see them as indications of pathologies of the imagination; indications that the imagination possesses a pathological side. In Part Three, 'Engagements', we'll enter into some of those dark pathologies.

LUCID DREAMING

The imagination with, before and beyond memory (and working with the senses) reworks, reactivates, but also forges new neurological channels. The imagination, like memory, is primed – the reverberations of a single note, the tonality of a colour in relation to other colours, a single frame of a film; each trigger new connections along neural paths. These paths are then received and recorded in the brains of audiences, viewers or readers; hooking up to their own neural networks in individual ways. These networks operate according to a similar logic in dreaming, but artists and audiences are not dreaming; you need to be awake to be imaginatively creative, as you need to be awake to be imaginatively appreciative. Nietzsche knew: 'the lovely semblance of dream is the precondition of all arts of image-making', but the 'semblance' both stops and starts with the degree of conscious activity in the imagining.

There are two particular points where dreaming and the creative imagination come closest. The first is in stage 1 sleep, with its hypnogogic activities where there is a wake–dream continuum; and the second appears in what is called 'lucid dreaming'. This is a technical name given to those dream episodes in which the dreamer knows he or she is dreaming. They witness their own dreaming. Certain Buddhist mediation practices like 'dream yoga' disciplines the imaginative work in lucid dreaming as it crosses from waking states to dream states and back again. It attempts to determine changes to the dreamscape from within it. By controlling the dreaming they believe they are able to enter even deeper states of consciousness. Film has often explored and exploited its association with lucid dreaming. Christopher Nolan's *Inception* is a case in point.

In the late 1950s when, as we have seen, sleep science began to emerge and psychology separated itself as a science from 'free association', dream symbolism and ink-blots, it wasn't only Hitchcock who was exploring this domain. Empirical data and behaviourism may have monopolized the capturing of government grants, but the domesticity of TV offered a subversive undercurrent to the cultural imagination. *The Twilight Zone* ran for five seasons on CBS from 1959 to 1964. Two of its most famous episodes were psychological dramas around dreaming. One, 'Nightmare at 20,000 feet', has become a classic. But in the first series there was another classic, broadcast in late November 1959: 'Perchance to Dream'. This programme explores lucid dreaming and it effects upon the dreamer.

Edward Hall, the protagonist, meets Maya, the Cat Girl, 'who knows a lot of things', in a dream. 'This is a dream. I'm not here. I'm at home asleep and you're part of that dream.' Maya answers, simply, 'I know that.' Edward is convinced Maya is trying to kill him by getting him to jump from a fairground ride and tries to stay awake. But because of a heart condition he is caught in a double bind: he'll die of heart failure if he cannot sleep and if he sleeps Maya will get him to jump. The double bind is scientifically accurate. We need to sleep and we need to dream. Those with a chronic inability to sleep because the chemical and physiological mechanisms for sleep have been damaged die within ten to fourteen days. For Edward the consequences of lucid dreaming have none of the Buddhist karma about it. He dives out of the window of the psychiatrist's office to the pavement below. Or so it seems – for in the last scene we're back with the psychiatrist who is sitting quietly in the office, while Hall lies dead on his couch, his heart having failed. The double bind is played out both ways, suggesting the average American in the late 1950s is caught between the illusions he's fed and the illusions he conjures. The question is which is the lucid dream. A voice-over concludes: 'They say a dream takes only a second or so. And yet in that second a man can live a lifetime. He can suffer and die and who's to say which is the greater reality: about the one we know or the one in dreams, between heaven, the sky and the earth in the twilight zone.'

Lucid dreaming takes place in what is known as a 'phasic' period of REM sleep where there are sharp spikes or sudden depressions in the levels of brain activity. It's an excitable and complex brain event. It seems to tap into primitive levels of mindfulness and coming-to-self-consciousness. In lucid dreaming this is the consciousness of being conscious *in* a dreamstate; dreamers being able to reflect upon their own dreaming.

It's not just that 'Perchance to Dream' plays with the real and the imaginary as it pertains to psychology. It certainly does that. Like the *Twilight Zone* series as a whole, the programme (aired late at night when people are preparing to go to bed and therefore entering the forecourts of hypnogogic sleep) treats the paranormal as alternative states that we all experience and are all aware of, and to which we are perennially prey. It doesn't just treat; it attempts to induce an alternative state in ways that disrupt everyday perception. Dream and reality are two sides of a Möbius strip here. Hall's recognition that the imagination can make you see things that are not there is a reflection upon both the programme and the conception behind the series. *The Twilight Zone* offers scenarios in which imagination examines its own productions, processes and powers. While questioning the dominant philosophies (of positivism) and the post-World War II veneration of science (and its appeal to the objectivity of empirical evidence), it explores Cold War fears. Reality may deal with brittle and plastic surfaces, but to go beneath them and enter psychological phantasmagorias of the mind or to go beyond them and entertain the extraterrestrial, is to head straight into the cultural paranoia generated by the post-Truman era.

Fear and paranoia go back to simple memory tracks of primal conditions in which we had to find ways of surviving; they go back to traumas. In trauma we are attracted to the very terror we're denying. This is *making sense* in exposed and precarious conditions – conditions existing as much in hominid hunters as Cold War America. In fact, precariousness itself reactivates and rehearses all the conditions in which we learned and recalled fear. Friction-free utopias flourish alongside apocalyptic fantasies; this is the sign of a culture in crisis. Both are imagined states governed by death.

CONCLUSION

As we come to the close of Part Two, on the mental and physical architectures of the imagination that exist in close association with memory and dreaming, let's return to Freud so we can orientate ourselves for further travel. As I pointed out in the Introduction, in turning from his early studies in neurology to psychoanalysis, Freud ventured upon the imaginative and the unknown. He introduced into his study, and lay upon his analyst's couch, a cast of characters whom he got to perform for him. We enter *his* imagination with every interpretation of what is happening inside the heads of the Wolf Man, the Rat Man, Little Hans, Anna, Dora, King Lear, Hamlet and Dostoevsky. And he took an evident delight in writing down the narrative accounts of his explorations. The findings of medical science since his time reveal how much we have yet to learn about the deep mind, the nature of consciousness and the actions of uncharted purposefulness executed beneath the rational. They draw attention to primal propulsions from our evolutionary heritage – aggression, fear, hunger and sex – that can totally overwhelm processes of socialization. Freud saw dreaming as wish fulfilment, and that has been debunked or put into a far wider panoply of affect and predisposition through the experiments of cognitive psychologists and neuroscientists. That said, Freud's anthropological curiosity remains. Imagination is always probing the unimaginable as its source and as its goal.

Caught between the infinities of wonder and the nihilisms of horror, the question posed is what it is we long for. Imagination forages the depths of this question. Dreaming is associated here with what we hope, desire, want, need and crave. The ancient Hebrew psalm writer tells of how Yahweh will 'give you the desires of your heart' (Psalm 37.4). But who can name what they really desire? Dreaming is an altered state of consciousness or subconsciousness or preconsciousness or unconsciousness – since we have no spatial maps, dimensions or measurements for this *terra incognita* of human consciousness. We have only placeholders for what we have yet to understand. Dreaming is an altered state of consciousness that raises existential questions about who we are and the recognition that I, ego, self, me is not the entire answer; for there are continents and islands of incomprehensibility within that I, ego, self, me. What happens then when that I, ego, self, me is not in control and currents of appetite and predilection take over? Dreaming is a permanent insistence that we are not what we hold ourselves to be – there is something more that moves and disturbs and wonders and mystifies and frightens; something as unimaginable as it is ungraspable. And when engaged it dispossesses us.

The creative imagination pushes into the hinterlands of the unfamiliar. We can call it 'primitive' if you like, but that puts us on a timescale; even if that is a long evolutionary timescale. And we can conjure primal scenes of terror and sacrifice, chaos and murderous violence, out of which order and cosmos and chronological time emerge. I don't find such scenarios particularly comforting, though they may point to a profound fragility that inhabits all our experience of what's real; the extraordinary we live with so quietly can be forgotten. The scenarios may be true – many anthropologists accept them as the basis for myth, ritual, religion and art. But when I look upon those cave paintings and portable images from the ice age, I recognize something familiar, even celebratory. I don't see unmitigated terror or what Conrad's Marlow in *Heart of Darkness* describes as 'The horror! The horror!'

As we fathom below the vivid fragments of dreams, something stirs, driven by the basic biological currents of survival: energy, and the throb of reproductive living. It's desire, it's affect, it's fear, it's pleasure, it's longing, it's hunger, it's violence – as profoundly physical as mental. On the semipermeable perimeters of the unimaginable belief arises, inchoate beliefs that all of us live with. They are not necessarily religious. These are not belief systems, but impressions, images, iterations, intuitions, echoes and memories; jarring and associating, condensing and displacing. Indeed, nothing shows the close association pertaining between imagination and belief more than dreaming: we cannot *not* believe in our dreams. We, as a latest *Homo* species, have become dependent upon these filaments of sense and sense-making. From them arise the thoughts, intentions and multiplicity of ways in which we communicate to each other. We form cultures; we build civilizations. But our experience is so much older. Without beliefs we are adrift. Adrift not necessarily on some nihilistic flux, but adrift on the fears of what is unknown, the immensity of that unknown. The raised hand with the extended index finger is not pointing at either atrocity or meaningless indifference. It is pointing at the ultimate and frightening difference that remains unrecognizable and overwhelming. Our need is nameless.

PART THREE

ENGAGEMENTS

VI

Myth-Making

The Marina Bay Sands Hotel was designed by the secular Jewish architect Moshe Safdie. It's the focal point for downtown Singapore: a magnificent awarding-winning building standing on the edge of land reclaimed from the sea. The land has only recently been reclaimed, and the hotel has only recently been built. It's one of the most extravagant and imaginative pieces of contemporary architecture I have ever seen. Given isolated prominence by being surrounded by much lower buildings, gardens and an esplanade, and the backdrop of the Indian Ocean, it comprises three towers. Each tower is in the form of an Egyptian Ankh, or two playing cards resting against each other. So from six split bases the hotel rises seventy stories, forming three free-standing plinths. Resting across these plinths, at the highest elevation of the building, is an ocean liner. The prow and the stern of the liner overhang either end of the plinths. The whole spectacular complex of Marina Bay Sands houses multiple bars, restaurants, a museum, two theatres, a conference centre, a vast 2,500-roomed hotel and a casino. It rises from sea level to a 2.5-acre SkyPark almost 700 feet above the city, with its own jogging paths and a vast infinity pool lined with palm trees and sunbeds. At night the mythological resonance of the architecture sings across the city and its skyline: three gargantuan pillars upon which a ship sails through the vast constellations of the universe framed by the dark stretches of the Indian Ocean and the cosmos. Of course the liner goes nowhere, but among the passing clouds or the shifting moon and stars it appears to be sailing through time and space – indifferent to both.

Its technological ingenuity (using gravity to offset the effects of high winds and seismic effects) is built on money (over $5 billion). It's built to generate more money, and it's locked into Singapore's tourist economy – not least because the huge and controversial casino it lodges has certain tax exemptions on winnings. It's an icon of modern progressivism gazing confidently into the economic future of South East Asia. But what is most evident in the whole of its form and activities is a yearning to transcend the labours and belittlements of quotidian existence that sprawl diminutively below it. It's a yearning for escape into more enchanted realities; to escape war and famine and migrant crises and economic depressions and homelessness and sickness and mental frailties. On the day I visited in February 2016, the harbour it overlooks and dominates was full of ships lying idle because trading was so poor due to the glut in the global oil market, the slowdown in Chinese productivity and the surplus of manufactured goods in the region. But at night, with a vodka martini costing you an eye-watering amount of Singaporean dollars, you can sit in a balmy breeze coming off an ocean warmed by an equatorial sun and fanned by tropical trade winds. You stare out across the infinities of space as the earth turns slowly and the planets circle. The more vodka martinis, the deeper the experience of transcendence – such that one might imagine a new religion being born here or the consummation of all religious longing. Imagine, that is, until you get your next credit card statement; because of course all this comes at a very high price. But it's not the price so much that interests me. Or the fact that such experiences are reserved for a tiny portion of the world's population. In a sense, just by this place being there, even if you can't afford it, you might nevertheless dream of experiencing it. The secular imagination doesn't need money, but it does need dreams and blue-sky thinking; because even the destitute can dream. Below it are public parks and spaces for public meetings. People can look up, and transcend the materialities of a diurnal 'getting by' through imagining the lifestyle that had been architecturally imagined so many years prior to its construction. But then people have been dreaming of this building for centuries. It is this that gives it its mythic resonance.

In this final part of our exploration, we leave behind the palaeontology, archaeology, biology, physiology and psychology of the imagination to examine how it engages with the world we have constructed; how it is foundational to that construction. In the West, we have lived through a time since the Enlightenment in which we believed that all that is cultural, social, political and economic in our world is, or should be, based upon reason and rational determinations. But this is not so; for reasoning itself is rooted in the imagination. The notion of 'progress' so central to modernity's projects is itself an expression of a modern myth. We have seen that the power of the imagination over us lies in its ancient evolutionary development, its profound association with sensory processes, affect, memories, our need for sleep and dreaming, and our hunger to *make sense*. We need to appreciate how that power manifests itself not just in the metaphors by which we live, but the myths that haunt us.

The Sands SkyPark is just one contemporary example. It is a landscaped space that strains to be beyond space (utopia). It is timeless and detached. Even though it is only made possible through all the servile and material practices that give rise to it, maintain it, and produce it. There is nothing explicitly religious about the way it stands guardian to the city, beyond the mythic resonances in the architecture itself that, as I said, could just be a luxury cruiser standing on three pairs of playing cards. But it provides an imaginative and material image of what it is that people with or without religious allegiances dream of, hope for and aspire to: a paradise of rest beyond unceasing restlessness. A paradise without walls – given that the word is taken from the Persian *pari-dae za*, which is a walled-in garden. The mythic resonances of the building are attuned to the local. Through migration and colonization, Singapore is a city where Western and Eastern religions meet and overlap. The building situates its paradise above and beyond the terrestrial and outside time. It offers release from the burdens and vagaries of history; a transcendence of the human lot through the material consummation of those ancient human desires recorded in those ancient sacred texts cited at the end of Chapter V. If this architectural configuration recalls the innocence of origins in the monotheistic faiths, it also recalls the Hindu and Buddhist ideals of escaping from the cyclic time of birth, death and rebirth.

The architecture gives expression to an observation made about myth and secularism by the anthropologist Mircea Eliade: 'in the great majority of individuals who do not participate in any authentic religious experience, the mythical attitude can be discerned in their distractions [or ways of being entertained], as well as in their unconscious psychic activity (dreams, fantasies, nostalgias, etc.)'.

MYTHIC RESONANCE

But what exactly constitutes the 'mythic resonances' I have described? I used this phrase earlier in appreciating the paintings found in rock shelters and the carving of ice age art. I observed there that the mythic sensibility that gave rise to these fabrications and that haunts them still is prior to religion, and so the use of religious language to describe them (or the effects they have upon us) is anachronistic. The mythic sensibility arises with the awakening of consciousness to the landscape within which it is immersed, and the stirring of the imagination to engage with it; the point where human creativity encounters and responds to creation, and is itself involved in that creation. The nature of living is made more expansive, immediate and ambivalent. The senses are dilated. The psychological and the physical come together in ways not yet susceptible to reflective analysis, but imaged thought stirs the blood and sparks the electrobiologies that make living possible. So we strike out here into the mystery not just of imaginative creativity, but also creation. We encounter complex, relational sympathies, empathies and dissonances. And in striking out into the mystery 'spirit' as that which animates both mind and matter, human creativity and creation comes to the fore in forms that give it expression. In that expression a chord is struck in which mythic sensibility becomes mythic resonance.

Let me be clear. There is no going back to Neanderthal mythical or religious consciousness. There is too little evidence – of speech, for example. But what does remain undisputed is their burials and whatever interpretation we give to these (and we do not need to imagine their beliefs in an afterlife or any developed rituals), these carefully laid-out skeletons (frequently in a foetal position) are a response to both a change (from life to death) and a metamorphosis. A corpse is materially different from the human being who was alive and its difference registers complex affects because of the kind of consciousness (with memory) possessed by those who gather round it. Animals experience these complex affects. There are documented cases of elephants and monkeys as they respond to the death of one of their species. They gather round. The corpse is not a material object like any other material object because its past state still haunts its present condition. It is perceived differently.

There have been attempts to trace back mythological thinking to possibly the 'African Eve' and the broken continent of Gondwana. But the mythical sensibility I am arguing for does not need us to discover the historical origins of myth-making. For my claim is that the awakening of the imagination that takes so powerful an effect in mythic sensibility is always available. Whatever the evidence, it was available to Neanderthal hominids, and their burials express that sensibility. It was available to those who worked the carvings and paintings that we see now at Chauvet (however developed or undeveloped their mythical and religious consciousness may have been). It is always available: there are times when the world discloses something to us that makes us stop in our tracks and experience. Like that adolescent moment on a summer's night, in the grounds of the ruined abbey at Walsingham, when I stared up into a black hole and, for a moment, couldn't breathe.

THE MYTHIC SENSIBILITY: WONDER

Imagination arises as mythic sensibility dawns – milky like moonstones and opals. With opals you look for the hidden flame. Poets, musicians and painters have attempted to give form to the nakedness of this sensibility. To reduce experience of the world to its simplest, a naivety is sought by these artists; a way of seeing that aspires to innocence and purity. *Innocence* is a Latin word at root. *Noxia* is 'injury' or 'hurt', and it has it own mythic resonance because it's related to *nox* ('night'). The suffix *in* is what grammarians call a privative. It negates the meaning of the word and, by implication, reverses its sense. So innocence was, by Latin association, related to light, and light expressed that which was ungraspable and so ineffable. Several such words, derived from Latin in this way, carry a transcendent gravity. Like *in*finite, where the boundaries

157

(*fines*) marking out a space dissolve, so space is everywhere and endless. Like *infans*, a Latin adjective meaning 'unable to speak', that by extension became infant or a little child. Semantically, *infans* is close to *ineffabilis* that becomes *ineffable* – that of which nothing can be said; the point where words fall silent.

Beginning in the mid-seventeenth century, English and Welsh poets like Thomas Traherne and Henry Vaughan used the figure of the child as a way of giving expression to this fold in the ineffable from which the spoken might emerge. They did this within the framework of the Jewish creation myth: Adam, Eve and Eden. Religions and their sacred writings are flooded with mythic sensibility, resonance and consciousness. What these poets were exploring was how we might appreciate again, by going back to a fundamental intuition that they imaged as the child's (or childlike), what it is to be a creature. Their concerns were as much anthropological as theological. For Traherne, in particular, this 'infant' (in all its Latin and English senses) perspective offered a view of perceiving creation differently: 'a Tree set on fire with invisible flame, that Illuminateth all the World' is how he described the Cross on which Christ died. 'The corn was orient and immortal wheat, which never should be reaped, nor was ever sown. I thought it had stood from everlasting to everlasting', he recalls from his own childhood. It was experiencing the world around him that developed Traherne's mythic sensibility. In the same *Meditation* he continues:

> The dust and stones of the street were as precious as gold: the gates were at first the end of the world. The green trees when I saw them first through one of the gates transported and ravished me, their sweetness and unusual beauty made my heart to leap, and almost mad with ecstasy, they were such strange and wonderful things.

A new creation could be glimpsed 'Where all his [the human creature's] Body Shall be purified/Flesh turnd to Sense, and Sense be DEIFIED.' In later terms, taken from the poet William Blake, the myth detailed a movement from innocence to experience, and the advance towards *being godlike* ('DEIFIED').

Traherne's experiences share an epiphanic quality with lucid dreaming and hallucination. They disclose things in the world that demand and capture the attention. The object and the image coalesce; the image does not represent – it simply *is*. And what takes place cannot be denied because we are captured by it.

In the closing years of World War II, the Jewish agnostic composer, Gerard Finzi, took up Traherne's poetry in a five-movement cantata entitled *Dies Natalis*. Finzi's work bears no relation to his own childhood, which was fissured by the death of his father, three of his brothers and his favourite music teacher. He had been composing settings for poems by Vaughan and Traherne (among others by Hardy and Masefield) since 1923. Traherne's poetry had only been available from 1903, after a notebook was found on a market stall by Bertrand Dobell. Traherne's great prose work, *Centuries*, was only published in 1908. Finzi was the first to set Traherne's great lyrical outpouring. Three of the five movements of *Dies Natalis* (the title is Finzi's) were written in 1926.

The cantata launches swiftly into a sweep of feathery strings playing *andante con moto* until a solo violin ascends like a skylark. The music of the *Intrada* comes in waves and flows as the signature melodies of the first song that follows are rehearsed and modulated. It sails, it soars, it swoops and gathers taking the strings to a high-pitched crescendo and dropping them into a reflective *poco meno mosso*. And with the smallest intervals between a stepwise movement the first words of 'Rhapsody' are sung *recitativo stromentato*. That is, as if language itself was not yet fully formed, the word not yet flesh, the voice of creation only just beginning to announce itself: 'Will you see the infancy of this sublime and celestial greatness?' Every one of Traherne's words is emphasized with Finzi's usual one-note, one-syllable setting, and a shift from major to minor mode gives them a fresh tonality. But 'this' refers now to what we heard in the *Intrada*, and we iterate again the dip into G with 'knowledge' to ascend from C to D on 'divine'. If that D is maintained for a bar, then there is breathing space for the tenor and a modulation of tone; not grand exclamation now, but small and intimate. 'I was entertained like an angel.' Then we enter top E and F sharp, only to mount higher, moving from a low E when singing about the 'works of God *in their*' to a top G sharp on the first syllable of '*splen*dour' and '*gl*ory'. Then in the quiet *liberamente* and tones of rapt reminiscence the affective expresses the mythic: 'certainly Adam in paradise had not more sweet and curious apprehensions than I'. On 'I' the accompaniment has nosedived to D flat. There's a pause before we are back with 'glorious', the first syllable on a top A flat. I pass by Traherne's famous lines about the corn and wheat, the exquisite phrasing for 'seraphic piece of life and beauty' and 'all in the peace of Eden' to the hushed *molto mono mosso* of 'All was at rest, free and immortal.' A luminous visibility is caught through hearing what no one else could hear – an orchestration of the sensed.

There are three songs that follow – 'The Rapture', 'Wonder' ('and everything which I did see did with me talk') and 'The Salutation' ('so many thousand, thousand years beneath the dust did I in a Chaos lie [...] from out of dust I rise and out of nothing awake'). Traherne is filleted to fit what Finzi seeks: a lyrical intensity and an emotional force that eschews the darknesses of late Beethoven and Wagner as much as it eschews the sentimentalities and coyness of the Romantic child. The pauses, the vibrancy of the strings, the crafted mood-changes from the allegro of 'The Rhapsody' and the dancing energies of 'The Rapture' to the introspection of 'Wonder', enables *Dies Natalis* to avoid indulgence and strip back any possible nostalgia. What is left is the sheer beholding of creation, being created and being creative ('my new made tongue'). Wonder sings out as pure perception of what is imperceptible: the divinely giftedness of all things straining to express itself. The music takes any soloist (tenor or soprano) into the highest reaches of his or her range; it demands superhuman breathing discipline. One of Finzi's inspirations was a visit to a church in the fenlands of Cambridgeshire and observing three ranks of angels with outspreading wings on its roof. Another was Botticelli's *Mystic Nativity*, with its circling seraphs above the oxen stall. This is one of the effects of mythic sensibility when it finds acute and almost adequate expression: it generates and expands its transforming dynamics. 'Natality is the route to transcendence', the contemporary Jewish theologian and philosopher, Michael Fishbane, writes, affirming a perennial and primordial perception. This sensibility is not necessarily theological; just a metamorphosis of the everyday – the simple things on which the beautiful is built.

The epiphanic quality of mythic sensibility that so arrests is first only attested, not ascribed. And it is not confined to either literature or music.

It can emerge from dance, film and painting. Although the work of Paul Gauguin is often appreciated as an example of primitivism, the true primitivism of mythic sensibility is much more apparent in the paintings of Van Gogh, and particularly those works done in the years he spent in Arles and Saint-Rémy. Paintings like *Sower with the Setting Sun* (1888), *Starry Night* (1889), the *Sunflower* sequence he painted for Gauguin's bedroom when they lived together (1888–9) and *Wheatfield with the Crows* (1890) are all startling not just in their colour, texture and form, but in the lucidity of the experiences they present.

Standing before the *Sower with the Setting Sun* in the Rijksmuseum there is just delight and radiance, wonder and surprise. Yes, a few crows are picking up the seed, filaments of darkness, but the yellow sun beats and burns with the blues and mauves, softening its intensity. The sower's arm is extended generously across the field. The dry clay path loses its way towards the light, but the wheat behind the sower *is* orient and immortal – as the man is, buried in the textures of the land, and the great circle of fire setting beyond the fields. The painting throbs with simplicity, plenitude and life. The sower, like the painter, like the viewer, is eclipsed by a oneness that doesn't erase the solid house in the corner, but rather situates it. Everything is rooted in the specificities of location such that details are infused with the timeless, the transfigured and the cosmic. The sun *is* setting: it is low in the sky and the scene has that golden intensity at the end of the day, not the pearl and rose of dawn. It holds everything in a healing, salvific light so that the distance of the perspective is suspended in the overwhelming experience of proximity – the proximity of warmth. Space and time become mythological as we are poised here between day and night, dark and light, summer and autumn. The cyclic has, for an intense moment, gathered everything to itself in one concrete experience of generation.

Our response to what is elemental here feebly gropes for names. 'Sublime' won't help. It's dogged down now in philosophical niceties. But Traherne's 'ravishment' is suggestive – for it has the immediacy of the unimaginable; capturing that moment as it excites the imagination. Sensing (*aesthesis*) opens into aesthetics, and immediately the effect is a transformation not just of perspective but also of the way existence is experienced: gusto, ravishment, wonder, delight are the affective registers of beauty.

MYTHIC SENSIBILITY: HORROR

There is, though, another side to mythic sensibility; and I did say in Chapter V that we would have to encounter the pathologies of the imagination. Traherne and Finzi register the shadow side as everything they are *not* engaged with, but those dark crows in Van Gogh sometimes overwhelm him. 'Be afraid', the journalist Veronica Quaif tells the scientist Seth Brundle in David Cronenberg's film *The Fly* (1986). 'Be very afraid.'

It's a close evening in Lagos, the capital city in Nigeria, and I am feverish. On returning to the UK I will be taken directly to a unit for tropical medicine in a hospital in the Midlands, and isolated. This might help to explain things – though not everything. Night falls quickly in West Africa and with a weight – the air is sultry, stale, sticky and sweet with the kerosene fuelling thousands of storm lanterns. And although Lagos is on the coast there is no cool breeze off the ocean. The salt, like sweat, just adds to the stickiness. Where I am we have the luxury of electricity, though not air conditioning. Even in the diplomatic quarter only a few buildings have air conditioning. But at least there's light.

I'm twenty and coming to the end of a period of working in a Bible School in Benin, and then following up the work back in makeshift churches in the remote bush. I had already been well out of my depth on any numbers of occasions – a night sharing a bed with a man who had just told me he had been a hired assassin during the Biafra War; an encounter with a magician in a market who challenged me to put a scarf he held over my face and he would disfigure me for life. But the experience tonight was to be of a different magnitude altogether. This was the final night when the team recruited from churches across Britain to do this summer school would be reunited in Lagos ready for an early flight in the morning.

I don't know who made the arrangements. Connections, favours, a gift of some anonymous churchgoer? I never discovered. I'm not sure I asked. But this was the residence of someone important in the government, a mansion house, newly built with marble steps, terracotta floors, huge leather sofas with deep matching armchairs, stunning chandeliers, gilt taps in the bathroom and showers that didn't work. There was a man on guard at the entrance, armed, and a high wall surmounted with broken glass. The man of importance was not at home. It didn't look as though he was ever at home. There were no pictures anywhere, or rugs, or wall-hangings. The two large rooms on the first floor we were shown to, one for the women and one for the men, were empty. We would sleep on roll mats. The only item in the fridge was bottled water. And there were no servants. No one but the man who had organized everything for us on the Nigerian side. And he was an American. We must have eaten somewhere else – probably on the flight from Benin. I was grateful for the water. Everywhere else we'd had to boil it and then let it freeze.

Throughout our time in Nigeria, whether alone or in small groups, we would begin and end the day with Bible readings and prayer. So it was far from unusual before we turned in for the night that we were shown a large, sparsely furnished but elegantly shaped room for evening prayers along the corridor from where we were sleeping. It was brightly lit with expensive-looking crystal chandeliers. I don't know whether he was in there when we arrived, I only recall that, when we were sat on the floor in our usual circle, he introduced himself as a Nigerian soldier or perhaps an American soldier stationed in Nigeria. His English had a US twang. Even sitting down he was a large, tightly formed and imposing man, dressed in civvies. Then the meeting began: singing choruses from memory, clapping, raising hands, speaking in tongues, prophesying, readings from Scripture, testimonies – all very 1 Corinthians stuff. It was the kind of church I belonged to back then. All very normal, of a sort – until the soldier began moaning and rolling his head. Then the moaning became a groaning and he keeled forward. His body contorted and writhed on the floor. When he sat up suddenly, his face was a mask of pain and there was foam coming from his mouth. I immediately thought epilepsy, but when I moved the leader of the team put his hand up and signalled for me to remain seated. We didn't try to continue. We just watched. And then it happened: his eyes rolling up and down and side to side and voices, hideous, awful, terrifying voices coming from somewhere deep inside him. I froze – unable to move, unable to speak. I suppose we all did, though I have no memory of looking at the others. I was in the grip of my own horror; the air was thick and my chest tight with it.

It was at that point that the leader stood quickly, moved to tower over the man and took control of what suddenly had become an exorcism. I was sweating and trembling uncontrollably. I had never seen anything like this; though in southern Nigeria there was a lot of talk of witchcraft. We were told to sing, to sing loud, to praise loud, in, an attempt to drown, I think, the sounds coming from the soldier, the violence racking his body. The leader stretched out his hand above the man and started shouting, 'Come out of him, Satan!' 'In the name of Jesus I command you to leave him!' We stopped singing. The silence was awful. I was on the brink of panic. Maybe the others were too because then the leader abruptly ordered us to leave the room. Two older males remained with him, the soldier screaming and writhing at their feet. The rest of us tore out of the room and ran down the marble stairs to the kitchen.

We avoided looking at each other. We avoided any mention of what we had all just witnessed. We were all locked into a silence that may have been prayer, only it didn't come from worship. It came from trauma. Time passed; the howling upstairs continued. I don't know how much time passed. I remember someone thrusting a bottle of chilled water from the fridge into my hands. I remember suddenly everything went quiet. From the open kitchen door several us saw the two older men with the solider walk down the stairs to leave. He walked in strong, measured steps that made the visit seem routine, normal. The front door shut. The leader came down soon afterwards and said we should get to bed; we had to leave the house early for the airport.

There is dark and there is dark; dark matters within and dark matters without. I pass no judgement on what I saw and experienced. The team had been comprised of volunteers. I spent four or five days in the isolation ward and when I left hospital there was no one around who had shared that experience. Exorcisms were not uncommon in charismatic circles. When I talked about the experience with other Christian friends they accepted it as evidence for what they already believed in: the power of Satan at work in the world. At that time I shared those beliefs, but after that night in Lagos I saw them in a different way. I saw them through

William Peter Blatty's novel *The Exorcist* (which we were not supposed to read), and the film by William Friedkin that was made of it. I saw them through a glimpse of the depths of being human, being me, that I had never encountered before; a glimpse of raw and primeval terror.

In this glimpse the awesome becomes the awful, the orders of experiencing the world are rent and what is disclosed is just too fearful to be fascinating. This isn't Voldemort or Vladimir Nosferatu, Grendel or Grendel's mother – though it might be where Moloch was conceived or the ferocious Leviathan. Mythology and religion teem with monsters, hybrids, aliens and misfits. My name is Legion, the demoniac tells Christ as he struggles, manacled and naked among the graves, cutting himself with stones (Gospel of Mark 5.1–17). Legion – many. The experience of terror turns our realities into paper decorations blown into chaos. Christ casts out the demons, giving them permission to inhabit not the uncleanness of sarcophagi with their stench of liquefying flesh, but the uncleanness (for Jews) of pigs. Then the pigs hurl themselves over a cliff into the sea – that ancient symbol of primordial chaos. News spread, the people from the town and villages around it came out to see what had taken place. They found the demoniac 'sitting clothed and in his right mind'. Job done; order restored. Not quite. The folk turn to Jesus. They turn to him probably like the disciples later in the Gospel will turn to him when they witnessed him walking in a storm across the waters of Galilee towards the little boat they're struggling to control: they were terrified. The folk 'begged [*parakalein*] Jesus to leave the district [*tōn oriōn autōn*]'. There's an insistence and resistance in *parakalein* – an invocation and a demand. 'Get away from here!' Jesus should do more than leave Galilee. He should go beyond the mountain range or horizons marking their geographical location. Over four centuries later, at the Council of Chalcedon, the gathered bishops may have bent Greek and Latin in their contorted attempts to identify this man with 'two natures', but among these Galileans the experience of frightening strangeness was much more palpable. Given the demoniac and the Christ, the demoniac they could live with, had lived with (after a fashion).

Nietzsche is right when he tells us how Raphael turns the troublesome nature of Christ and the demoniac into 'the illusion of illusion'. In *Transfiguration*, a demoniac in the right-hand corner of the painting is held back by his parents and pointed out by someone in the crowd. The boy writhes in the shadows with what Nietzsche calls 'eternal, primal suffering'. But the whole painting is orientated towards the light emanating from the transfigured Christ. And Christ is portrayed in Apollonian ecstasy, his eyes lifted in beatific splendour, remote from the mass of bodies crowded into a dark rock shelter beneath the mountain. Nietzsche fails to notice the way the arm of the demoniac is clawing at the air that separates him from the transfigured Christ, but this is a small point. Throughout his writing Nietzsche was unable to appreciate the Dionysian elements in Christ, only the embrace of infinite suffering that he identified with Dionysius the crucified. But his reading of Raphael's painting is astute, whatever the appeal of the demoniac, there is no dialogue between Christ and the demoniac in *Transfiguration*.

This is not Mark's story, for, irrespective of any historical basis, here is a profound encounter indeed, and one not simply between demonic darkness and divine light. Despite the prosaic, pared-down detail there is something of the clash of chthonic forces that opens clefts of bewilderment in the mythic sensibility of wondrous plenitude. There are darknesses and darknesses, some of them dazzle and some of them paralyse. There is the silence of ineffable awe and attunement, and being silenced by the terrifying. The journey to illumination is a journey into *tenebrae*. Imagination collapses into the unimaginable, and who is to say where holy madness becomes mental breakdown?

The imagination is born in, through and as mythic sensibility, and mythic sensibility issues from encounters with unimaginable plenitude or horror. We might call this an encounter with the 'numinous' or the *mysterium tremendum et fascinans*. But what we are treating here is the near edge of the unnameable that renders all our symbolic thinking and communication fragile and aporetic (from the Greek *aporia* – 'unthinkable impasse'). The ancient Greeks gave this another name also: *khôra*. *Khôra* goes back to Plato. It's neither being nor nonbeing. It's what lies outside the demarcations of the city and the social. These epithets at least indicate we are not just talking about a heart of darkness – there is a creativity here that can work for good or evil. There are rents in the fabric of the world itself. Quantum physicists have been exploring them for decades. The creative imagination has been exploring them without knowing what they were for a good deal longer. Joseph Conrad (through his inscrutable character Marlow in *Heart of Darkness*) describes it well:

> all that mysterious life of the wilderness that stirs in the forest, in the jungles, in the hearts of wild men. There's no initiation either into such mysteries. He has to live in the midst of the incomprehensible, which is also the detestable. And it has a fascination, too, that goes to work upon him. The fascination of the abomination – you know, imagine growing regrets, the longing to escape, the powerless disgust, the surrender, the hate.

The nameless and invisible is more terrifying than any face given to evil. Marlow looks down on the dying Kurtz whose last word is 'horror'. *He* is not the one whose soul was 'satiated with primitive emotions'. He is one who discovered after his encounter with Kurtz that 'it was my imagination that wanted soothing'.

MYTHIC RESONANCE

Whether as wonder or horror, mythic sensibility is the source of mythological thinking. It is imaginative activity encountering extreme affective states. Myths are not all about 'deeply felt meaning' (E. J. Witzel), but myth-making develops out of the imagination working upon this 'deeply felt meaning'. What is felt is mythic sensibility. It is from this experience of the affective as a kind of disclosure that myth voices those questions that haunt us: where do we come from, why are we here, where are we going? Before it becomes a literary genre, a musical composition or a painting, myth is a sensibility about being in the world registered in the awakening of the creative imagination and intensifying around objects – a tree, a lion, a bird, a river, the ocean, the sky – or phenomena – birth, death, sex, food, sleep. It invests these objects with communicative vibrations. It gives them mythic resonance. From these vibrations figures and eventually stories emerge as we *make sense* of them. The object becomes the symbol, the icon. It makes present that primordial encounter, which is both exchange and communication.

It focuses those relays of sympathy, empathy and dissonance. In the symbolizing processes of the imagination we become conscious of our own creativity and, by extension, creation itself. The reciprocal relationship between myth-making and language formation is a well-trodden philosophical track.

Mythic resonance is not about psychic archetypes in the Jungian unconscious: the Old Crone, the Ogre, the Father, the Hero, the Great Mother, the Trickster, for example. Neither is it about the employment of certain mythic motifs; so-called 'mythemes'. Such motifs – like the paradise of the Sands SkyPark – are forms in which the sensibility itself has become imagined in a specific, evocative and expository manner. But with what is the symbol saturated?

It is saturated with wonder or horror, intimations of primordial splendour or terror, presentiments of a transfigured, self-transcending order or monstrous and intolerable chaos. It is saturated with gifted surprise and response (gratitude or fear). However fabulous and 'unreal' myths-as-stories are, the stories are the final expression of a trajectory that begins with mythic sensibility. So there is something profoundly corporeal that the stories acknowledge. Hence the 'body' is one of the most intense sites for the investment of mythic consciousness. We will never understand its mysteries. This is why burial mattered even before *Homo sapiens* developed sophisticated forms of symbolic communication. Myths are not about ideals. They are '*extremely* real, *singularly* corporeal, and almost frighteningly material and physical' (Aleksei Fyodorovich Losev). We are seized by this saturation; its intensity possesses us.

We have to tread carefully here: philosophical battles have been fought over this terrain, and the landscape is littered with learned disquisitions by positivists and idealists, realists and nominalists, and several critical thinkers in-between. Modern philosophers are sceptical of words like 'presence'. That material existence of the world is received *via* the senses, even that the sensory drives are actively engaged in reaching out hungrily in order to receive, is accepted – otherwise we're all tumbling down Bottom's bottomless dreaming. But it's the access to the nakedness of what is given that is difficult. As I have repeated: we see *as*; we see imaginatively. We don't just see. But mythic sensibility tears away some veils of that seeing *as*.

168

Neuroscience tells us we can't possibly cope with all we sense. We are immersed, and have evolved to section, interpret and judge. There is no permanence – we *create* it because we need it in order to give our experience a structure. There is no unity to our experience – we *create* it continually as memory lays down a sense of ourselves. This self-making is also continuous. It doesn't deny the reality of me and you, but it suggests that in what I consider to be 'me' and what you consider to be 'you' there are any number of illusions, misrememberings, refashionings after the fact and areas of our mindfulness that we just don't have access to, though they shape and impact all notions of selfhood.

Because this is the human condition, we have limited admission to immediate experience and its translation into symbolic form. Cognitive science and neuroscience are still trying to piece together aspects of this processing and come up with how our embodiment, on all levels, processes our material existence. We have come a long way, but these sciences can only examine the effects of this processing, not the processing itself. The effects are captured on fMRI scans, as the results of cognitive experiments, and through the examination of patients with injuries to certain parts of their brains. These effects are then abstracted from the embodied people who experience them. They need supplementing and integrating into accounts of what it feels like to *have* this experience by those experiencing them. The expressions of the creative imagination can offer such accounts.

The firsthand supplement is needed because the imaginative experience of mythical sensibility, as Conrad's Marlow recognizes, has a powerful transformative impact *on our imaginations*. Affective, endocrinal and sensory motor effects are themselves effected by the operation of the imagination on the way we make sense of our experience. This is significant, because the transformation is not just on an individual level. The power of mythic sensibility to forge modes of mythic consciousness, even explicit mythopoetic acts, demonstrates that myth shapes the way cultures and societies view and express themselves. Myth is powerful collectively; that sensibility and resonance gets cascaded down. Through the imaginative encounters of Marlow, Conrad was attempting to change the way nineteenth-century bourgeois Britain, European empires and their colonial exploitations, and *fin de siècle* optimism with its trifling decadences understood themselves. The novel has had a major literary impact: Orson Welles adapted and starred in it for radio in 1938; it became a television play in 1958; it sparked an important debate in post-colonial theory in 1975; it was adapted for film by Francis Ford Coppola in 1979 as *Apocalypse Now*; and in 2011 the opera by Tarik O'Regan and Tom Phillips premiered in London. Mythic sensibility generates transformative mythic resonance as imaginations are fired by it, rather than 'soothed'. The forms mythic resonance takes are then themselves communicatively vibrant and ferment further forms that do not repeat identically but nevertheless transpose that sensibility.

Trauma lies at the vital core of mythic sensibility. As I said: there is a surprising disclosure – something was not expected. And yet to see *as* means we select and modify our perceptions. So why do we make the selections we do make? What is the basis of our selection? It can only be that *this* is significant while *that* is not. Significant of what though? We *make sense* of our experiences so that they become meaningful, but mythic sensibility experiences significance *prior* to anything becoming meaningful. In mythic sensibility a selection is made for us: the world has disclosed something to us and we are suddenly, and dramatically, arrested by it. There is a quality in such experiences comparable to that in lucid dreams and hallucinations – our attention is demanded and captured by what has been presented to us. In the experience it is not just that fragments of the world reveal a significance or are charged with a significance, but more that our whole perception of things is transformed by such a disclosure. The intensity of the significance 'appears', and in that appearance cause is totally consumed in effect.

Mythic sensibility is not an alienation from whatever has given rise to it. It's a participation in the unfolding of what has arisen. As such the sensibility doesn't transcend the material world; it amplifies the experience of being in that world, as forests deepen and amplify wind currents passing through the trees. So mythic sensibility cannot be reduced to psychology. It's about existence itself. Existence that refuses the constraints of the meanings we give it. So mythic sensibility bears a close resemblance to epiphany: the sudden and even confrontational surprise. One can understand how such encounters can take the charge of the religious, the numinous. But, as I said, the mythic sensibility is prior to religion.

The tension in the unexpected, which is somehow still what is known or has been known or known to be knowable, is evident in Singapore's ship of dreams sailing through the cosmos but actually going nowhere; promising rest in the endless restlessness of the cosmic cycle, equatorial weather systems and the geopolitics of commercial trade. What is reanimated in the mythic resonance is a remembrance, as present now as in ages past, of what is prior to memory because it gave rise to memory or belongs to collective memories into which we are each born. Traditions are not just passed-down transmissions of histories through the spoken and the written. They are *lived* histories. As we saw in Chapter IV on memory, neurological tracts are laid down by the ways we have experienced those histories and made them meaningful. Our brains and their processing have been shaped by such traditions, and such neurological work is part of our genetic heritage. Mythic sensibility at the awakening of imagination, at the awakening of wonder and terror, invokes memories of pasts we have never lived.

So, returning to the question of 'presence': mythic sensibility is the nearest we can ever come to the immediacy of experiencing; a point where imagination is touched and invoked *by* that which transfigures, transcends and immerses it. It is that point where consciousness registers what only self-consciousness can evaluate – not the indifference of all that is available to be sensed, but rather the definitiveness, the facticity, of *something* that was sensed and in being sensed appreciated (positively or negatively): this tree, that snake, this light, that moon, this atmosphere, that mood. The objects of myth stand out because the experience of them remains unnameable at this point. A sensuous, material force and its undeniable presentation excites our imaginations.

THE MATERIAL TRANSFIGURED

With the Marina Bay Sands Hotel, three forms bear the charge of the mythic resonance: the triple nature of the plinths; the ocean liner that rests upon them; and the garden in the sky. Let's take each in turn. We are familiar with threeness from kindergarten counting and fairy stories. But it goes deeper because three has always attracted mythic and religious significance: the three *lokas* of the Hindu tradition (Earth, Atmosphere,

Heaven), the three *trailokya* of the Buddhist tradition (the world of desire, the gods relieved of desire and the perfection of formlessness), the threefold deity of Diana (divine Huntress, goddess of the Moon and goddess of the underworld) or Christian Trinitarianism. 'Three' has significance in mathematics (as a complex prime number), and in palaeoanthropology because there is some evidence that early human beings counted 'one', 'two', 'three' and then 'many'.

We are also familiar with ocean-going vessels and their associations with luxury cruising and exalted social class. But the mythic core in crossing water, and any marine craft involved in this crossing, is the experience of initiation and transition; movement from one domain to another entirely distinct one: from life to death (Charon the ferryman) and from death to the afterlife (Egyptian funeral boats buried with pharaohs, the ship burials of Sutton Hoo and Oseberg). Boats are associated with the crossing of thresholds, with rites of passage, with the sea as an ancient symbol of chaos.

And, finally, there's the garden where the sacred and unpolluted is enclosed from outside threats, violence, ageing and sickness; a site of delight and innocence and eternal reward (the Elysian Fields, Valhalla, Eden). The garden becomes a locus of nostalgic intensity in those cultures where it characterized a golden age in the past – a past now lost.

When combined, the mythic resonances in the Marina Bay Sands Hotel, best appreciated at night, prime emotions and promise a lifestyle. But it is a lifestyle keyed into memories, cultural associations and ancient longings.

In myth the relationship between content and form is not arbitrary because it's concrete and material. And anything can become the bearer of such a sensibility – a Neolithic hand-axe, for example. Priests and poets have always known this. Designers, market developers and advertisers know it also. Traherne could rhapsodize that the 'corn was orient and immortal wheat', but the same mythic sensibility can invest a hotel and a casino.

What persists, when the sensibility finds expression, is aura (Benjamin) or communicative vibration. Mythic resonance is the lingering, creative and transformative trace of this communicative vibration in symbolic form; a vibration that is before the form but persisting at one level of intensity or another in it. It is the impress in the representative material of mythic sensibility: the still very concrete timbre of its tonality. It has the persistence of that quietness that can sometimes be known on a summer's evening in the country: the frogs croak, the crickets scratch, the nightjars warble, a bat flits and a mole screams, but there is a settlement of the land as rocks cool and trees rest back on their roots that communicates something like 'abiding'. It is something apprehended more than comprehended.

As I said, resonances are not references back to mythic motifs – like a lost paradise with respect to the SkyPark or the crucifixion in Traherne's perception of the Cross. They offer a participation; they prime for a participation – not just a passive contemplation. In brief: the line between resting in the land of promise (paradise) and self-indulgent somnambulance in the land of the lotos-eaters makes the SkyPark a complex cultural experience to evaluate. What we appreciate is *living*, *being alive*.

It is this sensibility, and the resonances it affords, that prevents myth being something in the past, something 'pre-scientific' that belonged in primitive societies who needed to explain forces they could not control. Myths are not allegories of origins like Kipling's 'Just So' stories. Neither are they metaphysics posing as poetry. Banishing, vanquishing, explaining away the mythic from the Enlightenment and on into the twentieth century is part of an attempt to create a pure realm of nature that natural science could scrutinize and its laws explain. But with science today the mythic has not been expunged. As scientists push investigations further they only raise more questions. Questions to delight us as the mystery expands. All the complex mathematics of Einstein's general relativity gives way to 'black holes' and 'wormholes' – things not just predicted but imagined *before* we could find them out there. All of us continually stand on the frontiers of the inexplicable, the unknown and the mysterious. In contemporary cosmology, science is working with the astonishing, the wondrous and the unseen: the theoretical physics of nothingness, gravity waves and dark energy. Today what is natural about 'nature' is captured in words like 'regularities', 'emergent properties' and 'plasticity'. In the quantum world there's a whole transfiguration of material existence as 'foam', 'spin', 'lattices' and 'clouds'.

The mythological is being intensely and energetically cultivated in any number of contemporary locations, from actual wars and cultural wars to *Stars Wars*. We live in and alongside the virtual and the simulated where the mythological is ineradicable. Its resonances echo and reverberate. The mythological is most hidden when it is most naturalized – that is, passed off as the unquestionable way that things are. Myth that forgets itself and closes critical reflection becomes ideology.

We *are* myth-makers – that is the point. We don't just produce mythologies; we are creatures created in and through our mythologies. We are our own deepest mythology because we imagine, understanding ourselves and the world around us through *being* imaginative.

MYTHICAL THINKING AND THE CREATIVE IMAGINATION

Mythic resonances change – as certain forms bearing the mythic charge get used, reused, thrown out and recycled in a culture's history. But because mythic sensibility is so chthonic and rooted, it's pervasive and ineradicable.

Today the mythopoetic dominates many cultural forms, from the novel (the *Twilight* series), TV (*Game of Thrones*, *Vikings*), art (the video installations of Bill Viola, the evocative sculptures of Anthony Gormley and Geoffrey Gorman), film (the work of Christopher Nolan and Terrence Malik) and digital games (*Doom*, *Final Fantasy*, *Dark Souls*).

But the mythopoetic has never been neglected – from the Scottish fairy tales so prevalent in oral culture in the eighteenth century, the philosophy of Nietzsche, the operas of Wagner, the poetry of the Romantics and the American transcendentalists, to Tolkien and Marvel Comics. In the past, such mythopoeisis had to fight for its cultural importance (beyond its mere entertainment value) against science. Today we are elsewhere. But what does this cultural shift towards the mythopoetic reveal about us now, and reveal about the nature of being human now? For having explored the material depths at which the imagination operates we need to be clear: in turning us away from Enlightenment transparencies to the profound roots of our personal and collective psyches, this is a new exercise of imagination's power. We are committing ourselves more and more into the hands of the imaginary.

KNOTTED ASSOCIATIONS

Evidently, there is a wide spectrum of emotional intensity between wonder and horror, and so a spectrum of mythic sensibility. The wonder or fear and the surprise or shock they engender head all the lists of the basic emotions. And Jane Goodall is right: these are not just human emotions, though there is greater consciousness of these emotions in human beings. Imagination amplifies these sensibilities. We might conceive wonder and horror as the extremes of mythic sensibility and, as affective extremes, the most disclosive of relations between human beings and what is given in the world in which they are immersed.

A similar spectrum pertains to mythic resonance, but this spectrum is not between two extremities with numerous gradations in-between, but rather between the strength and weakness of the communicative vibration. That vibration is between the mythical sensibility and its expression. Both spectrums are concerned with the power to affect and effect. That power will either generate further imaginative actions as others pick up the resonance and it goes viral, or it will gain very little traction and be forgotten. The spectrum of mythic resonance concerns the power of imaginative association and the way one collection of associations can energize further collections.

From the eighteenth century it has long been recognized that one of the potencies of the imagination was its ability to associate impressions and images. The creative and productive power of the imagination lay in its ability to generate associations. It teemed with blind intuitions in something like Brownian motion and, in flashes, it synthesized. The power of mythic resonance lies in this imaginative and creative knotting of association into a complex form and movement (a poem, a picture, a dance, etc.). This knotting is not always either unifying or synthetic. It is shot through with dissonances and paradoxes; fissured with ambiguities and indeterminacies. As I said, Conrad's *Heart of Darkness* generated adaptations, modifying and transposing the mythic sensibility it keyed into. This ability to generate is the index of the strength of the mythic resonance, the rich complexity of its knotted associations. Advertisers and designers know well the power of imaginative association and the use of mythic resonance. In a world continually being marketed for our consumption, appeal to mythic resonance is an appeal to associate the product with a much wider and more powerful set of ideas, even a lifestyle. The logos of commercial companies as they vie with each other for trade, float like Platonic ideas far above the material contents they are selling (coffee, trainers, holidays, computers). The SkyPark at the summit of the Marina Bay Sands Hotel, while not a logo, draws upon a weak mythic resonance. (Though here the resonance can gain in intensity as the alcohol is served from rooftop bars, a tropical night sets in, the moon is mirrored in the infinity pool, and the constellations pulse.) The ascendency of contemporary mythopoeisis owes much to the commercialization of mythic resonance. So, in concluding this chapter, let's explore that distinction between strong and weak mythic resonance.

THE SPECTRUM OF MYTHIC RESONANCE, OR THE STORY OF TWO BULLS

The bull is an ancient mythic figure. It is found early and pervasively in Neolithic cultures and remains iconic in Xhosa culture today. It gives expression to a complex set of mythic sensibilities and religious sensitivities that become transposed into priestcrafts and liturgical sacrifices. The bull/bison turns up everywhere from the caves of Lascaux to mythologies from Iran, Ireland, Japan, India, Greece and Egypt. The bull/bison/buffalo cult has global reach and it's of ancient origin. There are bull deities like the Egyptian Apis, or bulls' affiliation with deities such as Zeus, Mithra, Anu and Shiva.

The logo of two bulls charging each other against the backdrop of a large golden sun was registered in 1984 by Dietrich Mateschitz when he co-founded Red Bull GmbH. Red Bull is now the highest-grossing energy drink in the world, selling to almost 200 countries in the world – including Thailand, where a slightly different drink was first produced called *Krating Daeng*. It was this Thai drink, consumed by truck and taxi drivers to keep them awake, that inspired Mateschitz following a long-haul flight. Strange things happen to the mind on long-haul flights. All the elements of its logo have mythic resonance – the bulls, the charging, the colour red, the sun – but although the drink has certainly encouraged other companies to imitate it and the sale of energy drinks more widely, it does not exploit its mythical references. In fact, its slogan – 'it gives you wings' – and its use of a cartoon winged bull in its advertising, diminishes the impact of its mythic resonance. Its appeal is to young men, particularly those involved in extreme sports. It acts as a major sponsor for a number of these sports. Clearly, it associates bulls with energy, adrenaline, testosterone and hypermasculinity. But given the power of its mythic sensibility and the history of the figure in mythological thinking and religious cult – *that* is it. Nietzsche would say here that myth 'is thoroughly paralyzed', trading in the seductions of illusion and pandering to a culture greedy for opiates and consolations. Maybe he's right.

Now compare this to the water buffalo (carabao) butchered in the ruins of an ancient Cambodian temple in the closing scenes of *Apocalypse Now*, intercut with the machete attack by Willard as he assassinates Kurtz. It might be viewed as one more act of gratuitous violence among many such acts in Coppola's depiction of the Vietnam War. Kurtz's base camp is strewn with dead and mutilated corpses killed at the whim of the colonel's mood. Yes, through the cutting, the animal is associated with Kurtz, and Kurtz *is* the heart of darkness, beyond good and evil, beyond judgement – a terrifying Nietzschean *Übermensch*. But something more is going on in the butchering of this animal that lifts the terrifying vision at the end of the film into a mythic and almost liturgical dimension. It is both well known and well documented that Coppola wrestled with the making of this film (and particularly the way it would end). He turned Conrad's exploration of the social psyche of late Victorian colonialism into a personal exploration of his own American psyche following the end, in April 1975, of the Vietnam War. In fact, Coppola began shooting the film, on location in the Philippines, in March 1976.

In his gargantuan attempt at authenticity, Coppola had a massive set for the temple constructed outside Pagsanjan. The set was strewn with dead bodies, severed heads and body parts, and the blood runs everywhere. There were even corpses brought in inside body bags that were set on fire to complement the work of the special effects team. This is where Willard (Martin Sheen) would encounter Kurtz (Marlon Brando). What would happen in that encounter, and how the two characters would interact, kept the two actors and Coppola in long talks day and night between shoots, reshoots, torrential downpours and a vast cast of extras drawn from the

Ifugao tribe. In Conrad's novel, Marlow takes the sick Kurtz on to his boat to return to England, and Kurtz dies there. In the film, Willard meets Kurtz as the deep shadow side of himself it is tempting to entertain; a side, given the blistering ironies of the war, that Coppola portrays so masterly. Killing Kurtz is killing part of himself, and Brando's huge, mythical figuring of Kurtz shows Willard that. The killing would be no triumph of good over evil, civilization over barbarity, or a hygienic sweep-up by the American forces before heading home.

So the killing itself would cleanse nothing, and walking away back to the boat to leave the place afterwards wouldn't end the deep brutality of human existence portrayed in the Cambodian temple – only ignore it. Willard does walk away, finally, but the walking away is just stepping back on to a surface routine that plays out the domestic games of soap opera. So the intercut of the sacrifice plays an important part in transforming the contagion of violence, because with the ritual butchering of a water buffalo (a real not staged action) by the Ifugao on the Temple set, the killing is given a terrifying sacred profundity. The film ends, is consecrated almost, by the bloodletting. We don't really see Kurtz being cut up. We do see the carabao butchered as it stands. We see every hack into its flesh by the howling mob, until it falls and its sad, confused and disappointed eyes stare back at the audience. The blue-brown glazes. For the Ifugao, the carabao was a symbol of Spanish colonial power.

The scene of the slaughter wasn't in the script. Eleanor, Francis's wife, took him to see priests performing the ritual when they arrived at the camp built to house them for the denouement. It was Coppola's imagination that made the connection. Brando had returned to the USA. The stature he gave to Kurtz at the climax of the film and Willard's journey into himself and the American psyche, is as troubling as it is immense – total war, total dictatorship, absolute tragedy, the destructive anarchy at the heart of being human that not even Hobbes had imagined. Apparently Brando commented that he wanted to play Kurtz how Conrad imagined him. The ritual slaughtering of the bull universalizes – it's difficult to use the word 'spiritualizes' – the mythic sensibilities persistent through the stark ironies of the film. It universalizes it viscerally. It orchestrates what otherwise would be and would provoke insanity. The experience of watching the ending of *Apocalypse Now* is elemental.

Before the film fades out there is an amazing sequence: Willard comes to stand above the Ifugao tribe in the Temple with the machete that has killed Kurtz in his hand, and they slowly bow before him in recognition that he is their new god. As he walks among them, deserting American soldiers standing prominently blond and tall in their number, they drop their weapons. He moves to the boat holding the hand of one of the crew members who had given himself up to what Willard whispers, echoing Conrad's Marlow, 'the horror, the horror'. The last shots reinforce a sacral obscenity as a close-up of Willard's face, shots of the turning boat and the face of the Temple goddess are superimposed upon each other. Only ritual can handle, compose and contain the resonances of such unimaginable inhumanity. Only myth can conceive of such inhumanity; that is why it is needed and why the need for it is tragic, because it points to a profound discordance in being human. 'If we could imagine dissonance becoming man — and what else is man? — then in order to stay alive that dissonance would need a wonderful illusion, covering its own being with a veil of beauty' (Nietzsche). Ritual allows both a participation and recognition of that dissonance and its ordered 'covering'. Film imitates ritual here, as *Apocalypse Now* dissolves into Aeschylean tragedy.

The spectrum of weak and strong mythic resonance points up the complexity of what we call 'reality', and it's irreducible. The very attempt to erase the mythic in the nineteenth century was an indication of a culture's sickness.

> Without myth all culture loses its healthy and natural creative power [...] Myth alone rescues all the powers of the imagination [...] The images of myth must be the daemonic guardians, omnipresent and unnoticed, which protect the growth of the young mind, and guide man's interpretation of his life and struggles. The state itself has no unwritten laws more powerful than the mythical foundation that guarantees its connection with religion and its growth out of mythical representations (Nietzsche).

We have to come to terms with the mythic not just aesthetically, but socially and politically. Its power to heal or destroy us is formidable.

VII

The Cultural Imagination

We exist in time and, however much we might wish, we cannot freeze-frame. We are immersed in processes material, emotional and cognitive that exceed us, transgressing our perceived boundaries and identities. We do not belong to ourselves, however much we might cultivate the illusions of such ownership. This is the transcorporeality of our condition (Chapter II). We ingest the world around us continually and our presence is itself ingested by that world continually. Our bodies overlap with, underlie and are superimposed upon other bodies physiologically, socially (civic bodies, institutional corporations) and culturally (there are bodies of ideas). We process this transcorporeality unconsciously (through breathing, endocrinal, digestive and immune systems), affectively (through moods, perceptions and emotions), intellectually (through thought, interpretation, translation and language) and effectively (through habits, behaviours, practices and actions). What we call our 'self' just as much as what we call our 'nation' is a perpetual construction site – an assembly of practices and performances and the interplay of multiple modes of memory.

ASSEMBLIES

Imagination expresses, explores and progresses these assemblages. In expression: it takes what's available, it clusters associations, it improvises, experiments and, finally, innovates. In exploration: it probes, questions and interrogates the corporate psyche and its collective dreams. Famously, Francis Ford Coppola said of *Apocalypse Now*, 'My film isn't about Vietnam. It is Vietnam.' There have been a number of films about the war in Vietnam, some of them cutting-edge and established landmarks in Anglo-American cinema – like Stanley Kubrick's *Full Metal Jacket* (1987). The cinematic innovations these films make possible arise from the urgency of going beyond representations of the war ('My film isn't about ... ') in order to enter the communicative vibrations, the mythic sensibilities and resonances of war itself ('It is Vietnam'). The film expresses and explores constructing something novel in the cultural imagination.

As an art of assembling, film production offers a good example for what goes on in the cultural imagination. Coppola wrestled with something he experienced when he first read a screenplay based on Conrad's novella. He then wrote and rewrote the dialogue, often with the main actors involved. He thrashed out the atmosphere he wanted to create with his cameramen, set designers and the composer and special effects team. He was working with intuitions, inchoate suggestions and his own conflicting responses to war – concretely the Vietnam War, but imaginatively any and every war. The struggle was not simply with what he wanted to say. Of course there was an anger and a protest with respect to American involvement in a war that had just ended. But what he struggled with was what he *needed* to say. Or rather, what the whole situation was saying to him. At its most productive and creative, at the level where to express and explore is a *need*, imagination is sparked by the elemental. And the elemental doesn't just arrive for you to tap into. It has to be listened for. The clamour of other claims on attention, especially in the aftermath of a devastating war, needs to be silenced so something can be distilled, heard; something that almost seems to come up from the soil and cling to the palm trees. That's why being on location was essential for Coppola; it enabled him to grope his way into the film.

What this implies is that imagination – which is never just individual, but always socially and culturally located – is most energized in times of 'dis-ease', dissonance. Alone at night, the house dark because you are waiting for someone to return who should already have returned and is now several hours late, the imagination goes into overdrive, feeding on anxiety and fear. It heightens perception, sharpening the edges of alertness, sensitivity and attentiveness. It fastens on to what is being perceived, not always consciously, *as* it is being perceived – in that lies its immediacy. It is the urgency of this immediacy that imagination needs to communicate when it engages the kinetic – in an act of writing, painting, dancing, filming, etc. It is in this manner that the apprehended mythic sensibility is passed on, in a transfigured way. And what is passed on is that mythic resonance apprehending far more than it comprehends; but always groping for more, for a greater amplification of the resonance.

In the land of the lotos-eaters, 'A land where all things seem'd the same', the imagination is torpid, as Tennyson understood. Compared to the 'roar of waters, torrents, steams/Innumerable' in Wordsworth's figure of the imagination in the *Prelude* or Alph the sacred river running 'Through caverns measureless to man/Down to a sunless sea' in Coleridge's figure of the imagination in 'Kubla Khan', in the land of the lotos-eaters (where it seemed 'always afternoon') 'like a downward smoke, the slender stream/Along the cliff to fall and pause and fall did seem.' And the people inhabiting this land looked with a 'mild-eyed melancholy', enthralled by the stare of death. Contentment is not a good climate for creative imagination – it flourishes best on the 'event horizon' of the unimaginable. Invoked by the gravitation of the unimaginable its activity is viral, vital.

PATHOLOGIES OF THE IMAGINATION

The imagination is only psychological insofar as individuals doing the imagining exercise it. But the contents with which these individuals work are the piles of various images and their endless associations provided by the cultures (their pasts, presents and projected futures) in which they are situated and educated. From this swirling biotic and psychotic mélange of images, preconscious and consciousness, perceived and imagined, entry is made into the symbolic. The symbolic structures this amorphousness in concrete ways that ultimately lie to or deceive us. So we have two levels: the ideologically laden symbolic codes we have learned and the unconsciousness itself, which is much more febrile, unstable and occult. Though the boundaries between these levels are fluid and porous, the imagination is a sphere of complex associative activities assembling complex forms.

At times, the imagination takes something of the shape of that exotic indoor pool in the Bond film *You Only Live Twice* (1967). A pool teeming with piranha fish that 'can strip a man to the bone in thirty seconds' (Blofeld). At times it takes the shape of that deep rock pool in a cave into which the hero plunges in Robert Zemeckis's computer animation of *Beowulf* (2007). On coming up, he is met by Grendel's mother ascending naked, golden and seductive like a sexually provocative Aphrodite. The imagination is the space of promise and birth, aggressive urges, guilt, fears, desires, hopes and aspirations. It's a vast, energetic deposit of half-beliefs, images, associations, drives, dispositions, intuitions and instincts – biological, somatic, psychological, affective – from which the conscious mind emerges as cognition that is best lit. Here is housed what Nietzsche termed 'the innermost core of things' that enabled Freud to conclude that 'human nature has a far greater capacity, both for good and evil, than it thinks it has, i.e. than it is aware of through the conscious perceptions of the ego'.

It is not just the self that that imagination gives birth to; civilization too issues from the collective psyche and cultural memory. For Freud, *Kultur* is never happy with itself. Towards the end of *Civilization and its Discontents* he begins a reflection on 'cultural urges' and the work of the super-ego 'under whose influence cultural development proceeds', speculating that one day some one 'will venture to embark upon a pathology of cultural communities'. That there is a pathology directly concerns the cultural imagination and how it becomes expressed, displaced and sublimated in any number of material and institutional expressions. I'll treat the institutional expressions in Chapter VIII when we explore the social imagination.

We are the inheritors of the way our minds have been shaped. That's why, however strange it might seem (and did seem at the time), Freud's investigations into the early murder of the father by his primitive sons – and the origin of remorse, guilt and the super-ego – were attempts to track back to what human beings inherited from their earliest development. We are the inheritors of whatever was experienced in pasts we have never lived, but through which our species lived – particularly fears, anxieties

183

and pleasures. We are inheritors of instincts, forces and potencies not remembered and yet transposed. To these are added our own experiences as they are filtered through our families, our friends, the things we have learned, the beliefs we hold and the sensibilities cultivated in the way we have been socialized. From these, and within these inheritances and personal experiences, the imagination generates fields of embryonic meaningfulness – as perceptions, feelings and thoughts are repressed, suppressed, sublimated and displaced. This is the way we cope with, make sense of and even flourish in the surges of stimulation that comes to us internally and externally. The imagination is not chaotic, as biological life is not chaotic. Certainly, it's opportunistic as it gropes and ferrets out the most favourable and meaningful circumstances, and as it moves towards or away from some ideal attunement between inner propulsions and outer habitats. As with biological life generally, all its movements are aspirational – for optimal flourishing and survival. Pushing to express itself, imagination may not perceive the way ahead or what it wants clearly; it may not even understand its own compulsions – but it *is* directed, not blind.

IMAGINATIVE PURSUITS

Exploring the imagination enables us to assess what is going on in a given cultural situation; what is going on beneath and yet through the symbolic. The imagination admits no boundaries. It infiltrates all human understanding. It's like those granular clouds of space-time in accounts of quantum gravity. These 'clouds' are thick with energetic and interactive relations, giving rise to spontaneous and indeterminate connections. Maybe imagination brings the very fabric of the universe to human consciousness. Spatial terms become too awkward to describe it; the imagination is febrile, breathing. But all the potential for the future (for good or bad) and all our creations of the past lie in present imaginative pursuits. Our imagination maintains the possibilities for our cultural well-being today and tomorrow.

I suggest there are three identifiable levels of this imaginative pursuit in which we are each and always embroiled, individually and collectively. There's the cultural imagination as a vast deposit of possibilities. There's the cultural values or ethos that emerges from engaging this imagination. And then there's the ways we institutionalize and organize these imaginative pursuits – the social imagination. Each level is shot through with the activities and dynamics of the other levels. Each level is propelled by the need to *make sense* – propelled to assemble models of reality out of symbolic resources that are readily at hand and primed to associate. The levels are not hierarchically ordered: the cultural imagination feeds and ferments our cultural values, and the cultural values open the space for ongoing creative expression. These expressions then become sedimented as the cultures in which we live and in our unreflective habits of thought. And since all of this expressiveness is material and embodied, the cultural imagination and the cultural ethos impact every concept we have of social relations and social organization. In this way the social imagination emerges from within the activities of the cultural imagination and the cultural values it generates.

Graphically, the Marina Bay Sands Hotel again provides an illustration: the SkyPark is the domain of the mythic just as the pursuit of indulged leisure is the visual key to the architectural concept and functions of the building. What is generated throughout the building is a certain *ethos* that guides the kind of values to be lived out: values like service, hospitality, pleasure-seeking, courtesy, toleration and civic responsibility. Its website advertises the hotel's concern with 'portions of the local community that are currently underserved'. This ethos is established and maintained by socio-economic activities from laundry-handling to parking, bartending to entertainment management. These activities are the focus for the corporate vision of several intersecting elements – the hotel, the casino, the franchised restaurants, etc. – each of which come under specific national legislature: tax laws, health and safety regulations, gambling rules, and so on. The cohesive vision is for a certain social order that has to live within a wider social, civic and, for Singapore, national order. This social ordering and the vision for its management and maintenance is what I will call the social imagination. But it is evident even in this small illustration how cultural imagination, cultural values and the social imagination work together.

ICONOCLASH AND CULTURAL ETHOS

While paying attention to the animal within us, Freud's account of the psychic perturbations of the id tends to eliminate the positive and accentuate the negative (because psychoanalysis dealt with pathologies). Culture is not all consolation, and beauty is not something we create to dress up remorse. There is delight, like the late clarinet concerto by Mozart, where the clarinet is flighty, playful and effervescent even in the face of the ephemeral. But the imagination remains a site of assembly where processes collide and collude, receive and respond. In shape-shifting between the formless and the informed it is continually in a state of metamorphosis. If it's a realm for burials it is also a realm where things are born; the home of hubris, humility and humiliation – because whatever its fragility the ego can assert itself, live with all its illusions and impose them on others. The imagination's creativity has the spontaneity of muscular reflexes; it's all awareness and attention, alertness and possibility. It can possess or attune. There is dissonance and contradiction, but there is life and startling insight also. Fuelled by passion, the imagination lives by what Nietzsche called the 'intense capacity to suffer', as an activity at the intersection of an infinite number of relations with itself and the outside world.

It is too simplistic to conclude that either the Dionysian or Nietzsche's philosophy are nihilistic. That's like bluntly claiming all those who enjoy extreme sports have a death wish. While the subterranean dynamics beneath symbolic form are agonistic, their antagonisms can be generative. Nietzsche assaults us with a Promethean question: 'do you *dare* to live?'

Recall the *pasodoble*, a dance frequently associated with and staged as a bullfight. The violence and aggression expressed take years of disciplined practice, because the steps have to be stiletto sharp, the turns and twists precisely timed, the arm, finger, leg and feet positions poised and tense with defiance. Destructive, murderous resilience is fused with an erotic intimacy locked into survival. Each dancer is at once totally possessive and totally at war with the other. The movements of a Spanish or Portuguese matador facing and taunting a charging bull may have inspired the way the dance is now performed. But the dance expresses what is more primitive, way more primitive than any bullfight. It draws upon more visceral and older combats – between humans and powerful animals, and between humans and other humans, between men and women, brother and sibling. It draws upon the profound attraction and terror the participants feel for each other. These steps were stamped into dust aeons old; rhythms and drumbeats found and ritualized in our elemental prehistories. However much evolution had diminished our sense of smell, the smell of fear, sex and dominance remain pungent and arousing. The bodies of the dancers have to inhabit their animality like a shaman does his totem, not just perform animal gestures. Arms have to become horns; fingers have to become claws and talons; and heels have to become hooves or blades. Flesh will be torn and the victim despoiled.

The tension in the dance is not just between the partners; it is also within each partner – an inner fight between the disciplined body and the emotional expression. This is an important element of the cultural imagination, for it stores any number of images, associative patterns and indeterminate events within it. But as the true poet knows in writing, the true painter in painting, the true musician in composing and the true dancer in dancing, the expressive force has to take over in order to break through to a new, that is, authentic form of expression. Otherwise there are only clichés and betrayal of the mythic sensibility. So the imagination is in conflict with what comes most easily to the fore as it struggles to renew the language of the medium and strike out authentically. This striking out for the authentic must forge new neural tracks of sensibility, new networks between affect, imaging and memory. There is Dionysian destructiveness, in finding this expression, but it is not iconoclasm. We might call it, after the French philosopher Bruno Latour and the Austrian artist Peter Weibel, iconoclash.

Where iconoclasm means the destruction and defacement of art, iconoclash is more ambivalent towards what that destructive engagement might mean productively. There is an encounter and there is a conflict, but what might be affected by that encounter and conflict is unpredictable. The violence and intimacy of *pasodoble* is a form of iconoclash.

What comes to the fore in the dynamic struggles within the cultural imagination is the propelling and compulsive need to give the expression priority, because the expressive will propels towards something authentic. We might see this activity in the concerto, where the individual instrument – the violin, the clarinet or the piano – is pitched against the orchestra. In the struggle for a new expressiveness its individual music emerges and usually, by the end of the third movement, the orchestra is being led by the inventive play of the soloist towards a new and energizing integration. Brahms's Violin Concerto comes to mind.

What the cultural imagination struggles against are all the old and familiar ways in which feelings and intuitions resist the vibrant communication of the mythic. What is fought for is a new equation between reality and articulation that *makes sense*. Giambattista Vico, in developing his understanding of poetic wisdom, writes about richer and more condensed forms of expression that have emerged historically and 'are more beautiful because they are more expressive; and that because they are more expressive they are truer and more faithful'. Every artist has to fight to find his or her distinctive voice, but it is not just an individual voice. It is rather a voice that seeks to challenge what is culturally available in any given location and time, and communicate afresh. The violin (or the clarinet or the piano) in a concerto doesn't want to abandon the orchestra. It wants to lead it into new directions. In poetry, the voice often issues from reflections in the writing of the wrestling to create the poem. We sense the naked urgency of this need to find expression in Zbigniew Herbert's 'I Would Like to Describe':

> I would give all metaphors
> In return for one word
> Drawn out of my breast like a rib
> For one word
> Contained within the boundaries
> Of my skin.

Although there is a lonely, visionary quality to what the individual choreographer or poet or the solo instrument is doing, the wrestling isn't with themselves, and only to some extent is it with the medium they are working in – twisting and filleting it for their purpose. Finding that expressive idiosyncratic voice *is* vital; and so is the larger recognition and affirmation from those who have themselves submitted to the disciplines of dancing, say, or musical composition. The voice to be a voice has to be shared, shareable. The difference it makes, the novelty it sounds, has to be heard and understood to be more authentic, faithful, true. So their wrestling is with that authentic sensibility, sensed but somehow just out of reach. So they grope, fail and labour, and if they return from that wrestling with something they know *speaks*, something they know *communicates vibrantly* and faithfully, they are usually the first to be surprised by it. Like Rothko settling back on his chair and staring at the painting he has just completed. The artist wrestles with the imagination *in* the cultural imagination in an attempt to get beyond all it is offering to an unimaginable so palpable it's painful. This is a fight; a fight for transfiguration. And by speaking of artists I am not excluding scientists. They too are 'hunting for hidden beauties and mysteries' (Galfard). Maybe we are all on the same quest.

The artist's struggle is not with either himself or herself or the medium they are working in. The struggle is a labour to give birth to freshness that impregnates them; to *make sense* way beyond mere cleverness, virtuosity or technical perfection. It's a labour to be faithful *that must also be* technical perfection of a new kind. A gravity is felt in and through the mundane. It is not seen or heard; yet it touches. The dancer, the poet, and the soloist each know it. They feel it. They can't escape knowing and feeling it. But they don't know what it means. They only know that they have to make it meaningful because that's the only way they can live it and live with it.

CULTURAL ETHOS

There is no doubt the ego is involved here. The line between the confidence and self-belief necessary to embark on that solitary imaginative journey and cocky narcissism is difficult to draw. The felt need to excel and perfectly fuse skill with imaginative inventiveness, even risk, generates priorities and values. So what is expressed and achieved in execution emerges in, through and with a distinctive ethos. Ethos or cultural value is neither ethical prescription nor moral law – though these may follow and social norms may develop from it. Ethos emerges here in the value placed on courage, daring, determination, discipline, faithfulness, truth and a sense of the perfect being inseparable from a sense of the beautiful. The creative and imaginative act is not value-free nor beyond good and evil; it is value-laden and engenders shared emotions that are themselves value-laden. The crafting, tenacity and necessary self-denial can all be rewarded, and competition with others is part of the spurring and whetting of desire. Imagination is also key to that spurring and whetting; for the creative act is lived imaginatively in its perfection and triumph way before its execution.

Generating values is one of the cultural activities of the creative imagination. It is not that there were no values before; the imaginative act does not spring from a vacuum. The cultural imagination is already thick with dispositions, habits of mind and behavioural responses that have internalized the value systems that each of us lives. It is a fundamental element of cultural (and social) change that the creative expression injects new imaginative possibilities into the bloodstreams of social and cultural activity. All these possibilities have their own edginess. They are all political insofar as they resist Tennyson's torpor. In this way the cultural imagination, the imaginative expressions emerging from it and the ethos they generate constitute a dynamic for change; or a dynamic for counteractive repression. Even revolution. The boldness and originality of the act challenges the established – the governing politics and the structures of authority that police and enforce them.

CULTURAL MEMORY

Cultures as specific ways of imaginative living *do not* have geopolitical boundaries, though languages and ethnic vernaculars (and their histories) must certainly lend them distinctive shapes and sensibilities. Language use will impact upon social relations (like class and race) and the imagined possibilities of certain ways of symbolic thinking. But cultures as specific ways of living *do* have temporal strictures; they are vital, dying or dead. Either way, cultures issue, change and innovate through remembering and forgetting. As we saw in Chapter IV, imagination is older than memory. The mental facility to produce and process images must predate their recording; and the empathetic sensibility in embodied responses to the world must be in place prior to the mental facility to represent.

The repeated practising of those responses lays down the body's numerous forms of memory. In the same way, the cultural imagination is inseparable from cultural memory and its transgressive nature – bending and binding the given. It engages traditions (and the invention of traditions) that store knowledge and practices that maintain the corporate sense of our continuity.

It's spring, and all four seasons can be passed through in one day as we travel the twenty hours south from São Paulo to Rio Grande do Sul, the basal ganglia of Brazil. Along its western edge lies Argentina and across its southernmost bounds runs Uruguay. They have a saying down here: when God created the heavens and the earth in seven days, He spent six days down in the Rio Grande do Sul.

It's September in Porto Alegre and we're heading into the centre of town to the extensive Parque Harmonia because it's here amidst the *paraná* pine and several varieties of palm that an annual *festa* is held – the Acampamento Farroupilha. It commemorates, in part, a battle in which the *gaúchos* were defeated. It's implicated in a complex story not unlike that of Texas: a distinctive state with its idiosyncratic, cattle-rearing, cowboy culture who fought for independence from the empire of Brazil – and lost. Festivities reach their climax on 20 September when people (and horses!) congregate in public places throughout the Rio Grande do Sul, bands play, food is prepared (*comida campeira*), folksongs sung (*música campeira*) and dancing is compulsory. This is the day independence was declared; not the day when it was finally denied. It's a public holiday, with schools and offices closing and civic freedom enjoyed.

So you don't feel much loss and defeat as you enter the elaborate fabrication in wood of a small town, the Acampamento Farroupilha, for the weeklong event, there are makeshift bars and barns, homesteads (*galpão*) and stables, with working wood stoves and clay ovens for the baking of bread. These stage sets are worked and toured by women and girls in long hooped dresses and men and boys in pleated pants (*bombachas*), held up by broad leather belts (*guaiaca*) and stuffed into long leather boots. Some wear ponchos, some wear a *boina* (a wide-brimmed, sun-sheltering hat), and all wear neckerchiefs. Several shops in the township sell the distinctive costumes, the leatherwork, the metalwork and the icons of the tradition (like the cartwheel). Groups of men pass round one such icon, a drink called *chimarrão* made in a gourd (*cuia*) and drunk through a metal straw (*bomba*). The drink is made from water poured over a green canopy of herbs (*mate*). Hot water is poured on to the herbs and then the drink is passed from host to guest, hedged with an etiquette of right and wrong practice: the host pours the water and the *cuia* is always returned to him or her for any further water. Don't manhandle the *bomba*! In the intimacy of sharing the same cup social bonds are forged and maintained. In some of the groups younger men stand with lassoes circling above their heads. Tonight there'll be a rodeo in the central arena and a competitive trial of expertise. And everywhere is the smell of open fires on which racks of cow ribs slow-roast and thick skewers the length of rapiers are used to prepare beef, pork and chicken for the *churrasco*. As the fat from the meat drizzles and sizzles into deep troughs of charcoal, all local TV stations broadcast the festival live throughout the day.

Churches of all denominations join in with picnic lunches across the region, while in the Acampamento Farroupilha several local *gaucho* groups (*paquetes* and CTGs – Centers of Gaúcho Tradition) and larger regional associations (some for distinctive employment, like the police) have their own booths, saloons and restaurants. There are associations like these across the world meeting regularly to celebrate their culture and coming together annually for this week of *festa*. But in the Parque Harmonia the fair becomes a living 'museum' advertised by international tour agents and open to visits from local schools. The inverted commas are there because for some, who not only cook but also sleep there, it is a recreation of life in the *campos* (the grassland) that is sometimes taken up elsewhere for weekends during the year. For such people being *gaúcho* is close to an ethnic identity (as it is in Argentina); these people don't dress up as *gaúchos*, they *are gaúchos*. So 'museum' is not quite the right word. We'll encounter another Western word later, with which we have a similar problem: nostalgia. Some things *do* get lost in translation.

But for most today, Farroupilha is a living museum to a history passed down through the generations that few have directly experienced and certainly not experienced in the wild-west way it is presented or even lived at the weekends. And like all such museums it is a material exercise in memory and forgetting. What is remembered is solidarity, a shared past and a continuing tradition. What is forgotten is that such a life was very far from comfortable and that conditions were often basic. What is also forgotten is the colonialism and slavery such a past is built on. But unlike museums there's a vitality here that belies the scenery – an insistence as deep as personal identity itself. There is an existential urgency about the celebrations and coming together that museums lack. Diversion, entertainment, yes – but visceral too in its significance for a sense of belonging. To lose this cultural memory would be to lose a sense of place in life.

The festivities of the Semana Farroupilha are a distinctive 3D event, but there are any number of other constructions and reconstructions of *gaúcho* cultural memory – literature and folksong, painting, film, music and dancing. 'There's a popular TV Show on the local Globo TV (RBS TV – the largest media group in Brazil) called Galpão Crioulo that celebrates *gaúcho* culture with musical acts. This show is more than 30 years old, and the studio set is made as to resemble a *Galpão gaúcho*' (Tiago Garros in conversation). Nostalgia is too small a word to capture the emotional investment here; attachment is as strong as the smell of the acidic soil in tropical rain. Portuguese has its own word, *saudade*. It is frequently the timbre and tonality of *saudade* that can be heard in *música campeira*. The word expresses a longing that is quite distinct from nostalgia or even desire. Nostalgia idealizes and desire has an object. Longing, like the grasslands, exceeds any object that might figure in its expression. Longing is inexpressible; what is imagined is unimaginable.

The activities in the Acampamento Farroupilha clarifies the social mediation of a collective self-image. We are treating loss here, even mourning, that is bound up not just with a past flourishing between the mid-eighteenth to the mid-nineteenth century but with certain architectures, fashions, foodstuffs, music and lifestyles. But the imaginative re-enactment and institutionalization of what is lost fosters a continuity and communal celebration that comes close to being religious. That is, it requires participation in sets of agreed values, practices and festive and communal rites that not only translate the past into the present, but also transfigure the present through a certain suspension of time. The past is lived again only differently; and in being lived again it is given a certain mythological and transcendent quality.

In fact, religious affiliation, even syncretism, is not discouraged. The icons of the tradition are deployed and redeployed in acts of religious socialization and enculturation. The neckerchiefs, for example, are usually red or white. The red identified with the rebels and the white with their imperial enemies. At a Sunday service I attended in the city of São Leopoldo, just south of Porto Alegre, a short rite was performed in which two coloured neckerchiefs were knotted around a wooden cross in an affirmation of a continuing reconciliation. But the link between national and religious identification is made possible because they both share in an experience of the transfiguration of temporal conditions. The cross too is a mnemonic icon returning the Christian believer to events in Palestine in the early years of the first century CE. The icons cannot then be reduced to some theme park trade in simulacra. The reduction of a complex set of historical conditions for life to a series of interconnected and stabilized icons reveals the inner structure of a cultural sensibility: its felt or experiential structure (belonging, ethnic identity); its moral structure (tenacity, courage, independence and hospitality); its social structure (patriarchal, familial, polarized and static gender relations); and its spiritual or transcendental structure (the land, human–animal intra-dependence). While such traditions maintain their vitality and ability to attract high levels of affective engagement and participation then their future is guaranteed. They are, in fact, functioning as genuine 'traditions' – that is, handing on (from the Latin *traditio*, 'to deliver up') to the next generation. It is through such traditions that the cultural imagination is both energized (when the tradition lives) and enervated (when the tradition is dying or dead).

But something happens on 21 September: the complex facades of the Acampamento Farroupilha are dismantled and the Parque Harmonia returns to its everyday use. Lorries, vans and cars come and pack the show away, storing it somewhere for another year. For the cultural memory, reinvented with such intensity for that week, is an entirely imaginary project. It is an *image* of the past. On 21 September the lived event becomes a commemorative event – over for this year – as the quotidian is resumed and a distance from the past restored. A great deal has happened in Brazil and the Rio Grande do Sul since the Farroupilha Revolution and the fall of its strongholds in 1843 to the imperial Duke of Axias. The *paquetes* will continue to meet, as will the area associations; *gaúcho* culture will continue to be remembered and imagined as the practices of *chimarrão* and *churrasco* continue. But the imaginary and the remembered are lived differently now because Farroupilha has to be integrated into any number of other cultural memories. For each of us belongs to several self-images and memories. Some of these different collective and imagined identities will have no association with *gaúcho* culture. They will have different memories. Processes of explanation and interpretation may work across these matrices of cultural memory. It was through such processes that I, as a visitor and observer, could partially 'enter' into an understanding of *gaúcho* culture. But the cultural memories that constitute part of the cultural imagination I have come to inhabit will mean I *make sense* of it through different cross-references. Walking the streets of the Acampamento Farroupilha that September was, for me, like walking through a stage set for some wild-west movie erected in an MGM studio. It was *High Noon, Paint Your Wagon* and *Unforgiven*. I half-expected a camera crane and jib to soar above us at any moment and a director shout 'Action!' And I haven't even visited such a studio. Once more I am engaging the imagination. I can imagine such a set in such a studio because I've seen films in which such sets have been depicted. The imagination is then not just mine – it's shared because it's socially mediated. I can't even see the palm trees without thinking of David Hockney.

The point of all this is: the cultural imagination continually deploys and activates any number of cultural and collective memories. What it shapes emerges from a deeply poetic force, mythic in origin and not directly visible. The force is composed of magma flows and currents of imagery, affect, memory and misremembrance, conscious and uncon-scious. Societies live, and their institutions are created, collapse and transform in and through that living. So the cultural imagination cannot be divorced from the social imagination, though it is a great deal larger and more amorphous – while undergirding all social practices, relations and the establishment of institutions governing, disseminating and evaluating those relations and practices. Such practices and relations (and eventually the institutions they give rise to) emerge from the cultural ethos that promotes the norms, standards and values embedded in the social imagination.

More than this, the cultural imagination is lived, experienced and expressed differently by each individual because just as memories are individual so are imaginations. What I have lived and read and received and reflected upon is not the same as what you have lived, read, received and reflected upon. Hence, the cultural imagination is never there as such. It is always emerging *in* and *as* it is enacted, at once physiological and psychological, cultural, social and historical. From its formlessness and fluxes, form materializes in and through its symbol-shaping and meaning-making. And the mythic still plays within and upon all that is materialized. *Mythopoiesis*, we might say, sums up the entire work of the cultural imagination.

DIVINATION AND THE MANAGEMENT OF PERCEPTION

After the poem, the painting, the musical score, has been produced, then we can explore the cultural imagination more analytically. And such explorations can inform us about the things preoccupying us collectively; our shared pathologies. The explorations move us from the cultural to the social imagination; from the creative acts to the social realities they are responding to. Like those ancient priests poking among the entrails of slaughtered animals to inspect the state of their livers and, on that basis, make prognoses, these explorations into the cultural imagination are like the practices of divination. Of course, as with any act of augury we need to know what we are looking for. But there's no more mystique to this activity than there is to spin-doctoring.

Spin-doctoring reminds us that some cultural productions are intentionally undertaken to bend the way we might see things. They don't emerge from mythic sensibility or resonance and so lack any authenticity. They're mind games employed for political purposes. Artistic labours have been co-opted by political regimes from time immemorial *because* of the power that lies in myth-making and the creative imagination. Propaganda and censorship recognize that the imagination is powerful. An artist needs food, shelter and friendship like anyone else. Some of them, perhaps the best of them in the past, have had their patrons; patrons interested in what has been called, since the 1980s, 'perception management'.

'Perception management' has been defined by the US military as:

> Actions to convey and/or deny selected information and indicators to foreign audiences to influence their emotions, motives, and objective reasoning as well as to intelligence systems and leaders at all levels to influence official estimates, ultimately resulting in foreign behaviours and official actions favourable to the originator's objectives. In various ways, perception management combines truth projection, operations of security, cover and deception, and psychological operations (Department of Defense Dictionary of Military and Associated Terms).

It's a tool for controlling information, creatively, for the manipulation of public consciousness. Its aim is to transform, confuse and direct the cultural imagination. And as with many other research initiatives by the military, the tool was quickly taken up by image consultants, branding executives and PR managers.

At a recent executive meeting of one major international insurance company, the directors (I am told) sat down to discuss what future risks they should plan to insure against now – the risks that no one is yet aware of but which are already forming in the imaginations of peoples such that future fears are emerging. I said to the executive who told me about this meeting, 'You're actually one step away from giving those fears, that might not be even real, a shape they wouldn't necessary have and marketing miniscule risk as something maximally threatening.' He agreed. That's what risk management is all about at the level of insurance: success comes from getting a lot of people to insure against something minimally possible but the threat of which is much, much larger *in their imaginations*. Trying to persuade people that the risks are higher than they really are (statistically) is an exercise in belief formation and imagination-capture. Facts are not that important when it comes to fears.

Explorations of the cultural imagination can unravel the politics of its manipulation. Through the malleability of the cultural imagination we are not only able to diagnose future trajectories, we can form them. And that's what the executives at that board meeting were about: fear planning.

So what does our contemporary return to the mythic and epic reveal about our present cultural imagination – its hopes, its fears, its values, its dominant preoccupations?

I suggested earlier that film can be understood as a form of collective dreaming. It can also be viewed as a form of perception management: its power over the audience lies in its ability to capture the imagination. And so it's to film we will turn; in fact, to a series of films by the same director covering the period 2005–12. They each treat mythic material self-consciously and all three films were highly acclaimed with high gross earnings. That means: (1) they did the job – they captured the imagination; (2) they *made* us believe. Their success, then, is an indication that they struck a certain chord in a certain manner with an international public. I take popularity here as an indicator of a strong resonance with an underlying and shared cultural imagination *that can be captured*.

BATMAN AND BLACK HOLES

With Christopher Nolan's Batman films (*The Dark Knight Trilogy*: *Batman Begins*, *The Dark Knight* and *The Dark Knight Rises*) we enter the secular imagination. There is nothing explicitly religious about them. There are dizzying transcendences from skyscraper heights, but the mysteries they open for us are all within ourselves. Nolan plumbs the unimaginable, but that unimaginable is the endlessness of our own longings, fears, desires, hopes and damage. In *Interstellar* (2014 – not his best movie, though his most innovative cinematographically), the hero, Joseph Cooper, is only saved by submitting himself to the gravitational pull of the black hole Gargantua. There, in the kernel of an infinite density, he abandons his spacecraft and descends deep into the 'black mischief' only to find he is falling through a vast computer. In his accelerating descent he catches hold of what seems to be a shelf in a vertiginous library. Only it's *his* library. He floats at the back of the bookshelves in his study, and, on the other side, there is simultaneously both his daughter as a young girl and his daughter as an adult. This was the room in which in he abandoned his younger daughter in favour of a heroic world-saving quest. Both women are trying to understand why the books moved in the past, the past that initiated that quest, and what the 'ghostly' movements were trying to communicate. Cooper's radio link with the android in his spacecraft cuts in.

Cooper: We survived.
Android: Somewhere in their fifth dimension they saved us.
Cooper: Who the hell is 'they' and why would they want to help us?
Android: I don't know.

But providentially placed by an undefined 'they' (that could, given the science informing Nolan's script, be future scientists on earth) is a time-bending key to how Cooper will be able to return to earth. The omniscience of this providence, governing both past and future through harnessing gravity waves, navigates the complex plotting of the film script like the invisible hand of a divine and omnipotent director.

It is the vision behind Nolan's overriding sense of control – the director's control enforced over every frame, shot and edit – that is important; because this is where we enter *his* subconscious as it engages with the cultural imagination of twenty-first-century, Western realities. In this way, although Nolan is certainly one of the answers to Adriana's labyrinthine question to 'Dom' Cobb in *Inception* ('whose subconscious are we in?'), he is only *one* of the answers; because the subconscious is also collective, and participated in by audiences that appreciate Nolan's work. As with *Inception*, the dreams are shared – most particularly when Nolan takes on the Batman icon (almost eighty years in the making), his mythic battles with the inmate freaks of the Arkham Asylum and the commercial franchise that has grown up from his first appearances in DC Comics.

Nolan translates this older product of the cultural imagination into his own, playing with anxieties that have arisen through terrorism and mass surveillance, torture and a bubbling war between the haves and the have-nots. These anxieties, specifically male gendered (his female characters tend serve his studies of masculine pathologies), circulate around something more metaphysical, inexplicable and not altogether dark (while certainly being dark). There is a *film noir* edginess to his work, but also something extraordinary. Metaphysical enquiry (into truth, knowledge and identity) folds into and out beyond the pathological (lies, deceptions and betrayals) as Nolan's work treats split personalities, memory loss, obsession, paranoid fears, sleeplessness and trauma. Like Cooper, drawn into the gravity of that gargantuan hole, the hole similar to the one I was told about on that night in Norfolk, Nolan is fascinated by the enormous gaps in all our self-understanding and the way we *make* life experiences intelligible. He is fascinated by how what coheres is partial and fragile – opening possibilities for both comedy and tragedy. So he probes the hole in and beyond all our imagining that collapses the differences between real and fictional constructions; the imagination to be feared for its destructive and illusory productions and the imagination that can mend. By facing, entering and passing through the hole, some form of weak redemption is achieved. It's a redemption fraught with illusions, virtual and spliced realities, misperceptions and self-deceptions.

In *Batman Begins* the hole is the cave into which the young Bruce Wayne falls as a child in a game with the equally young love of his life, Rachel Dawes. Significantly, the scene in which this event is portrayed is both a dream and a flashback; at the level of imagination (and Nolan's cinematic art) there is no distinction. In the hole bats engulf Wayne, and this is the phobic trauma from which he has to be delivered if he is to emerge as a new kind of philanthropist following the murder of his parents at a charity function by a hapless and mentally unstable mugger. Fear, Batman's beginning, is an association of the chaotic circling of black wings and strident echoes with the arbitrary as violent, interruptive and meaningless. Nolan, a student of English literature at university and immersed in English film-making, would have known E. M. Forster's *Passage to India* and David Lean's adaptation in 1984 of the scene when Mrs Moore emerges panic-stricken from the echoes in the Marabar Caves. Her experience *is* metaphysical and her world view tragic in its modern valence: 'I suppose, like many old people,' she tells Adele, 'I sometimes think we are merely passing figures in a godless universe.' From that hole in the ground Wayne, with his butler, Alfred Pennyworth, and later his corporate employee, Lucius Fox, will create the techno arsenal of Batman's cave – from which Gotham's deliverance from public anarchy will emerge.

But prior to that reimagining of the cave, Wayne has to face his fears. In the Himalayas, under the training of Henri Ducard/Ra's al Ghul (whose name in Arabic means 'the head of the demons') and numbered among the League of Shadows, he learns to combat fear through obsessive bodily discipline and self-control. In this way, Nolan eschews the supernatural as a source of power for his superhero: Wayne's alter ego has a visceral realism centred on his physique; his body becomes his defence against psychosis, personal and social. Like the body of a suicide bomber (or bombs strapped to the bodies of victims by the Joker), Wayne's body becomes a lethal weapon. In the penultimate scene of the final film, *The Dark Knight Rises*, and in an ironic reversal of a suicide bomber's destructive task, Batman flies the nuclear bomb away from Gotham's cityscape to detonate it and himself in the blue yonder. Seemingly.

We are a long way from the Caped, even the camp, Crusader of the past and the immortal Ra's al Ghul of DC comics. Corporate billions facilitate the technology that extends Wayne's physical self-control and discipline. They extend it prosthetically. The prosthetics literally mask the truth of human fallibility. They may turn Wayne's body into a mythic fighting machine, but they also create the chink for Wayne's self-deception. Ducard/Ra's al Ghul is the first of many characters who seem one thing and turn out to be something else – like the Batman himself. Wayne rescues him only later to be betrayed by him. Ra's al Ghul's daughter, Talia, will seduce and then betray him in *The Dark Knight Rises*. So the demons are not so much exorcized as externalized by the mask. And the Batman himself is no countervailing angel. In *Batman Begins* he might pose as the deliverer of Gotham from the likes of Ra's al Ghul and the Scarecrow, but in not leaving Ducard to die when the training camp explodes in the Himalayas he has brought this on himself. And, in effect, in the end, he is forced to become Ducard's executioner, compromising his 'rules' and becoming a killer as he handcuffs Ducard to a train about to crash into its terminal, and escapes.

As the dark knight rises he becomes and remains an urban vigilante, one of the shadows even if not part of the League; entwined in anarchies involving impossible moral choices. He may be a vigilante with good intentions, even sacrificing his reputation (in *The Dark Knight*) and his life (in *The Dark Knight Rises*), but his chivalric rescuing is only partial (Rachel Dawes is murdered) and justice is achieved only through paradoxes of deception, theatrical fictions and a magician's acts of disappearance (he doesn't really die). So we're back with Plato's 'golden lie' that enables the stable and just order of the city state. Wayne's sense of social order, fed and maintained by such illusions, is pitched against the Joker's brutal honesty: 'I'm an agent of chaos [...] and you know the thing about chaos [...] it's fair.' Batman is no messianic figure like so many American heroes; but a new type of *Übermensch* upholding justice by placing himself outside the law and preying upon the fearful imaginations of the citizens of Gotham by employing technological means to effect a supernaturalism that is, in fact, the same conjuring trick explored in an earlier work by Nolan, *The Prestige* (2006). It is fear and the endless need for fictional redeemers that maintains the social order and, through the psychotic chemicals poured into Gotham's water system in *Batman Begins*, fear can also tear it apart. The need for fictional redeemers is a deeper and inerasable human pathology. The Batman is beyond fear like the Joker – his ultimate and final enemy in *The Dark Knight* – and both of them are totally captivated by the idea of being a fictional redeemer. The manipulations of fear and fiction, and a culture founded upon it, is the thematic focus of this film in which animal instinct meets ingenious intuition, and rational order struggles with its nemesis: the logical machinations of hyperintelligent insanity; the unleashing of a meaningless, violent depravity that is also at the heart of being human.

The question circulating throughout this trilogy concerns what is it to be human with respect to the animal and the transhuman (the technologically rebooted superman). Gyrating in this circulation are also questions and compromises concerning advanced corporate capitalism. So *homo economicus* meets *homo lupus*. Wayne Enterprises is a global business, and although Bruce himself is indifferent to either his business's success or bankruptcy (even naively handing over the reins to Gotham socialite Miranda/Talia al Ghul), corporate finance sustains his vigilante lifestyle *and* the lifestyle of his playboy alias. In fact, the critique of capitalist greed constitutes a theme throughout Nolan's other films (particularly *Memento* and *Inception*) while he remains entwined within the multi-billion-dollar

Warner Bros. empire, and nurtures that empire with his box office winners. The terrorism of all Batman's protagonists (Ra's al Ghul, the Joker, Talia and Bane) is fuelled by the attempt to terminate a material decadence in Gotham that has widened immensely the gaps between the super-rich, underworld exploitation and desperate poverty.

Selina Kyle (Catwoman) portrays the options in such a world for a resourceful and beautiful young woman. In the comics, though not in the film, there are suggestions of prostitution; in the film she and the Joker (if he is to be believed), share an abusive past associated with social deprivation. Significantly, the object of desire in *The Dark Knight Rises*, around which the vigilante and villains struggle, is a nuclear bomb manufactured (albeit for energy-saving and eco-friendly services) by the tech-savvy Wayne Enterprises. Salvation and destruction are two sides of the same coin; like the twinned sides of Harvey Dent's coin on the arbitrary flip of which he makes 'his own luck'. Ironically, Talia (a Batman nemesis whose real power lies in the seductiveness of *noir*'s *femme fatale*) stabs the penthouse superhero with a knife. She, like the Joker, is technologically unsophisticated. He murders one of his first victims with a sharpened pencil (the blunt end).

But unlike Talia, Bane, Scarecrow or Ra's al Ghul, there's no aim behind the Joker desire; no cause to fight. His presence bears a profundity deeper than all Batman's other villains – something of the mythic charge of the folkloric trickster and the Jungian archetype. He is the embodiment of transgression. We are confronted with a force that cannot be contained within the apocalyptic fantasies of either Ra's al Ghul or his daughter. We are confronted with chaos itself. The 'hole' in the moral and social universe, entered and exited in the cave of *Batman Begins*, appears again as the pit in *The Dark Knight Rises*. Broken by Bane and betrayed by Catwoman, the unmasked Bruce Wayne is thrown into the pit from which only one other person has escaped, Talia al Ghul. The pit is full of the broken. They stare up a sheer rock shaft towards a daylight that is unobtainable; stare up at a transcending hope of deliverance where there is no hope. The pit is a contemporary cinematic trope for Dante's inferno, hung with a sign that reads: 'All hope abandon ye who enter here. Through me you pass into the city of woe: Through me you pass into eternal pain.' Wayne again ascends by confronting his fears and overcoming them.

But in *The Dark Knight* there is no 'hole' portrayed because a hole accords with the logics of space, even if it breaches them. 'Some men', as Alfred tells Bruce, 'are not looking for anything logical like money. They can't be bought, bullied, reasoned or negotiated with. Some men just want to watch the world burn.' 'Men' is a significant word in Nolan's movies. Women slip and swerve through the plots, sometimes subverting the stereotypes of saint, penitent and terrorizing witch. Wives are frequently dead, even murdered. Nolan's imagined worlds are manmade, and so the traumas and pathologies in such worlds emasculate. His Batman might not be camp, but his masculinity is at breaking point and his sexuality a parade of heteronormative clichés. The 'hole' in *The Dark Knight* is Gotham City itself viewed from its towering pinnacles in those IMAX shots of Batman looking down like a bird of prey. In one particular shot, knowing his concealment behind the mask is responsible for several murders, he stands holding his head as a medley of voices circle schizophrenically around him. The vertigo, topographic and moral, is an inner state of the male mind, as it is in so many of Nolan's leading characters. 'You complete me', the Joker tells him, and as for all those living down there in the darkened riddle of streets, 'they are only as good as the world allows them to be'. And the world is a film set; its script running in several narrative directions simultaneously and on multiple levels, temporally and spatially.

Imagination, deeper than rational calculation, is conceived as the resource for utopian hopes, alter ego goods, the most cataclysmic chaos and predatory evils. And Nolan gives no answer to how one might predominate over the other. He can't: for as a film director he too is involved in manipulating while exploring the cultural imagination. The Batman trilogy, like so many of Nolan's films, treats the dark paradoxes of the film director's role with respect to that cultural imagination: he is conjuror and joker, he is *Übermensch* and entertainer, he is manipulator and saviour. Beneath the masks or make-up are unimaginable depths for good, evil and self-delusion captured in shots of underground warrens of intrigue, violence and violation, and the figure of the dark knight standing guard on the pinnacles of modern temples of commerce overlooking the city at night. He is tempter and temptation. Nolan is never sure whether he is part of the social problem or a contributor to its solution. Any transcending of this paradox is *through* immersion in his films. So are they means for escaping or entering more profoundly our social and moral pathologies? Either way, Nolan knows – and his films self-consciously portray this knowledge – that his illusion-manufacturing is not innocent. It paves an ambivalent way between utopia and dystopia, hope and terror, the aspirations of human love and its twisting disappointments and failings. And he is not confident there is any easy way through a maze of impossible moral choices. Nolan is himself Hollywood's dark knight, and the urban landscape is a film set that only glitters and soars seductively at night *if* the walls of Arkham Asylum can keep the anarchic other repressed and incarcerated.

Nolan didn't invent the asylum, that's part of DC mythology, but Nolan brings it into cinematic production as something terrible and terrorizing that lies just beneath the thin skin of the law-abiding. In fact, it is the presence of the law that reveals the dynamic power of transgression. The repressed, knowing itself to be repressed, returns, and what is policed haunts and infects those doing the policing. The meditation culminates in the consummate question: 'who can deliver us from this fascination with oblivion?' But there is no divine grace to answer this question for Nolan. The dark vigilante suspends the law in a state of exception, but he bears none of the marks of the messiah. In *Interstellar* the only hope for human survival is that there might be a 'they' who can save the day for us from out of a time beyond our time; in some indefinite future that can redeem the all-too-particular past. We are not able to do it ourselves.

TRANSITION

As I said at the beginning of this chapter, the cultural imagination and the cultural values that emerge as it is engaged cannot be separated from the social imagination. It creates, sustains, critiques, offers hope and harbours fears about the way we conceive ourselves in relation to others, and how we organize our shared existence. Film, like the other creative arts, is a bridge between our collective cultural subconscious and our social realities. There is little in the way of ordinary family life and domesticity in Nolan's work; he is wary of people and what they believe about themselves. There are moments of self-sacrifice, moments of altruism; there's a desire for justice and a shared social good. But the social world reflected in Nolan's films is one in which people are bewildered, fearful and isolated. Governance is riddled with criminality and compromise. It is compromised by its very willingness to be deceived, and to suspend our disbelief that the exercise of the imagination requires. Imagination is just as much a problem as a solution; an open wound as much as an antiseptic cream. In this situation, Nolan is a dream-planter like Cobb in *Inception*. But will the harvest fail (as in the opening scene of *Interstellar*) or flourish (as in the penultimate scenes of the same film)? Is the dream planted as part of a heist or part of a plan for deliverance? Nolan can't answer that question. He can only dream the dreams he dreams, and make them publicly available for consumption. But a flaw runs throughout his film-making: he is unsure this is either a worthwhile or meaningful enterprise. He can't commit to the projects without also undermining that commitment. The willing suspension of disbelief might ask too much; anaesthetise too much; and create the conditions for an ultimate betrayal. The films wait for the impossible 'they' – deferred endlessly – who might enable him to believe in himself. None of his male protagonists can believe in themselves. The terrorized and terrorizing worlds they inhabit foreclose on the option for foundations necessary for assurance and belief. They, Nolan, we who resonate with what his films communicate, are fragments of ego floating in a 'raw, infinite subconscious' (Cobb in *Inception*) – and we don't know whose.

Cultural productions like Nolan's Batman trilogy emerge from and develop the cultural imagination, and give expression to the cultural ethos of any social and historical moment. They are cultural events. But, launched into the public domain, the images, myths, narratives and values they communicate impact the social. Not all events are cultural, some of them are most certainly social – like worker strikes or the passing of laws, the coronation of monarchs or the declaration of war. Several film critics saw *The Dark Knight* as a post-9/11 allegory, but there is an enormous difference between Batman's descent into the criminal underworld (housed high in the financial towers of Hong Kong) and the attacks on the World Trade Center. Allegory is a product of the cultural imagination; the 9/11 attacks posed a challenge and an affront to a governing social imagination (American liberal democracy).

VIII

The Social Imagination

t's documented in photographs, videos and film because it was a national celebration: busloads of young men and children, laughing for cameras, jostling each other for a place at the window so they could be seen, singing like football supporters setting off to watch their home team play away in some big match. They're in T-shirts, many with the first flush of adolescence on their upper lips, several still not shaving. And they are all wide-eyed with expectation; playing it for the newsreels. There were female volunteers too; only they were not filmed. You can almost smell the sweat of these boys in their blind enthusiasm. Only these crowded buses were heading for the borders of Iran and Iraq and these were the *Basij* ('the Mobilization') − a cadre of mainly young but also some very old volunteers; paramilitaries primed for Shi'a martyrdom. They represented eighty-four per cent of the Iranian fighting force, according to 'official' statistics; and they composed almost fifty per cent of the country's 190,000 slain in that war alone. As I write they are still fighting in the conflict with Syria.

It's 1981, only months after Saddam Hussein had invaded Iran in September of the previous year. He was taking advantage of Iran's weakness following the revolution that overthrew the Shah and ushered in the Shi'a theocracy under the Grand Ayatollah Khomeini. While he wanted to seize control of the Shatt al-Arab waterway, Hussein was also responding to Khomeini's call for an Islamic revolution in Iraq; the call was inciting Shi'a enclaves in that Sunni-dominated country. Hussein was backed by the Americans, whose embassy in Tehran had been occupied in early November 1979. The Iranians still held fifty-five diplomats and American citizens hostage. The British, who had long-standing oil interests in the country, also backed him. Water and oil and devotion dispatched these busloads of young men and children as Khomeini's answer to Iraq's well-stocked and technologically advanced arsenal. They were Khomeini's answer to 'Westoxication' in general.

Along the borders the Iraqis had placed thousands of land mines and behind them squadrons of tanks. It was the God-commanded task of these volunteer recruits to walk into the minefields and carve a path for the Iranian advance – 10,000 children were sacrificed in that year alone, as they walked in waves into the line of Iraqi fire and detonated the mines with their bodies. Later in the struggle, when 'human waves' of up to a 1,000 volunteers were used to drive back the Iraqis, they were given blankets to wrap around them so the body parts of individual martyrs could be identified and sent back home packed into makeshift coffins. Christoph Reuter, a journalist for *Stern*, notes: 'By the mid-1980s there were already forty square kilometres of graves standing in dense rows, quickly weathered by the smog and by Teheran's harsh climate of piercingly cold winters and hot summers. Young people – twelve, fourteen, sixteen years old – watch you from photos on the headstones.'

THE KEYS TO PARADISE

Khomeini was a charismatic and forceful rhetorician, but something more its needed to trigger human sacrifice on such a staggering scale than the raw convictions of an Islamic cleric; a scale so impressive and unthinkable that it forged a new form of guerrilla warfare – the suicide bomber. We will explore in this chapter the profound associations of mythic resonance and the social imagination: the way we conceive of our collective lives, their meaning, their destinies and their organization. In the social imagination religion and power are inseparable; the sacred and the profane, the public and the private, are merely conceptual distinctions – they don't pertain to the way life is lived in and through the imagination, somatically, affectively and relationally. For Khomeini returned to Iran draped in a mythic thinking that he perpetrated but didn't create. He mobilized what was already there in the cultural imagination and ordered social life accordingly.

In Iran, traditionally, Shi'a Islam was not given to heroic uprisings; it was a quiet and interior piety. But its cultural memories were now reinvented, in part as a response to a colonial power that devalued their pre-colonial history and saw itself as bringing light into their barbaric darkness. Through the writings, lectures and seminars of Ali Shariati from the mid-1960s to his exile to Britain in 1977 (where he died), a generation was captivated by his imagined recreation of an authentic Shi'a Islam. With a Marxist and anti-clerical edge, he conjured his namesake the Caliph Ali, the son-in-law and cousin of the Prophet. It was Ali's son, Husayn ibn Ali, grandson of the Prophet, who fell in the Battle of Karbala. The battle took place in the seventh century CE (year 61 in the Islamic calendar) and Husayn was murdered by one Yazid I, the second caliph of the Umayyad Caliphate, with most of his family and friends (including his baby son). The Shi'a, who believe true Islam is to be passed down through the descendants of Mohammed, view this battle as decisive for the origins of their tradition and their sectarian differences with the Sunnis (who believe the caliph is to be elected by Muslims through representatives). In the Shi'a liturgical calendar, the Battle of Karbala and Husayn's murder are commemorated annually over ten official days. His death is seen as a sacrifice, and Shariati recruited a militia of guerrilla-martyrs to defy the Shah. 'Wage jihad,' he told them, 'and kill if you can, if you cannot, accept martyrdom and die.' In the process, Shariati turned the Arabic noun for 'struggle' that was inner, spiritual and strengthening to the moral fabric of a good Muslim society, into a word for war and revolution. The emotional and imaginative power of cultural memory, once invoked and inflamed, bears all before it. As Michel Foucault so aptly observed in the opening sentences of his essay 'Is it Useless to Revolt?', published in *Le Monde* on 11 May 1979: 'Last summer the Iranian said: "We are ready to die by the thousands in order to get the Shah to go". Today, it is the Ayatollah who says: "Let Iran bleed so that the revolution may be strong."'

The language of war, like the language involved in the waging of war, is viscous with mythic resonance. It becomes a language saturated with water, oil and blood. Paradise is pitched against perdition, good against evil, friend against enemy, Satan against God, and demons against angels. In the volleying from both sides, the conflagration becomes cosmic; words are turned into weapons: bullets, shrapnel, ballistic missiles, poison gas. An apocalyptic Gnosticism reigns, profoundly xenophobic, dark with animal instinct and blinding in its utopian brilliance. The power of the imagination is unleashed in unpredictable and vicious ways – in untrammelled violence and untrammelled heroics, and wildly contagious emotion. Khomeini rode and drove this ethos like an ancient prophet; a prophesied Imam returning for the end times. When the city of Abadan had been recaptured from the Iraqis in May 1982 and Saddam Hussein sued for peace in June, the Islamic Republic decided to launch a counter-offensive and invade Iraq. Six more years of war followed, with nothing gained and nothing but an immense number of human lives lost.

It is the imaginative power of myth, cultural memory and religious ideology (a lethal and explosive Molotov cocktail) that comes to the fore in any analysis of why those young men and children rocked the buses they boarded with their eagerness. A small amulet carried or worn around their necks leads us into the narratives, historical and religious, dense with mythical resonance, that Khomeini's Shi'a regime employed to capture the Iranian imagination. It was a tiny key to paradise given to each; metal to begin with, but as the war advanced, a gilded plastic or an image on a badge. This key was a potent symbol of a way of imagining social life under obedience to the Ayatollah, Sharia law and the sway of an historical, destined and divine imperative. It was a social life crowned with entry into an eternal life lived in watered gardens. In a flash we're back at the SkyPark and the Marina Bay Sands Hotel, but the cost of entry and habitation is obliteration; a suicidal martyrdom. Under the imaginative power of historical and religious narratives at the origin of Shi'a Islam, social relations were mythologized, and the relationship between this world and the next was marked out in carnage. In the very week the war ended, by the acceptance of a UN resolution (late July, 1988), Khomeini ordered the mass murder of political prisoners in Iran. The prisoners condemned to execution were offered walking on landmines in martyrdom as one of their options. I have not discovered whether any accepted the offer. They preferred to hang, six at a time from cranes especially driven into the prison compounds to do the work (because the noise of shooting them would draw too much public attention).

In an early scene from Nolan's *Inception*, 'Dom' Cobb explains one of his 'radical notions': 'What is the most resilient parasite? Bacteria? A virus? An intestinal worm? [...] An idea. Resilient. Highly contagious. Once an idea's taken hold of the brain it's almost impossible to eradicate. An idea that is fully formed, fully understood – that sticks.' I might change 'idea' for 'myth', but the sense of what Cobb is saying has been borne out on too many occasions in the chronicles of human time. According to Steve Biko's biographer, Xolela Mangcu, Nelson Mandela said something very similar about the Black Consciousness Movement: 'We know today that when, in the life of a nation, the time comes for an idea, nothing – not even murder – can kill the idea.' However much political and economic liberalism has taught the West to prize individuality, we are all part of someone else's dreams. Some myths have the imaginative power to counter the forces of evolution itself. People give up food, sex, sleep, livelihoods and survival itself. There is nothing unique about the brutality of Khomeini's theocratic power and the contagious myth legitimating it. Nothing, that is, except the period in world history when it was exercised; a period described by the social theorist, Charles Taylor, as the 'modern social imaginary'.

The atrocities perpetrated in the name of the divine have captured imaginations over aeons and left their deep scars in the religious traditions of every continent. Monopolies on the keys to paradise and promised rewards in an afterlife have been a characteristic of such rules on record since the Zhou monarchy in ancient China (*c.*1046–771 BCE). But we have to go far back into political history to find a social order in which the king, the kingdom and the deity are one; each legitimating the power, the glory and the authority of the other. Possibly the theocracies closest to that of the Iranian Islamic Republic under Ayatollah Khomeini were the absolute monarchies of Egypt under the Old Kingdom (2686–2125 BCE); monarchies at the dawn of political society where the ruler was the divine vice-regent.

In theocracies all social relations are power relations (based on proximity to the cult of the divine king) *and* cosmic relations. But no other ancient civilization other than Egypt under Amenemhat I identified kingship and divinity. The ancient Iranian people of what were once Mesopotamia, Assyria and Babylon held that kingship came down from heaven, but kings were not deified, and independent cities had their own gods. In ancient Judaism, the holy nation was Yahweh's nation, not the king's; the people (including the king) were all under Yahweh's Law. Kingship was permitted, but not sanctified, and not sacred – and oh how James VI had his translators squirm around that one in the Preface to his authorized version of the Bible!

Nevertheless, the iron bonds binding religion to social life – the religious orientations of social values, activities and organizations – make manifest how deeply invested the social imagination is with religion. The central questions of sovereignty and its legitimation that are evoked by any notion of social order can never be finally resolved. So the spectres of absolutism haunt not only the history of political thought, they haunt our cultural memories as messianic hopes or demonic threats, eschatological utopias and apocalyptic terrors. And secularism is no bulwark against this. In fact, secularism only offers itself as another system of beliefs, liturgies, pieties and values; and its fragility lies in the fact that it is entirely manmade. It stands and falls by its declarations of human rights – and whether they can ever be implemented. Church/state polities and the divine right of kings may have been archived in Europe and *laïcité* as state measure or judicial procedure established, but neither the political nor the social cast off their religious coats of many mythical colours so easily. As secular ideology marched strongly under the banner of progress throughout the twentieth century, voices as different as Eric Voegelin and Carl Schmitt drew attention not just to the religious traditions upon which it stood, but the religious textures and tinctures it still maintained.

LEVIATHAN MARK I

In his *Autobiographical Reflections*, Eric Voegelin expresses total surprise at Hitler's annexation of Austria in 1938. By the time he came to write his *Reflections* he was living in San Francisco; at the time of the *Anschluss* he was an adjunct professor of law at the university of Vienna. Austria was the road to occupying Czechoslovakia and the formation of a formidable

Central European power bloc. Voegelin genuinely believed the Western democracies would not allow this to happen; they would not hold back and just observe Germany's expansion. They would surely intervene and prevent any Nazi consolidation of power. But the Western democracies did not intervene; they did observe. No one relished another world war. Germany entered Austria in March. Voegelin was already being watched because of his explicit criticism of National Socialism. He had another book in press in Vienna, *Die politischen Religionen*. It was published in April, and by the end of the month he was stopped from teaching. On 17 May he lost his job. Although critics outside Germany thought the book should have been more trenchant in its criticism of Hitler's regime, and although, as a scholar, Voegelin's work could be historically cavalier even if often brilliantly perceptive, *Die politischen Religionen* was provocative. Voegelin had to flee. And it was not going to be easy.

Voegelin's book was provocative on several fronts. First, it recognized that the National Socialist state, in 'decapitating' God, set itself up as an object of worship. Then he proceeded to show how the demand for racial purification created a world that was closed in upon itself; where truth can only be understood in terms that promote it as the chosen race and demonize everything alien to it. In doing this, the state maintained the eschatological, end-time desire for redemption and earthly perfection. Only now the language and symbols of the 'transcendent end realm' were accommodated to secular and political purposes. Then, finally and most provocatively, Voegelin's book revealed the key mechanism behind this nationalist hysteria; a mechanism that could be made utterly rational, objective, instrumental and scientific within its own 'organic' (totalitarian) conception of truth. And that key was the imaginative power of myth.

With his notion of 'political religion', Voegelin provided an early analysis of how people bind themselves to a mythical political body and barricade their faith in this pseudo-religion from being disrupted. And they do this *even while recognizing* the psychological techniques used for creating the myths and *recognizing* the mechanics of propaganda. What is being sought in this uncritical and deeply emotional affiliation, he claims, is entirely similar to what mystics once sought in their absorption into the divine: the disintegration of the self into a collective person, the commonwealth – Thomas Hobbes's Leviathan.

This political model may be secular and inner-worldly, but its appeal, Voegelin argues, is profoundly spiritual because the aspirations it invokes are religious. 'The formation of the myth and its propaganda by means of newspapers and radio, the speeches and its celebrations, the assemblies and parades, the planning and the death in battle, make up the inner-worldly forms of the *unio mystica*.' People bought into the myth of the *Volk* knowing it to be a myth because the experience of the belonging, peace and stability it promised was addictive. The Führer gave this collective persona a concrete, historical incarnation; he embodied the mystical personification of this new form of *ecclesia*. As such the authoritarian state provided a secularized form of the older *cuius regio eius religio*. In his military uniform, the Führer became the voice not of a transcendent deity (like Amenemhat I – who Voegelin compares him to), but an immanent, inner-worldly deity. And, as such, he embodied the eschatological destiny of the *Volk*.

Later, living among a number of other exiled intellectuals in the USA, Voegelin could never understand those people (like Hannah Arendt) who asked him why he needed to flee. After all, they argued, he was Catholic and married – not Jewish, not gypsy, not gay. But in a totalitarian regime there are many ways in which to be 'othered'. In May 1938 in Vienna, the immediate question was where to flee and how. Switzerland was a possibility, but there was a question of money. He traded salaries with a Swiss journalist friend so that he could access money accumulated in a Swiss bank account. Then the Gestapo arrived wanting to seize his passport. His wife Lissy was alone in the apartment at the time and the passport was with the Austrian police with his application for an exit visa. The Gestapo left knowing they could pick up the passport from the police. Voegelin quickly mobilized friends so that in a single day he obtained the visa and his passport and jumped on a train to Zurich – leaving his wife in the apartment as a decoy. He describes, briefly, his fear of being arrested by the Gestapo at the border, but he wasn't arrested. He telegrammed Lissy that evening from Zurich and she left the apartment immediately to stay with her parents. In Zurich a letter from Harvard arrived at the American embassy that offered him a part-time appointment in the Department of Government. He and his wife left for the USA, settling in Cambridge, Massachusetts by Christmas.

It was over that Christmas that Voegelin wrote what I consider to be one of the most insightful pieces for understanding both the strong association between myth, religious imagination and politics in political life and the role of religion generally in the mobilization of the social imagination. It comes in his Preface to a new edition of his *Die politischen Religionen* to be published the following year in Stockholm. He begins by explaining why his approach to the Nazi regime does not take 'the form of ethical counter-propaganda'. Such an approach, he believes, would only mask a 'deeper and much more dangerous evil' and in doing this be simply ineffective. What needs to be tackled is 'the *radix*, the root in religiousness'.

> When considering National Socialism from a religious standpoint, one should be able to proceed on the assumption that there is evil in the world and, moreover, that evil is not only a deficient mode of being, a negative element, but also a real substance and force that is effective in the world. Resistance against a satanical substance that is not only morally but also religiously evil can only be derived from an equally strong, religiously good force. One cannot fight a satanical force with morality and humanity alone.

Putting aside, for a moment, Voegelin's own religious convictions (which no doubt inform this position) what he recognizes is that mythic thinking cannot be argued against, rationalized and explained away on the basis of secular, liberal humanism and its exaltation of human rights. Such humanism is itself a Promethean myth, the secularization of which has greatly diluted its imaginative power to move, compel and convict. Mythic thinking can only be challenged by an alternative form of mythic thinking that retains its imaginative power to affect, to capture and to bind. In this case an evil myth can only be countered by a myth of the good. The monster-state, Leviathan, is a 'closed cosmos' in which all contrary opinion to its rules is not just censored but silenced. Its rule, the logic of its sovereignty, ensures the unity of the commonwealth. It speaks and commands the true because any claims appearing to disrupt the peace of the community are automatically false. So Leviathan can only be countered by another powerful symbol of the common good.

But where is this to be found? For Voegelin it is clear that the alternative was the Christian Church, but he is honest enough to admit that in the course of European history the Church itself became 'closed, inner-worldly and also gave rise to the corresponding empires of Satan'.

But there is a deeper problem than finding a counter-myth that is registered here in the Preface. While recognizing that secularism is no bulwark against the mythic – since the mythic as it strongly works in the cultural imagination will always draw religion into the social and the political – to counter an 'axis of evil' with an 'axis of good' only perpetuates Gnostic myths of eternal conflict. So countering Leviathan's absolutism with the myth of enlightened, liberal democracy, the mythic sovereignty of the 'mortal god' with the mythic sovereignty of the people, will only perpetuate the ongoing war. Leviathans will fight each other in open total war. Voegelin sets out to his own solution:

> the world is experiencing a serious crisis, is undergoing a process of withering, which has its origins in the secularization of the soul and in the ensuing severance of a consequently purely secular soul from its roots in religiousness [...] it does not know that recovery can only be achieved through religious renewal, be it within the framework of the historical churches, be it outside this framework. Such a renewal, to a large extent, can only be initiated by great religious personalities.

Voegelin's call for 'great religious personalities' imitates the ancient cry of the Hebrew prophets looking for the Messiah. Too many 'personalities' have stepped up to the podium to face banks of press cameras and make their messianic claims – the Ayatollah Khomeini among them. And the world is still 'experiencing a serious crisis'. In fact, the crisis has deepened because while perpetuating a mythic association between religion and violence to enforce a separation between the political and the theological, the secular has never been able to privatize the religious. The crisis has also deepened because from the time of Iranian Revolution, the secular has been on the defensive; its presence understood as a Western ideology that is fundamentally Christian. The religious, mythic resonances have prevailed globally over the purisms of positivism and empiricism.

And this is profoundly impacting the contemporary social and cultural imagination.

LEVIATHAN MARK II

In the summer of 1938, in another part of the Third Reich (Berlin), Carl Schmitt was finishing his own meditations on Hobbes' *Leviathan* to be published later that year. He too was frightened and sensed his life was threatened. He didn't flee. He couldn't; he was too deeply involved with the Nazi Party, with a file kept open on him by the SS. His relations with National Socialism were complex and strained, in part because he was a complex man keenly sensitive to insecurity and so all too prone to arrogance and self-delusion. A short, handsome, stocky figure, in the early 1930s he had been courted by the likes of Hindenburg and Göring as a brilliant constitutional lawyer; and Schmitt liked to move in celebrity circles. Like Voegelin, Schmitt was a Roman Catholic, although as a divorced and remarried man he was ecclesiastically compromised. Nevertheless, he revitalized a tradition of intellectual enquiry following World War I in his book *Political Theology*, which reminded the human sciences (law, politics and sociology, in particular) that they were trading in secularized theological concepts. The religious was not erased, it was just transferred from an ecclesial framework to the apparatus of the nation state. Furthermore, those concepts still bore their mythical weight. Published in the autumn of 1938, *The Leviathan in the State Theory of Thomas Hobbes* parades its academic distance and erudite scholarship. But given the context in which it was written – the annexation of Austria, the persecution of the Jews, Hitler's violent and despotic seizure of sovereign power, and the aggressive foreign policy that seemed bent on international warfare – it makes uncomfortable reading. The takeover, colonization or enforced 'protection' of weaker states unable to manage themselves efficiently is a Leviathan logic that Schmitt justifies in the book, appealing to a convention made by the Geneva League of Nations. And although he may not have embraced the Nazi racial myth, his anti-Semitism emerges clearly. The Jewish philosophers Spinoza and Moses Mendelsohn, and the nineteenth-century consti-tutional lawyer Friedrich Stahl-Jolson (who converted to Christianity) are each blamed for their contributions to the collapse of the Hobbesian 'positive' understanding of the absolute state into the listless, talkative anarchies of liberal democracy. And international warring among different Leviathans is a constant possibility that cannot be submitted to any overriding rationality and legality; for each state is a law unto itself. So the only just war 'is the true "total" war'.

Scholarship is divided as to what Schmitt is attempting to argue (and for whom) in this book. That Hobbes' mechanical state and 'mortal god', Leviathan, has come of age is paramount. But so too is his own recognition that Nazi Germany was transferring the symbolic capital of ecclesial power to statecraft. Like Voegelin, the state is understood as a 'temporal divinity' in which religion and nation are brought together. Although Schmitt recognizes that the sovereignty of the 'new god', while transcending all other contracted parties, is juridical, not metaphysical. In a passage that is remarkable for its intertextual weaving of Hobbes's mid-seventeenth century and Schmitt's contemporary situation, it is claimed Hobbes: 'restored the old and eternal relationships between protection and obedience, command and the assumption of emergency action, power and responsibility against distinctions and pseudo-concepts of a *potestas indirecta*'. What Schmitt means by 'indirect powers' is the right of other parties (likes churches and communists) to exist and have their critical interventions heard. But this is the 'right' that the 'Night of the Long Knives' (June, 1934) savagely curtailed, when Hitler's secret police murdered possibly hundreds of political opponents. Nevertheless, we sense the freshly minted mythic appeal in the rhetoric of restoring the 'old and eternal'.

As with Voegelin, only now understood *positively*, the sovereign representative person of this contract and covenant, the Führer, establishes this artificially constructed deity by giving it 'soul'. He guarantees the security, peace and freedom of individuals who, by nature, would simply tear each other apart. But he can only do this only on the basis of blind obedience and the renunciation of every right of resistance to the closed, legalized police state. All of which sounds like an opportunistic *apologia* for National Socialism and its operations. But the refrain throughout the book is that such a state can only be maintained *if* that security and protection is deliverable. The concluding sentence of the volume sounds like a warning: Hobbes's '"deus mortalis" is a machine whose "mortality" is based on the fact that one day it may be shattered by civil war or rebellion'. Such war or rebellion is realizable when the state of nature, the fear of which drove people to form the Leviathan, reasserts itself, and in doing so proves how ineffective the 'mortal god' is to guaranteeing peace and security. So, as some have argued, is Schmitt wishing to remind the ruling party that the basis of the positive understanding of Hobbes's political myth, and its rational unity, is a liberal democratic proviso? Maybe.

Having joined the party in 1933, by December 1936 Schmitt was the focus of a series of caustic attacks made by the SS that ousted him. In 1938 he stood in the vacuum-vortex of a political maelstrom. Someone of his ability and temperament could not just quietly return to a university career. His post in the university was underwritten by his allegiances to the state – as Voegelin found with respect to his own university post in Vienna. But given the book's insistence upon total obedience and the right to resist, then what space could even a cunning and brilliant lawyer create for critique? For a man who only flourished when he could make political instability work in his favour, his position was extremely precarious; as precarious as Voegelin's – although for entirely different reasons. In 1947, when Schmitt was arrested and interviewed as part of the Nuremburg Trials, two of the prominent foci of the interviews were the questions: to what extent did Schmitt's 1939 argument for 'greater space' further Hitler's policy of German expansion? And to what extent did Schmitt participate in the preparation for an aggressive war and the subsequent crimes to which it led?

For our exploration of the social imagination we need not resolve, if they can ever be resolved, the ambiguous tones and tensions in Schmitt's argument. In contrast to Voegelin (whose work on the state Schmitt knew and even cites), Schmitt accepts the secularization of theological notions and recognizes that Hobbes redefines Calvin's omnipotent deity in terms of a deified state; just as the theological notion of 'covenant' becomes the juristic notion of 'contract'. He recognized that the same theological and mythical anthropology remains firmly in place – namely, Calvin's dark understanding of the natural and unredeemed human condition; the antithesis of liberal humanism's anthropology. Schmitt's secularism is, through and through, religious in texture and tincture – and self-consciously so as the state is both a mechanical and spiritual entity; technically constructed, transcendent while being fully immanent. This is not a secularism that can act as a bulwark against political religions. It is in fact itself – on Schmitt's own understanding of the term – a political theology. After the light and progress metaphors of the Enlightenment, secularism was symbolically anaemic and had as much intellectual presence as ether. Only raucous, God-cursing atheism could give it any colour – and that was much, much later. Imaginatively, secularism lacks the power to enthral and capture, so it's forced to fall back on the claw-hammer approach of legal positivism. Schmitt's religious secularism explicitly recreates a political mythology, spiked and spired with gothic warnings:

> When an author employs an image like that of the leviathan, he enters a domain in which word and language are no mere counters that can be used to calculate worth and purchasing power. In this domain mere 'values' do not 'hold true'; what effectively govern are force and power, throne and master [...] No clear chain of thought can stand up against the force of genuine, mythical images [...] Whoever utilizes such images, easily glides into the role of a magician who summons forces that cannot be matched by his arm, his eye, or any other measure of his human ability. He runs the risk that instead of encountering an ally he will meet a heartless demon who will deliver him into the hands of his enemies.

Schmitt was a connoisseur of the mythical and the cabbalistic, and a great manipulator of the social imagination. Here, for all the possible warnings and disclaimers, there is also a magician's seduction. Schmitt is conjuring *his* myth of Leviathan, and the echoes of *Faust* would not be lost on a National Socialism fermented by Joseph Goebbels' mythopoetic imagination. Its material culture was saturated with the Aryan, the Teutonic, the pre-Christian, the Celtic and the Roman. It flooded the social imagination with runes, emblems and mandalas like thunderbolts, the hammer and sword, and the Black Sun. Through an omnipresent cultural machinery it created an immersive but entirely imaginary community. Here was 'perception management' at its most lethal – demanding and cultivating strong imaginative participation in not simply a national identity, but a national destiny. The nation was the religious object for adoration. National Socialism promised to make Germany great again.

There is something to be learned here.

What appears difficult to understand for the 'outsider' (the person not locked into the imaginative world of the political myth and its state machinery; or the person looking back to a time when this occurred) is how intelligent, questioning, curious people can submit themselves so totally to such an ideology that they are unable to critique it. Even when many of them knew and attested to the fact it was an ideology. How could so many commit their hearts and minds to the totalitarian sway of Khomeini's, or Hitler's or Mussolini's storytelling? What happens to the ability to be critical and resist the imaginative currents of the myth? Of course, there were resistance movements (just as much as there was a violent policing of such movements) within the First Iranian Republic and Nazi Germany. But untold thousands of critically aware people did not resist. So we have to push deeper here into the operations of the social imagination.

THE IDOL IN OUR HEADS

In 1933 a young Jewish journalist in Berlin, Charlotte Beradt, began collecting dream-scripts. She encountered enormous fear and resistance among those who wrote down their dreams for her collection. She transcribed them into a code and dispatched them in letters to other people. In 1966 she brought together this collection of dreams by Nazi Germans between 1933 and 1939, publishing them with a commentary. Details of who dreamed them are thin and there is no way now of assessing how representative the people who provided her with their scripts are, or even authenticating the scripts themselves. But these dream-scripts say something about the close relationship between dreams and social reality. What the dreams convey is the way the social imagination becomes saturated and captivated by the cultural machinery constructing what Voegelin and Schmitt identify as the Leviathan.

A middle-aged housewife dreamed:

> A Storm Trooper was standing by the large, old-fashioned, blue-tiled Dutch oven that stands in the corner of our living room, where we always sit and talk in the evening. He opened the oven door and it began to talk in a harsh and penetrating voice [the Voice, reminiscent of the one heard over the loudspeaker during the day]. It repeated every joke we had told and every word we had said against the government. I thought, 'Good Lord, what's it going to tell next – all my snide remarks about Goebbels?' But at that moment I realized that one sentence more or less would make no difference – simply everything we have ever thought or said among ourselves is known.

The enormous fear is a product of the vast ear tuning in to thoughts and feelings. Nazi propaganda (the loudspeaker during the day) is internalized. The voice summons me to account, and it's both nowhere and everywhere. It makes no sense to ask who is speaking. The divine Judge, the alpha and omega of authority – transcendent, omnipresent. It is also omniscient – 'everything we have ever thought or said among ourselves is known': It occupies the very centre of what is private and intimate – the living room – and it urges confession. The confession shames and humiliates. We are not told that the 'blue-tiled Dutch oven' (which is in fact a porcelain stove) is lit, but it is implied in the way the oven is the focus of family life. The oven takes on the gothic horrors of the fairy-tale oven in Hansel and Gretel – a traditional German folk story recorded by the Brothers Grimm – and the ovens used in the extermination camps. Innocence is consumed in its flames, and so is resistance – 'all my snide remarks about Goebbels'. Betrayal is possible even among family members. The appeal to a transcendent 'Good Lord' may be a throwaway exclamation. It is not a prayer. While the adjective 'good' attests to a counter-myth. But the counter-myth only initiates the recognition of total defeat – 'I realized that one sentence more or less would make no difference.'

The insistences upon omnipresence, omniscience, judgement and confession are an index of how deeply the questions of authority, legitimacy, transparency and sovereignty in modern secular politics are entangled with religion. The transcendent suffuses the smallness of the domestic space. It is a transcendent that offers no hope of redemption. There's only claustrophobic paranoia. In the presence of the Storm Trooper (an ensign of the transcendent) and the magical oven, there is nowhere to hide and no one to trust – least of all oneself. The imagination has been captured; it dreams only what it is allowed to dream. And what it dreams is pathological – like the social reality it is immersed in.

Myth has the power to paralyse, to conflate the real and the imaginary, and create somnambulists, *Schlafwandlers*, sleepwalkers. We have entered Dr Caligari's cabinet where the idolized is in our heads and hearts, controlling what we see and think, feel and do. But it can only get there because of some close association between the imagination, mythic sensibility and the religious.

THE MODERN SOCIAL IMAGINARY

If totalitarianisms remind us of the mythic and religious roots of the social and political, and we find such mythic and religious roots troubling today, then that's because the West is invested in a different social imagination. An imagination strongly orientated towards the freedom and autonomy of the individual, humanism (and universal human rights) and liberal democracy. Dictatorships and totalitarianisms are boogie men stalking its nightmares. It wasn't always so. Even Schmitt's approbation of the state as a 'mortal deity' is shot through with aspects of the social imagination that are distinctly modern: consensual contracts among individual citizens framed by an overarching constitution; the law as circumscribing the limits and liberties of civic society; and the view that political authority, even absolute authority, is there to safeguard peace and security. These all have a history, a place in the movements of time, historical processes and cultural responses that followed the European Reformation. The 'Reformation' was not a monolithic event. It's just a convenient benchmark for a time when religion and politics were inseparable.

Voegelin's social imagination is even more thoroughly modern – where 'modern' is almost synonymous with moral and political liberalism:

freedom of expression and critical reflection, toleration of social and political difference, and the state as the guarantor and facilitator of 'the open society' (Karl Popper). This provides the imaginative bulwark against state domination. This modern social imagination arose out of a public sphere free from state interference. But as Voegelin and Schmitt realize, the secular has never been secular enough. Religion in the modern social imagination (along with public institutions like education, the police, the army, the law courts) assisted in developing the self-disciplines that provided 'the sanctification of ordinary life' with moral backbone (Taylor). Religion, that is, fostered the cultural values internalized by citizens that enabled the free flow of exchanges and respect. With such an ethos governance could be light-touch.

Of course, this liberalism compromised the value of equality to some extent because each of these institutions developed and was seen to require hierarchies: a man had to know his place (and a woman her place in a man's world). So there were class and gender tensions, later aggravated further by racial and religious tensions. But the peace, security and well-being of the people, championed, pursued and idealized, was the peace, security and well-being of the public sphere as a common and democratizing space. The state defended the privacy and freedoms of the individual, the public sphere and the freedom of the press, creating, imaginatively, a common space. It is the lack of this independence of the media (for Voegelin) and the necessary evisceration of this independence of the media (for Schmitt) that fundamentally divides them; because, at heart, they both want the same thing: national peace and security.

The mediations that construct the sense of a common space – which modern urban planners sculptured into public squares and public parks – develop imagined communities, and spaces of social and political hope. Justice was the name given to that hope. Justice was the optimistic goal of the free cultivation of public opinion. Such mediations are all projections of the social and cultural imagination; and that imagination can be captivated, as we have seen, by resonances mythic in origin and metaphoric in expression. And such resonances can impact, for good or evil, public reason.

In the histories of societies and nations there are too many accounts of alliances between imagination and power to ignore or diminish the seizures of public reasoning that can take place. The imagination has a great deal more power than rational deliberation. Reasoning itself is informed by and depends upon it. That doesn't necessarily mean that public opinion cannot rule the day. But the formation and strength of public opinion (which returns us to the management of perception) is very delicate and always involves the cultural and social imagination. The public sphere is, through and through, an act of the imagination requiring for its maintenance and participation further acts of the imagination. Its existence is a constantly emerging and shape-shifting virtual entity like a bubble. While the bubble lasts it endures. But, in the free market of opinion, arguments can multiply to such an extent (like the media points that disseminate it) that in the proliferation of reasonings (and their levels of being well informed or ill informed) the bubble pops. Social difference becomes social dissonance becomes social paralysis; social interest and concern turn to social confusion and indifference. The social imagination is overwhelmed by the plethora of imagined possibilities.

MAMMON

These possibilities become compounded when 'interests' – which go deep into the emotional and pre-reflective, the pre-political and the pre-social, and so are not at all easily assessed or accessible – are given another, complex, modern twist. For there is something missing from the modern social imagination as it finds expression in the political fears, critiques and visions of Voegelin and Schmitt. What is missing makes its appearance at an international (not the national) level in the Iranian Revolution: the seductive pulls of economic interests. The myth of Mammon stands alongside the myth of Leviathan and, as capitalism developed in the wake of sixteenth- and seventeenth-century mercantile expansion, the two monsters became increasingly one hybrid. The war between Iran and Iraq, and all the subsequent wars within that region (up to and including the Syrian civil war) draw international attention in a global market, draw allies and enemies, because of oil resources as much as humanitarian crises.

This is something new. Hobbes's wolverine man is defensively concerned with what is his, including his livelihood and property, but he is not ravenous for riches. Even the wealth production of Adam Smith's gentleman squire is recognized as a contribution to the prosperity of the common weal. Though Smith is all too aware of greedy and exploitative landlords who 'had not the least intention to serve the publick' and for whom '[t]o gratify the most childish vanity was the sole motive'. But his very tone acknowledges that such rampant, selfish wealth accumulation was not just morally offensive but corrosive of good government. Parsimony is a virtue and the lupercal tendencies of certain human beings should be curbed by the natural urge to better one's condition through mutual relations within a grand exchange of services in which the poor are protected.

But while the Adam Smith Institute was being founded in 1977 and postwar socialism was exiting the social imagination as a credible political possibility, a new breed of Leviathan was incubating.

The modern and Western social imagination is a swirl of ideas and images, remembered and misremembered, categories and classifications; with beliefs in certain structures, processes and practices on their way to being or already existing as institutions concerned with social order. The swirl is continuously undergoing change, with ideas and images interacting and transitioning. It's subject to creative forgetting and preoccupied as much with fears as ideals, dystopian scenarios as well as utopian will-o'-the-wisps, scapegoated gorgons as much as iron ladies and handsome superheroes. We are all now in the grips of this imagination, both colonized and post-colonized, from the socially abject to the socially celebrated. We are all caught up with trying to *make sense*, and (more or less) facilitate and enable.

Not every possibility for combination and change in the social imagination is activated at any given time; the contingency of circumstance and context cannot pull just anything from a society's political repertoire. Even if it is part of the repertoire of a nation's history it may not be credibly reinstitutionalized.

For a long time, the development of social stability was understood in terms of 'progress'. But the notion of 'progress' is increasingly exiting the contemporary social imagination in the face of so much fire-fighting pragmatism. At one time the pre-political and pre-social might be located in the intimacy and privacy of the family and universal human rights guaranteed by notions of natural law. But the private world of the family is increasingly under pressure from the public world of politics and surveillance. And human rights have themselves become battle-grounds – not least because many are negative rights (deterring damage), or impossible rights in a market-driven economy (the right to employment), and the cry goes up only in their infringement and violation.

So there is a struggle to locate any social and moral order – particularly where the political is *maintained* by the economic. In a time and space ordered by the flatline immanence of secularism, where might the possibilities of the pre-political and pre-social be found? There is no view that doesn't come from somewhere. If the sovereignty of the people can only have credibility when people imagine they belong to something, then what constitutes our imagined corporate belonging beyond our passports? We are all, increasingly, immersed in the political; where the political (after Schmitt) can no longer be identified according to the friend and enemy distinction. We are no longer certain we can identify either the friend or the enemy; a lot of contenders for either designation fill our newspapers every day. Today, any moral economy based on the just and the normative is overwhelmed by the market mantras of supply and demand, scarcity and glut.

The new, incubating Leviathan has come of age; and a hybrid Leviathan and Mammon rules.

THE NEW LEVIATHAN

The Barents Sea is part of the Arctic Ocean between Norway and Russia. In the small fishing port of Teriberka, the Russian film director Andrey Zvyagintsev shot the haunting external scenes for *Leviathan* (2014). Zvyagintsev co-wrote the screenplay based in part on a novella by Heinrich von Kleist, the friend of Goethe and Schiller; in part based on biblical stories of greed, the unjust possession of someone else's land and livelihood, rage and revenge; and in part based on the true story of Marvin Heemeyer, an American who, in 2004, went on the rampage with a bulldozer in the town of Great Lake, Colorado. Surrounded by a SWAT team, Heemeyer shot himself in the head.

Kolya is uncut malachite: a buff, rough, semi-precious stone with a short fuse and a friendly, generous heart. As a mechanic he runs a garage from his home at the edge of a post-industrial wasteland where fishing vessels stand rusting in the harbour, and seems to get paid mainly in vodka. He's also a minnow caught in the jaws of a voracious new Leviathan with several heads – political, economic and religious. The mayor of the town (Vadim) wants Kolya's property in order to build a telecommunications tower, but the compensation he is offered is diminutive. Vadim has set in motion a compulsory purchase order for its possession and Vadim has the town and its civil service under his thumb – they all owe him their livelihoods. Kolya's appeal fails. He calls in a lawyer friend in Moscow (Dima) to fight his legal case. With powerful connections of his own, Dima creates a file revealing the extent of Vadim's corrupt practices and scandalous activities. He uses this to blackmail Vadim into paying the full compensation. But in the process Dima becomes involved with Kolya's wife, Lilya. Threatened, the mammoth head of Leviathan rises.

In the mayoral office Vadim sits across a table from the Metropolitan Orthodox bishop. We have met the Metropolitan in an earlier scene. He is receiving funds for the Church from the mayor. Vadim is unsure how to respond to Dima's revelations, though is inclined to the thuggery he knows best. The Metropolitan asks him if he is attending church regularly. Vadim prevaricates. The Metropolitan asks him if he has a confessor. Vadim tells him vaguely about a priest the Metropolitan had recommended. A name is mentioned. An exchange ensues that blurs all the lines between political religion and political theology:

Bishop: Get a hold of yourself, Vadim. And don't worry, you are doing God's work. It is said that good deeds are done happily and with ease. But don't forget. The enemy is ever ready and does not sleep.

Vadim: That's the thing. You know ... it's like everything is going wrong. I'm uneasy. What's happening is ...

Bishop: Don't reveal anything to me. You're not at confession. You and I may be working for the same cause, but you've got your territory and I've got mine.

Vadim: I understand that. I just feel ill at ease.

Bishop: ... All power is from God. Where there's power there's might. If you hold power in your territory, solve the issues yourself with all your might. Don't go looking for help or the enemy will think you are weak.

The scene ends with the giving of a blessing and fades out as the camera moves in for a close-up of a miniature bust on the mantelpiece of Christ as the man of sorrows. We're not sure who's being or about to be crucified here. It looks like everyone – bar the Metropolitan. In another room, as we know from previous scenes, the ever-watchful eye of President Putin stares, askance.

Beaten and threatened by Vadim, Dima returns to Moscow; Lilya commits suicide by throwing herself into a sea where we have seen the frolicking of a mighty fish; Kolya is sent to prison for what the authorities claim (including his police friends) is the murder of his wife; and the bulldozers move in, crashing through the house like large metallic sea serpents. Vadim plans his new building and a church service is held in which the Metropolitan speaks of God and truth and the reawakening of the Russian soul through the Orthodox Church.

Zvyagintsev employs no filmic tricks. There is no music soundtrack until a series of closing shots of the harbour where the twisted iron and steel of old boats rust and the whitened bones of a monster fish lie sunken in the silt. The events of Kolya's dispossession unfold in a landscape and a seascape beneath a raw Arctic sky where the light is flat. The village is dilapidated; people struggle to keep warm, fed, employed and laughing. In the evenings disaffected youth stand drinking round a fire lit in the ruined apse of a church where an altar would have stood. The new Leviathan arises in all its political, economic and religious power where the pickings are paltry and people are already being punished. God answers in the hurricane, as a priest tells Kolya (citing the story of Job), but there is no restoration.

Paradise like Pandemonium has been hardwired into us by evolution. Through adaptation our physiologies (not just our brains) have become honed for expectation and anticipation. The future is not at all abstract. It lives already within us. Utopia is not at all abstract – in and beyond our materiality we imagine what would make us most happy; what the conditions might be for maximal flourishing. Carl Schmitt reminds us that the Leviathan's task is to create arcadia: the paradise of peace and leisure far above the instabilities of economic and political life. And the Marina Bay Sands Hotel shows us that the mechanics of global capitalism and its crusading democratic polity still chases the same dream – of rest beyond restlessness. One Leviathan gives way to another.

CODA

The mythic will not go away. Imagination will always assert itself – even where deprivation rules. Religion still remains a fundamental source of imaginative alternatives, but it is not without its terrifying dangers. It's a cultural production, and so embedded in and expressive of the cultural imagination. As an actor within and both an organizer and valoriser of relations (in terms of community building) it is also implicated in social life – even under the ideological pressures of secularism that wishes to reduce religion to the private realm and subjective experience. Mythic resonance is clearly associated with religious experience and liturgical worship. Myth nurtures it and it nurtures myth. For many people the most dominant and persistent forms of cultural memory are religious traditions. These traditions have shaped and valued specific forms of affect galvanizing the activity of the cultural imaginary – what is to be feared, what is to be hoped for, what is desirable etc.

In the West, whatever our debates about or analyses of secularism (and its possible implosion), there's no getting away from how our social imagination is deeply indebted to religious traditions. There's no getting away either from the scapegoating of religion in the modern social imagination by allying it with violence and irrationality; as if we haven't lived with decades if not centuries of secular violence perpetrated by nation states blind to the profound religious investments in nationalism. No one has clean hands here. Religious narratives, mythologies and practices have shaped and still shape the way in which we relate to each other and the world; and the ideals of how we should relate. They have invested those relations with convictions and values far deeper than any secular moral order, legal prescriptions and a sense of civic responsibilities. This is not an unmitigated good. Neither is it a colossal evil. It's the way things are. With their languages of power, dominion and kingdom; with their hierarchies of created and uncreated, bestial, demonic and angelic; with their metaphors of light and darkness, gardens of delight and seas of chaos – they have bequeathed a cosmological understanding of ourselves, our obligations, our governance and our being governed. Before we ever launched rockets towards the moon and captured photographs of the blue-green earth, they instructed us to think globally, to think universally, to imagine as God or the gods imagined. They provoked us to think imaginatively. They developed our imaginative capacities. For religions were themselves a product of that imagination, and cultivated it. We conceived models of reality that sacralised space and divinized time, and placed us between the grasses and the stars.

And from the beginning as hominids and *Homos* we were restless and curious. Adapting and adaptive, we walked, ran, climbed, beachcombed – as migrants and migratory. As we saw, all of our earlier species became extinct in the process. Nevertheless, whatever the climatic conditions, we explored our planet insatiably, and religious traditions informed us what we were searching for; they provided an object for our inextinguishable cravings. We are planted in sand, and we hope it's home.

I'm in the Forbidden City in Beijing; Tiananmen Square lies just outside its precincts. It's a night in late November and I'm one of many foreign guests at a state banquet given by the minister for education. The city is closed to visitors and a large supper of ten courses is prepared in a newly and magnificently restored Hall of the Supreme Harmony. The hall, on its raised marbled steps, is the only illuminated building in the dark complex. The sound of flowing water outside melds with the sounds of traditional Chinese music from a small group playing within. The moon appears from time to time between banks of clouds and snow is falling lightly. It's a recess between courses, and I stand with my Chinese translator on the marble terrace gazing into the magic of the occasion and the courtyard separating the hall from the Gate of Supreme Harmony. She is a woman in her forties, unmarried, who had studied for a year at a British university. Her English is flawless, and over the time I have been in China she has become a friend. It is difficult to comprehend the recent history of this country and the lavish cultural investments it is now making in reinventing its imperial past. The dissonance seems summed up in a city not just dedicated to but an embodiment of celestial harmony – that is also forbidden. I say as much, my words melting in the darkness like the snowflakes. At first she is silent, slowly moving us to the far edge of the terrace where we stand alone in the company of the Roof Guardians. She acknowledges my incomprehension, and she shares something of it. She has vivid memories as a child, she tells me, of her parents whispering to each other as they lay on the floor on their mattresses and thought she was asleep. They whispered secret and perhaps seditious thoughts; private thoughts uttered in a culture paralysed by fear. Neighbours might be listening; family might be listening. Tomorrow their conversation could be reported to the officials, and then there would be trouble. It seems she still lives with Beradt's enormous fear of the omnipotent ear. This is a different world, I said, but not half as sure as I wish I could have been for her sake. She agreed. But the habit was deep and remained: our voices were very low, and we both glanced around without turning our heads before exchanging a smile.

There are other stories and other politics. Kolya was betrayed by his friend; but there are friendships that outlast betrayals. Kolya was betrayed by his wife; but it is his wife who returns and asks him if he wants another child, and the day after she returns Kolya tells his angry son to forgive. Only Lilya can't forgive herself. There are depths in human beings that survive even the worst that can happen to them. The silk of spiders it is said is stronger than steel; and connections between human beings can also outlive life. People live in me who are long dead. Why should I not also live in them – wherever they are? Do they think and dream of me as I of them? There are other polities and a vision of social relations and their organization centred upon friendship, trust, mutuality and benevolence. Plato, Aristotle, Augustine and Aquinas all stand testimony to them. These sensibilities of being human are powerful too, and communicate powerfully, often without words, frequently across distances. Instances of intimacy can remain in the body's memory. Friendship, trust, mutuality and benevolence – they sound utopian. In fact they are written deep into all our utopian fantasies: there is no paradise without *convivium*, and the architectures of our most civic halls are all utopian. Maybe in a time when so much social interaction is online and so little face to face they increasingly seem utopian. What is it to confirm a friendship on Facebook? But that doesn't invalidate love, friendship and shared intimacies as creative, life-giving possibilities in the social imagination. Imagination awakens with empathy. Even though it may develop solipsistically, empathy is as old as fear and betrayal.

There are certain relations in the social imagination that resist being colonized by Leviathan ideologies because they too bear a mythic sensibility – a profound and transfiguring elusiveness. We may search down every street and city for months, for years, hearing seductive calls from every door and window. But the mystery of these relations is that they find us, and take us ... elsewhere.

ECCE HOMO

I stand at the earth's extremity – Cape Agulhas, the southernmost tip of southern Africa, where the Atlantic becomes the Indian Ocean. I have trekked here along age-worn paths. This is a country of strong colours and strong contrasts. It may have given birth to humankind, but in its interior and along its edges one comes to terms with failure or one sinks into fantasies. Daybreak generates creativity; the afternoon saps it dry. The land and all that dwells here is sunstroked. Achievements are hard won and may or may not be sustainable. Life lives on the brink. Illusions are unforgiving; but without illusions life is impossible. In summer the semi-arid veldt becomes a wilderness of scorched rock, thorn trees and aloes. And in the wilderness, as the Israelites learned, wild, untrammelled desires are stirred; lusts for water, food, shade and companionship. Stripped to basics, the testing begins. Land, sky, searing sun and reflective whispers pose ancient questions: what are you? How did you come here? Where are you going? What do you hope for? Why? Now, the exhausted sun sinks, there is no moon and the darkness is so deep the Milky Way is a rack of smoking stars. Clashing tides snarl as they snarled when the first human beings beachcombed the rocks and shale below. Numbed by a stiff westerly wind, lines from Shakespeare percolate. Particularly his sense of an ending: 'the great globe itself/Yea, all which it inherit, shall dissolve.' The awkward syntax and staccato dance of 'i' sounds deliquesces. Out here on the edge of a continent I struggle to put the world, my life, my work, this book into some perspective – 'some' perspective: I'm not seeking a comprehensive vision. I just want to make some sense out of what I sense: the stark, ungraspable beauty; the raw, defenceless horror. What are we?

We are not the centre of anything. So that Enlightenment myth has to bite the dust. We have no origin – notwithstanding Darwin – unless it's the stars. And despite sophisticated attempts to create synthetic life that would assist in enabling us to understand the origin of life; despite evolutionary biology, genetics and epigenetics; despite palaeontology, the searches for and discoveries of missing links, and debates about the 'out of Africa' thesis – despite all of these scientific quests, 'man' 'is the being without origin, who never has "neither country or date", whose birth is never accessible because it never took "place" [. . .] man is cut off from the origin that would make him contemporaneous with his own existence' (Michel Foucault, *The Order of Things*). For Foucault this is where human beings have to confront what is 'unthought'. For me this is where human beings have to confront the 'unbelievable' and the 'unimaginable' because these are on the very frontiers of the 'unthought'.

The visible and the invisible cling closely to each other – from the three sides of a cube that cannot be fully seen and the wave function of the quantum universe, to the cliff in Edgar's mind which Lear depicts in detail, watching as Edgar pitches himself into its illusion. We not only live this invisibility from moment to moment – the very means by which this living is possible is through the invisible constructive processes of our mind and the very visible actions of our bodies. We are amphibious – living on the air of ideas and submerged in all the material immediacies of our environment. Those very stirrings that enable us to function as creatures among other creatures – desire, hope, belief, sympathy, imagination, intellect – are secreted away within us, unseen though not unperceived. This is who we are as poets and lovers, lunatics, partners and enemies, ruled and rulers – of imagination all compact. We are creatures created by what has stimulated us to become, and we crave such stimulations, though they have the potential both to enhance and destroy our abilities to act – particularly to act well. In the Great Chain of Being, we are a little lower than the angels, but with a responsibility towards and affinity with all that comes beneath us. Many have put the angels aside with the other Christmas decorations, but the responsibilities remain for all of that, and our dependencies likewise.

Some nameless, unknown hominid from a half-a-million years ago may have stumbled upon his reflection in a still rock pool and stared with wonder, fear and the sense of being in this skin for so many years and still encountering the unknown. Is my knowledge superior to his? In his book *Awakenings*, Oliver Sacks describes a frightening bestiality unleashed when patients with *encephalitis lethargica* were injected with L-Dopa in the late 1960s. The cries, jerks and compulsive noises that emerged in the side-effects were 'of a most primitive and primordial sort [...] jungle noises, noises of almost unimaginable bestiality'. Sacks, reflecting on his experiences many years later, concludes: 'What we see here are genuine ancestral instincts and behaviours which have been summoned from the depths, the phylogenetic depths which all of us carry in our persons.'

As a planet approaches the 'event horizon' of a black hole everything is stripped from it – atmosphere, liquids of any kind, life. It becomes a magma fireball on the edge of disintegration. Imagination can 'amend': it can compensate for the raw woundedness of our animality and be a means of escaping it. Imagination can also indulge that animality, giving it viscous, indiscriminate and destructive form. It can also heal. It can resolve. Black holes have taught me how small we are in the vastness of what is beyond us and what has happened so far. So small we might think we, and all our questions about ourselves, are insignificant; all our vices and virtues a mummer's play pitched out there along the trajectories of light years, borne away on waves of gravity we can't see towards strings and branes that are unimaginable. But we *are* significant. We are significant to each other; the mysteries we hold out to each other in every encounter; the mysteries in which we are immersed that still call out to our curiosity to understand. We claim much, but know so little of what is significant and why. Knowledge of the significance of what we say or do is so very limited – effects are incalculable. We are fragile, dwelling in a fragile life-system made entirely possible by being where earth is in a solar system at the quiet edge of a galaxy. We may be alone. We may not. This may not be the only universe. But if we have neighbours out there then there's a whole lot of emptiness between us. Nevertheless, staring into the piercing brightness of the stars none of this reduces our significance or the significance of what surrounds us. Astronomers are right to say that the shapes of constellations we see are just paths we make between disparate lights in an immense vacuum. But they still dazzle me with a sense of intelligence and intelligibility. I may stand alone on this finger of land stretching down towards the Antarctic, but I can never be lonely looking at the stars, staring into their inter- and extragalactic presence. Because it is just that – a wondrous presence. It puts all things on earth in their place and perspective. And like the light travelling from all those distant stars, light going back billions of years, everything we do here is beamed out there announcing 'we are here'; everything good and everything bad. In this way we fill the universe or one of the many multiverses with the particles of energies science is still exploring, saying 'Ecce homo – behold humankind, the worlds we have created, and what we have come to understand by daring to imagine.'

Whatever memorials we leave, our stories, births and deaths, are not written in stone. They are composed of dust, rain and ice crystals; sucrose, proteins and fatty acids. That doesn't mean our living makes no difference. That doesn't mean the world out there is indifferent to our difference. It can't be; what is out there has come to need us too. What it means is that we are not what we tell ourselves – for all the complexity of our biographical experiences. We *are* important; just not *all*-important.

Arguments should come to a conclusion; something should have been learned. Explorations should come to places of discovery or return home to display the trophies won in the journey to a far-off country. There are things I hope I've shown. Not just facts. Knowledge I hope I have communicated that is more than information. I recognize the terrain we have explored is my own imagination. But the exercise of my imagination as a writer is an invitation to exercise your imagination as a reader. And what sticks as we imagine is often what is shared: I am haunted like others by images of victims – the photograph of the girl running burned and terrified from the Napalm bombing of a village in Vietnam; footage of a coach shaking with boisterous young men being delivered to martyrdom on the borders of Iran; clips of people dropping like over-ripe fruit from the roof of the World Trade Center. I am haunted also, hopefully more so, by images of the magical: the delight on the face of a student who makes a breakthrough; movements in Beethoven's quartets that shudder with complex inventive flights; the anonymous gift of a smile from a stranger; the predawn call to prayer that stirs the insomniac;

words that ring well; the curve of a green hill towards a sparkling sea; an ice-cold beer shared with a friend on a hot, dry day. Boundaries are crossed and recrossed continually. The landscape is replete with invisible topographies. These boundaries have been recurrent themes, the movement in, out and among bodies affected, and the porous membranes offering frail distinction and separation. The imagination can conceive cosmologies and conflagration; landscaped gardens as an index of our civilization and ingenious tortures as an index of our barbarity. It is the poet and prophet Apollo who slays Achilles, as his mother Thetis opines. The power of the imagination can destroy us, but it can also save us – or, at least, create both spaces in which hope does not die and futures in which friendship can flourish on more than consolation. It's up to us, and the people we elect to make decisions on our behalf.

In the summer of 1974, five adolescent friends lying in a mown field in Norfolk, gaze up into a clear night sky and face what they cannot see: the unimaginable.

We are *amazing*.

BIBLIOGRAPHY

Agee, James, *Collected Poems* (New Haven, CT: Yale University Press, 1969).

Ahmed, Sara, *The Cultural Politics of Emotion* (Edinburgh: Edinburgh University Press, 2004).

Asad, Talal, *Formations of the Secular: Christianity, Islam, Modernity* (Stanford, CT: Stanford University Press, 2003).

Assmann, Jan, 'Communicative and Cultural Memory', in *Cultural Memory Studies: and International and Interdisciplinary Handbook*, eds Astrid Erll and Ansgar Nünning (Berlin: Walter de Gruyter, 2008), pp. 109–18.

Austin, J. L., *How to Do Things With Words* (Oxford: Clarendon Press, 1962).

Bartlett, Frederic C., *Remembering: A Study in Experimental and Social Psychology* (Cambridge: Cambridge University Press, 1932).

Bashō, Matsuo, *On Love and Barley: The Haiku of Basho*, trans. Lucien Stryk (London: Penguin Books, 1985).

Beowulf, trans. Frances B. Grummere (Cambridge, MA: Harvard University Press, 1910).

Beradt, Charlotte, *The Third Reich Dreams: The Nightmares of a Nation 1933–39*, trans. A. Gottwald (Chicago: Quadrangle Books, 1966).

Bitbol, Michael and Pier Luigi Luisi, 'Autopoiesis With or Without Cognition: Defining Life at its Edge', *Journal of the Royal Society Interface* (2004) 1: 99–107.

Black, Antony, *A World History of Ancient Political Thought* (Oxford: Oxford University Press, 2009).

Blanke, Olaf and Silvio Ionta, 'The Brain Network Reflecting Bodily Self-Consciousness: A Functional Connectivity Study', *Social Cognitive and Affective Neuroscience* (2014) 9(12): 1904–13.

Bourgine, P. and J. Stewart, 'Autopoiesis and Cognition', *Artificial Life* (2004) 10(3): 327–45.

Breslin, James E. B., *Mark Rothko: A Biography* (Chicago: University of Chicago Press, 1993).

Brown, Peter, *Augustine of Hippo: A Biography* (University of California Press, 1967).

Buber, Martin, *On Judaism* (New York: Schocken Books Inc., 1967).

Bulkeley, Kelly, *Big Dreams: The Science of Dreaming and the Origins of Religion* (Oxford: Oxford University Press, 2016).

Calasso, Roberto, *The Marriage of Cadmus and Harmony*, trans. Tim Parks (London: Vintage, 1994).

Cartwright, Rosalind D., *The Twenty-Four-Hour Mind: The Role of Sleep and Dreaming in Our Emotional Lives* (Oxford: Oxford University Press, 2010).

Cassirer, Ernst, *The Philosophy of Symbolic Forms*, volume II, trans. Ralph Mannheim (New Haven, CT: Yale University Press, 1966).

Castoriadis, Cornelius, *The Imaginary Institution of Society*, trans. Kathleen Blamey (Boston: MIT Press, 1998).

Cavafy, C. P., *The Collected Poems*, trans. Evangelos Sachperoglou (Oxford: Oxford University Press, 2007).

Cavanaugh, William T., *The Myth of Religious Violence: Secular Ideology and the Roots of Modern Conflict* (Oxford: Oxford University Press, 2009).

Cheyne, J. Allan, 'The Ominous Numinous: Sensed Presence And "Other" Hallucinations', *Journal of Consciousness Studies* (2001) 8: 5–7.

Cocking, J. M., *Imagination: A Study in the History of Ideas* (London: Routledge, 1991).

Coetzee, J. M., *Summertime* (London: Vintage Books, 2010).

Cohen Dov and Angela K.-Y. Leung, 'The Hard Embodiment of Culture', *European Journal of Social Psychology* (2009) 39(7): 1278–89.

Coleridge, Samuel Taylor, *Collected Letters* (6 vols), ed. Earl Leslie Griggs (Oxford: Oxford University Press, 1951–71).

———, *The Notebooks*, volume 2, ed. K. Coburn (New York: Pantheon Books, 1957).

———, *Coleridge's Notebooks: A Selection*, ed. Seamus Perry (Oxford: Oxford University Press, 2000).

———, *The Collected Works*, volume 16, *Poetical Works*, ed. J. C. C. Mays (Princeton, NJ: Princeton University Press, 2001).

———, *Biographia Literaria* (Auckland: The Floating Press, 2009).

Csikszentmihalyi, Mihaly, *The Flow: The Psychology of Happiness* (New York: Harper & Row, 1992).

Curtis, Gregory, *The Cave Painters: Probing the Mysteries of the World's First Artists* (New York: Anchor Books, 2006).

Damasio, Antonio, *The Feeling of What Happens: Body, Emotion, and the Making of Consciousness* (London: Vintage Books, 2000).

Davidson, Peter, *The Last of the Light: About Twilight* (London: Reaktion Books, 2015).

De Preester, Helena, 'Meaning, What's the Matter?', *Theoria et Historia Scientiarum – International Journal for Interdisciplinary Studies*, Special Issue: Embodiment and Awareness (2003) 7(1): 195–205.

Deacon, Terrence W., *Symbolic Species: The Co-Evolution of Language and the Brain* (New York: W.W. Norton & Company, 1997).

Dennett, Daniel C., *Consciousness Explained* (London: Penguin Books, 1993).

DeSalle, Robert and Ian Tattersall, *The Brain: Bing Bangs, Behaviors, and Beliefs* (New Haven, CT: Yale University Press, 2012).

Deutschländer, A., T. Stephan, K. Hüfner, J. Wagner, M. Wiesmann, M. Strupp, T. Brandt and K. Jahn, 'Imagined Locomotion in the Blind: An fMRI Study', *Neuroimage* (2009) 45(1): 122–8.

Dickens, Charles, *Bleak House* (London: Penguin Books, 1996).

Eliade, Mircea, *Myths, Dreams and Mysteries: The Encounter between Contemporary Faiths and Archaic Realities*, trans. Philip Mairet (New York: Harper Torchbooks, 1960).

Engell, James, *The Creative Imagination: Enlightenment to Romanticism* (Cambridge, MA: Harvard University Press, 1981).

Fanon, Frantz, *The Wretched of the Earth*, trans. Constance Farrington (London: Penguin Books, 1967).

Feinberg, Scott, 'Christopher Nolan on *Interstellar*, Critics, Making Original Films and Shunning Cellphone and Email', *Hollywood Reporter*, 3 January 2015.

Fenwick, Peter and Elizabeth Fenwick, *The Truth in the Light: Investigation of Over 300 Near Death Experiences* (Guildford: White Crow Books, 1996).

Feuerbach, Ludwig, *The Essence of Christianity* (published in 1841 and translated by George Eliot in 1854).

Fishbane, Michael, *Sacred Attunement: A Jewish Theology* (Chicago: University of Chicago Press, 2008).

Foucault, Michel, *The Order of Things: An Archaeology of the Human Sciences* (London: Tavistock Publications, 1970).

———, 'Is it Useless to Revolt?', in Jeremy Carrette, *Religion and Culture by Michel Foucault* (Manchester: Manchester University Press, 1999), pp. 131–4.

Freud, Sigmund, *The Ego and the Id*, trans. Joan Rivere (London: Hogarth Press, 1947).

———, *Moses and Monotheism*, trans. James Strachey, volume 13, *The Penguin Freud Library* (London: Penguin Books, 1990).

———, *Civilization and its Discontents*, trans. James Strachey, volume 12, *The Penguin Freud Library* (London: Penguin Books, 1991).

———, *The Interpretation of Dreams*, trans. James Strachey, volumes 4 and 5, *The Standard Edition of the Complete Works* (London: Vintage Books, 2001).

Galford, Christopher, *The Universe in Your Hand: A Journey through Space, Time and Beyond* (London: Pan Macmillan, 2015).

Gardner, Daniel, *The Science of Fear: How the Culture of Fear Manipulates Your Brain* (London: Penguin Books, 2009).

Garelli, Paul, 'L'E tat et la légitimité royale sous l'empire assyrien', in Morgens Trolle Larsen, *Power and Propaganda: A Symposium on Ancient Empires* (Copenhagen: Akademisk Forlag, 1979).

Garner, Alan, *Boneland* (London: Fourth Estate Ltd., 2013).

Gazzaniga, Michael, *Who's In Charge? Free Will and the Science of the Brain* (New York: HarperCollins, 2011).

Gerard, Alexander, *Essay on Taste* (Memphis, TN: General Books, 2017).

Goodall, Jane (with Philip Berman), *Reason for Hope: A Spiritual Journey* (New York: Soko Publications Ltd., 1999).

Goodall, Jane, Interview with Goodall in *A Communion of Subjects: Animals in Religion, Science and Ethics*, eds Paul Waldau and Kimberley Patton (New York: Columbia University Press, 2006), pp. 651–5.

Guthrie, R. Dale, *The Nature of Paleolithic Art* (Chicago: Chicago University Press, 2006).

Halbwachs, Maurice, *On Collective Memory*, trans. Lewis A. Coser (Chicago: University of Chicago Press, 1992).

Harris, Alexandra, *Weatherland: Writers and Artists under English Skies* (London: Thames & Hudson, 2015).

Harth, Dietrich, 'The Invention of Cultural Memory', in *Cultural Memory Studies: And International and Interdisciplinary Handbook*, eds Astrid Erll and Ansgar Nünning (Berlin: Walter de Gruyter, 2008), pp. 85–96.

Hazarika, Manjil, 'Homo Erectus/Ergaster and Out of Africa: Recent Developments in Paleoanthropology and Prehistoric Archaeology' (June 2007), http://www.himalayanlanguages.org/files/hazarika/Manjil %20Hazarika%20EAA.pdf.

Henshilwood, Christopher, 'Oldest Human Paint-Making Studio Discovered in Cave', *Live Science* (13 October 2011), http://www. livescience.com/16538-oldest-human-paint-studio.html.

Herbert, Zbigniew, *Selected Poems*, trans. Czeslow Milosz and Peter Dale Scott (Manchester: Carcanet, 1985).

Hirschfield, Jane, *Nine Gates: Entering the Mind of Poetry, Essays* (New York: Harper Perennial, 1998).

Humphrey, Nicholas, 'Cave Art, Autism, and the Evolution of the Human Mind', *Cambridge Archaeological Journal* (1998) 8(2): 165–91.

Hunt, Gavin R., 'Manufacture and Use of Hook Tools by New Caledonian Crows', *Nature* (1996) 379: 249–51.

Hunt, Gavin R., Michael C. Corballis and Russell D. Gray, 'Laterality in Tool Manufacture by Crows', *Nature* (2001) 414: 707.

Huntley, B. and J. M. Allen, 'Glacial Environments III. Palaeovegetation Patterns in Late Glacial Europe', in *Neanderthals and Modern Humans in the European Landscape during the Last Glaciation*, eds T. H. Van Andel and W. Davies (Cambridge: McDonald Institute for Archaeological Research, 2003), pp. 79–102.

Ingold, Tim, *The Perception of the Environment: Essays on Livelihood, Dwelling and Skill* (London: Routledge, 2000).

Jeffers, Robinson, *The Selected Poetry of Robinson Jeffers*, ed. Tim Hunt (Stanford: Stanford University Press, 2002).

Joy, Stuart, 'Dreaming a Little Bigger, Darling', in *The Cinema of Christopher Nolan: Imagining the Impossible*, eds Jacqueline Furby and Stuart Joy (New York: Columbia University Press, 2015).

Keats, John, *The Letters of John Keats 1814–1821*, ed. Hyder Edward Rollins (Cambridge: Cambridge University Press, 1958).

———, *The Complete Poems* (London: Penguin Books, 1973).

Keller, Evelyn Fox, 'Genes, Genomes, and Genomics', *Biological Theory* (2011) 6(2): 132–40.

Killingsworth, Matthew A. and Daniel T. Gilbert, 'A Wandering Mind is an Unhappy Mind', *Science* (2010) 330: 932.

Kracauer, Siegfried, *Theory of Film: The Redemption of Physical Reality* (New York: Oxford University Press, 1960).

Kummer, Hans, *In Quest for the Sacred Baboon: A Scientist's Journey*, trans. M. Ann Biederman Thorson (Princeton, NJ: Princeton University Press, 1995).

Lakoff, George and Mark Johnson, *The Metaphors We Live By* (Chicago: Chicago University Press, 1980).

LaMothe, Kimerer, *Nietzsche's Dancers: Isadora Duncan, Martha Graham, and the Revaluation of Christian Values* (New York: Palgrave Macmillan, 2006).

Lane, Nick, *The Vital Question: Why is Life the Way it is?* (London: Profile Books, 2015).

Lang, Andrew, *Helen of Troy* (New York: Charles Scribner Ltd., 1882).

Latour, Bruno, *We Have Never Been Modern*, trans. Catherine Porter (Cambridge, MA: Harvard University Press, 1993).

Lawson, Andrew J., *Painted Caves: Paleolithic Rock Art in Western Europe* (Oxford: Oxford University Press, 2012).

Leverton, Denise, *The Life Around Us: Selected Poems on Nature* (New York: New Directions Books, 1997).

Lewis-Williams, David, *The Mind in the Cave: Consciousness and the Origins of Art* (London: Thames & Hudson, 2004).

Losev, Aleksei Fyodorovich, *The Dialectics of Myth*, trans. Vladimir Marchenov (New York: Routledge, 2014).

Luisi, Pier Luigi, *The Emergence of Life: From Chemical Origins to Synthetic Biology* (Cambridge: Cambridge University Press, 2006).

MacFarland, Robert, *The Old Ways: A Journey on Foot* (London: Penguin Books, 2012).

Maiese, Michelle, *Embodiment, Emotion, and Cognition* (New York: Palgrave Macmillan, 2011).

Margcu, Xolela, *Biko: A Life* (London: I.B.Tauris, 2014).

Marsh, Michael N., *Out of the Body and Near-Death Experiences: Brain State Phenomena or Glimpse of Immortality* (Oxford: Oxford University Press, 2010).

Maturana, H. R. and F. J. Varela, *Autopoiesis and Cognition: The Realization of Living* (Dortrecht: D. Reidel Publishing Company, 1980).

McGilchrist, Iain, *The Master and His Emissary: The Divided Brain and the Making of the Western World* (New Haven, CT: Yale University Press, 2012).

Merleau-Ponty, Maurice, *Phenomenology of Perception* (London: Routledge and Kegan Paul, 1962).

Miller, Stanley L., 'Current Status of the Prebiotic Synthesis of Small Molecules', *Chemica Scripta* (1986) 26(B): 5–11.

Mitchell, Peter, *The Archaeology of Southern Africa* (Cambridge: Cambridge University Press, 2002).

Morris, Simon Conway, *Life's Solution: Inevitable Humans in a Lonely Universe* (Cambridge: Cambridge University Press, 2003).

Moss, Lenny, 'Redundancy, Plasticity, and Detachment: The Implications of Comparative Genomics for Evolutionary Thinking', *Philosophy of Science* (2006) 73(5): 930–46.

Napier, John Russell, *Hands*, revised Russell H. Tuttle (Princeton, NJ: Princeton University Press, 1993).

Nietzsche, Friedrich, *The Birth of Tragedy*, trans. Shaun Whiteside (London: Penguin Books, 1993).

Otto, Rudolf, *The Idea of the Holy*, trans. John W. Harvey (Oxford: Oxford University Press, 1923).

Panksepp, Jaak, *Affective Neuroscience: The Foundations of Human and Animal Emotion* (Oxford: Oxford University Press, 2005).

Papagianni, Dimitra and Michael A. Morse, *The Neanderthals Rediscovered: How Modern Science is Rewriting their Story* (London: Thames & Hudson, 2015).

Pascal, Blaise, *Pensees*, trans. A. J. Krialsheimer (Harmondsworth: Penguin Classics, 1995).

Persinger, Michael A., 'Religious and Mystical Experiences as Artifacts of Temporal Lobe Function: A General Hypothesis', *Perceptual Motor Skills* (1983) 57: 1255–62.

Pfeiffer, John E., *Creative Explosion: An Inquiry into the Origins of Art and Religion* (New York: Harper and Row, 1982).

Popper, Karl, *The Open Society and Its Enemies* (London: Routledge, 2002).

Povinelli, Daniel J., *Folk Physics for Apes: The Chimpanzee's Theory of How the World Works* (Oxford: Oxford University Press, 2000).

Proust, Marcel, *Correspondance de Marcel Proust*, ed. Philip Kolb, volume 8V (Paris: Plon, 1970).

———, *Le Carnet de 1908*, ed. Philip Kolb (Paris: Gallimard, 1976).

———, *The Remembrance of Things Past*, 3 volumes (*Time Regained* is the last volume, trans. C. K. Scott Moncrief and Terence Kilmartin (Harmondsworth: Penguin Classics, 1983).

Rascaroli, Laura, 'Oneiric Metaphor in Film Theory', *Kinema* (2008), http://www.kinema.uwaterloo.ca/article.php?id=141.

Reuter, Christoph, *My Life is a Weapon: A Modern History of Suicide Bombing*, trans. Helena Ragg-Kirby (Princeton, NJ: Princeton University Press, 2004).

Sacks, Oliver, *Awakenings* (London: Duckworth, 1973).

———, *Hallucinations* (New York: Borzoi Book, 2012).

Sartre, Jean-Paul, *The Imaginary: A Phenomenological Psychology of the Imagination*, trans. Jonathan Webber (London: Routledge, 2004).

Schaeffer, Donovan, *Religious Affects: Animality, Evolution, and Power* (Durham, NC: Duke University Press, 2015).

Schmitt, Carl, *The Leviathan in the State Theory of Thomas Hobbes*, Forward by Georg Schwab, trans. George Schwab and Erna Hilfstein (Westport, CT: Greenwood Press, 1996).

———, *Political Theology: Four Chapters on the Concept of Sovereignty*, trans. George Schwab (Chicago: University of Chicago Press, 2006).

Secor, Laura, *The Children of Paradise: The Struggle for the Soul of Iran* (New York: Riverhead Book, 2016).

Shariati, Ali, *Martyrdom and Martyrdom*, trans. Ali Asghar Gassemy (Chicago: Kazi Publication, 1988).

Sheets-Johnstone, Maxine, *The Primacy of Movement* (Amsterdam: John Benjamins Publishing Company, 2011).

Shepherd, Nan, *The Living Mountain* (Edinburgh: Canongate Books, Ltd., 1996).

Sidney, Sir Philip, *An Apology for Poetry* (London: Thomas Nelson And Sons, 1965).

Smith, Adam, *An Inquiry into the Nature and Causes of the Wealth of Nations* (Oxford: Oxford University Press, 1993).

Solms, Mark, *The Neurophysiology of Dreams: A Clinico-Anatomical Study* (Abingdon: Routledge, 2016).

Squire, Larry and Eric Kandel, *Memory: From Mind to Molecules* (Englewood, CO: Roberts & Company, 2009).

Stewart, Kathleen, *Ordinary Affects* (Durham, NC: Duke University Press Books, 2007).

Stout, D. and T. Chaminade, 'Stone Tools, Language and the Brain in Human Evolution', *Philosophical Transactions of the Royal Society B: Biological Sciences* (2012) 367(1585): 75–87.

Stringer, Chris, *The Origin of Our Species* (London: Allen Lane, 2011).

Tallis, Raymond, *The Hand: A Philosophical Inquiry into Human Being* (Edinburgh: Edinburgh University Press, 2003).

———, *Michelangelo's Finger: An Exploration of Everyday Transcendence* (London: Atlantic Books, 2011).

Taylor, Charles, *Modern Social Imaginaries* (Durham, NC: Duke University Press, 2003).

Tennyson, Alfred Lord, *The Poems*, ed. Christopher Ricks (New York: W.W. Norton, 1972).

Thomas, Edward, *Collected Poems* (London: Faber and Faber, 2004).

Thompson, Evan, *Mind in Life: Biology, Phenomenology, and the Sciences of Mind* (New Haven, CT: Belknap Press, 2007).

———, *Waking, Dreaming, Being* (New York: Columbia University Press, 2015).

Traherne, Thomas, *Centuries* (London: The Faith Press, 1963).

———, *Selected Poems* (Charleston, SC: Nabu, 2014).

Türcke, Christoph, *The Philosophy of Dreams*, trans. Susan H. Gillespe (New Haven, CT: Yale University Press, 2013).

Tweed, Thomas, *Crossing and Dwelling: A Theory of Religion* (Cambridge, MA: Harvard University Press, 2006).

van Huyssteen, Wentzel, *Alone in the World? Human Uniqueness in Science and Theology* (Göttingen: Vandenhoeck & Ruprecht, 2006).

Vico, Giambattista, *New Science: Principles of the New Science Concerning the Common Nature of Nations*, trans. David Marsh (London: Penguin Books, 1999).

Voegelin, Eric, *Der authoritäre Staat: Ein Versuchüber das österreichische Staatsproblem* (Wein: Julius Springer, 1936).

———, *Die politischen Religionen*, translated as *Political Religions* in *Modernity Without Restraint*, volume 5 of *The Collected Works*, ed. Manfred Henningsen (Columbia, MO: University of Missouri Press, 1999).

———, Autobiographical Reflections, volume 34 of *The Collected Works*, ed. Ellis Sandoz (Columbia, MO: University of Missouri Press, 2006).

Warburton, Edward C., 'Of Meanings and Movements: Re-Languaging Embodiment in Dance Phenomenology and Cognition', *Dance Research Journal* (2011) 43(2).

Williams, Rowan, *The Edge of Words* (London: Bloomsbury, 2014).

Wilson, Edward O., *Biophilia* (Cambridge, MA: Harvard University Press, 1986).

Wilson, Frank R., *The Hand: How its Use Shapes the Brain, Language and Human Culture* (New York: Vintage Books, 1998).

Wittgenstein, Ludwig, *Philosophical Investigations* (Oxford: Basil Blackwell Ltd., 1953).

Witzel, E. J. Michael, *The Origins of the World's Mythologies* (Oxford: Oxford University Press, 2012).

Wunn, Ina, *Die Religionen in Vorgeschichtlicher Zeit (Die Religionen Der Menschheit)* (Stuttgart: Kohlhammer, 2005).

Wunn, Ina and Patrick Urban, *Götter – Gene – Genesis: Die Biologie der Religionsentstehung* (Berlin: Springer-Verlag, 2015).

Yates, Frances, *The Art of Memory* (London: Routledge, 1966).

Žižek, Slavoj, *Living in the End Times* (London: Verso, 2010).

INDEX